URBAN RISK
ASSESSMENTS

URBAN DEVELOPMENT SERIES

The Urban Development Series discusses the challenge of urbanization and what it will mean for developing countries in the decades ahead. The series delves substantively into the core issues framed by the World Bank's 2009 Urban Strategy, *Systems of Cities: Harnessing Urbanization for Growth and Poverty Alleviation.* Across the five domains of the Urban Strategy, the series provides a focal point for publications that seek to foster a better understanding of the core elements of the city system, pro-poor policies, city economies, urban land and housing markets, urban environments, and other issues germane to the agenda of sustainable urban development.

Titles in the series include:

Cities and Climate Change: Responding to an Urgent Agenda

Climate Change, Disaster Risk, and the Urban Poor: Cities Building Resilience for a Changing World

Urban Risk Assessments: An Approach for Understanding Disaster and Climate Risk in Cities

URBAN RISK ASSESSMENTS

Understanding Disaster and Climate Risk in Cities

Eric Dickson, Judy L. Baker, Daniel Hoornweg and Asmita Tiwari

THE WORLD BANK
Washington, D.C.

© 2012 International Bank for Reconstruction and Development / The World Bank
1818 H Street NW, Washington DC 20433
Telephone: 202-473-1000; Internet: www.worldbank.org

ISBN (paper): 978-0-8213-8962-1
ISBN (electronic): 978-0-8213-8963-8
DOI: 10.1596/978-0-8213-8962-1

Cover photo: istockphoto.com; *Cover design:* Debra Naylor, Naylor Design, Inc.

Library of Congress Cataloging-in-Publication Data

Urban risk assessments : an approach for understanding disaster and climate risk in cities.
    p. cm. — (Urban development)
  "The report was prepared by a Bank team comprised of Eric Dickson ... [et al.]."
  Includes bibliographical references and index.
  ISBN 978-0-8213-8962-1 — ISBN 978-0-8213-8963-8 (electronic)
1. Urban ecology (Sociology) 2. City planning—Environmental aspects. 3. Urban policy. 4. Natural disasters—Social aspects. 5. Climatic changes—Social aspects. 6. Risk assessment. 7. Environmental risk assessment. I. World Bank.
  HT241.U7273 2012
  307.760973—dc23
                                   2012014666

Contents

Tables

Acknowledgments

This report was prepared as part of a broader program addressing cities and climate change undertaken by the Urban Development and Local Government Unit of the World Bank. The development of the urban risk assessment (URA) is part of a memorandum of understanding on a joint Cities and Climate Change work program between UN-HABITAT, United Nations Environment Programme (UNEP), and the World Bank, supported by Cities Alliance. The report was prepared by a Bank team composed of Eric Dickson, Judy Baker, Daniel Hoornweg, and Asmita Tiwari. Catalina Ochoa developed the URA template, and Henry Jewell supported finalizing the document. The work was carried out under the overall guidance of Abha Joshi-Ghani (Sector Manager, Urban Development and Local Government Unit, FEUUR).

Among the people who provided guidance and contributions at various stages of the work were Abigail Baca, Abhas Jha, Alex H. Barbat, Andrew Norton, Anthony Bigio, Armando Guzman, Bianca Adam, Eddie Burgess, Fatima Shah, Federica Ranghieri, Fernando Ramirez, Francis Ghesquiere, Galen Evans, Glen Pearce-Oroz, Henry Jewell, Hyoung Gun Wang, Joaquin Toro, Margaret Arnold, Martha-Liliana Carreño, Niels Holm-Nielsen, Patricia Fernandes, Omar-Dario Cardona, Robert Kehew, Raf Tuts, Ricardo Jimenez Cruz, Saroj Jha, Sladjana Cosic, Soraya Samoun, Stuart Gill, Tiguist Fisseha, Uwe Deichmann, and Vijay Jagannathan. Any errors and omissions are solely the responsibility of the authors.

The work has been developed through the support and advice of various agencies, including Arizona State University, Association of American Geographers, Cisco Systems, Development Seed, the Environmental Systems Research Institute (ESRI), FortiusOne, GTZ (now GIZ, Deutsche Gesellschaft für Internationale Zusammenarbeit), International Development Research Centre, International

Institute for Environment and Development, ITHACA, Joint Research Commission, Munich Re, Office of Space and Advanced Technology (U.S. Department of State), United Nations Environment Programme, UN-HABITAT, United Nations Population Fund, and United Nations University.

Abbreviations

AAL	Average Annual Losses
BAP	Bali Action Plan
CAT DDO	Catastrophe Deferred Drawdown Option
CAPRA	Comprehensive Approach for Probabilistic Risk Assessment
CCA	Climate Change Adaptation
CDC	Centers for Disease Control and Prevention
CEPREDENAC	Centro de Coordinación para la Prevención de los Desastres Naturales en América Central
COP	UNFCCC Conference of Parties
DEM	Digital Elevation Models
DRM	Disaster Risk Management
DRR	Disaster Risk Reduction
DSM	Digital Surface Models
DTM	Digital Terrain Models
GCP	Ground Control Points
GFDRR	Global Facility for Disaster Risk and Recovery
GHG	Greenhouse Gases
GIS	Geographic Information System
GPS	Global Positioning System
HFA	Hyogo Framework for Action
ICSMD	International Charter on Space and Major Disasters
IPCC	Intergovernmental Panel on Climate Change
LEC	Loss Exceedance Curve
LECZ	Low Elevation Coastal Zone
MDG	Millennium Development Goals
MDR	Mean Damage Ratio

NAPA	National Adaptation Programs of Action
SA	Shelter Associates
UDRI	Urban Disaster Risk Index
UNEP	United Nation Environment Programme
UNFCCC	United Nations Framework Convention on Climate Change
UNISDR	United Nations International Strategy on Disaster Reduction
URA	Urban Risk Assessment
VHR	Very High Resolution
WHO	World Health Organization
WRI	World Resources Institute
WWTB	World Wide Typology of Buildings

Overview

The rapid and often unplanned expansion of cities is exposing more people and economic assets to the risk of disasters and the effects of climate change. For city governments, increased climate variability imposes additional challenges to effective urban management and the delivery of key services, while for residents it increasingly affects their lives and livelihoods due to more frequent floods, landslides, heat waves, droughts, and fires. There is an urgent need for cities to consider disaster and climate change by streamlining assessments of related risks in their planning and management as well as delivery of services.

This paper proposes a framework for carrying out urban risk assessment, and seeks to strengthen coherence and consensus in how cities can plan for natural disasters and climate change. The Urban Risk Assessment (URA) was developed by drawing on lessons from existing efforts to assess risk in cities as well as urban planning literature. It was vetted through consultation and collaboration with international development agencies, the public and private sectors, and nongovernmental organizations. It minimizes duplicative efforts, and brings convergence to related work undertaken by the World Bank and other key partners.[1] The target audience for this report includes: (1) decision makers such as city managers, mayors, and those involved in developing national and local policies related to urban development; (2) urban practitioners and technical staff at the municipal, regional, and national levels; and (3) international organizations.

The URA presents a flexible approach that project and city managers can use to identify feasible measures to assess a city's risk. It provides key information needed to consider appropriate city-level responses to the risks posed by natural hazards and increased climate variability. The assessment lays the groundwork for collaboration across multilateral agencies, the private sector, and city and national governments to begin benchmarking their own progress toward reducing urban risk. The goal is to establish a common foundation upon which urban risk assessments could periodically be performed, with the ultimate objectives being to quantify risk and monitor progress toward improved resilience. The URA methodology has been piloted in four cities (Mexico City, Jakarta, Dar es Salaam, and São Paulo) and will be further refined with the support and guidance of various international agencies as it is rolled out globally.

The proposed assessment methodology focuses on three reinforcing pillars that collectively contribute to understanding urban risk: A hazard impact assessment, an institutional assessment, and a socioeconomic assessment. The URA allows flexibility in how it is applied, depending on available financial resources, available data relating to hazards and its population, and institutional capacity of a given city. Through the URA's sequencing, which is linked to complexity and required investment, city managers may select subcomponents from each pillar that individually and collectively enhance the understanding of urban risk.

Based on the identified needs and priorities, city governments can select the most appropriate level of risk assessment. At the primary level, the assessment requires only limited financial resources and institutional capacity, and can help cities identify hazard-prone areas, basic climate change challenges, and capacity for disaster preparedness and response. At the secondary level, the assessment relies on techniques requiring more financial and technical resources to be able to develop actual risk mapping, resilience studies, and institutional gap analysis. At the tertiary level, the assessment will require greater resources, institutional capacity, and data availability to make use of advanced risk management tools and to undertake detailed disaster and climate change modeling.

The URA assists decision making, urban planning, and designing disaster and climate risk management programs. An important step toward this objective is streamlining data acquisition and management into an integrated system that can not only be updated and monitored easily, but that is also accessible to the various entities involved in city management. Recent technological advances, specifically those making the collection and sharing of hazard-related information more readily available through open-source software, will benefit emerging programs in the four phases of risk management (risk reduction, preparedness, response, and recovery) and in formulating programs to adapt to climate change. The same information can often be valuable to the design of traditional urban projects, such as poverty alleviation and housing or infrastructure upgrading.

An ancillary objective of the URA is to better position cities to absorb and allocate discrete adaptation funds, should they be available. Currently there are no direct linkages between city-level actions and National Adaptation Programs of Action (NAPA), and few funding schemes are in place to finance their implementation. When compared to other sectors such as forestry or agriculture that have typically received sizable allocations for climate adaptation funding, cities have lacked necessary mechanisms to begin addressing climate change and disaster management in a sustainable and unified manner. By identifying risks and vulnerabilities within urban areas, city authorities will be better positioned to address short-term disaster risk reduction as well as the longer-term impacts of climate change. National governments will also benefit by being better able to allocate adaptation funding based on multiple assessments across its cities.

This report (1) presents the case for the need to better understand risks related to natural hazards and climate change in cities; (2) proposes an integrated approach to practitioners for identifying areas, populations, and assets most at risk from the effects of disasters and climate change; and (3) provides preliminary suggestions for risk reduction by quantifying risk and implementing preventative programs. The report is divided into four chapters: Chapters 1 and 2 are aimed at policy makers with information on why and how to invest in measures that strengthen the understanding of urban risk. Chapter 1 provides background information on the growing importance of strategies for disaster risk management at the city level, and Chapter 2 provides guidance on how to operationalize and mainstream the URA with ongoing urban management and development activities. Chapters 3 and 4 are aimed at practitioners, and provide details on the conceptual approach, components, uses, and monitoring requirements related to the URA. This document does not provide a detailed discussion on each methodology presented, but rather an overview with selected resources for those wanting more information on specific approaches. Annexes provide detailed case studies and other useful resources.

Note

1. The development of the urban risk assessment is part of a Memorandum of Understanding on a joint Cities and Climate Change work program among UN-HABITAT, the United Nations Environment Programme (UNEP), and the World Bank, supported by Cities Alliance.

1

Need for an Urban Risk Assessment

Chapter Summary

- Cities in the developing world are facing increased risk of disasters, and the potential of economic and human losses from natural hazards is being exacerbated by the rate of unplanned urban expansion and influenced by the quality of urban management.
- Climate change brings additional challenges with a growing number and variety of impacts on cities, their critical ecosystems, and citizens' livelihoods.
- New residents and the urban poor living in peri-urban areas and informal settlements are particularly vulnerable to natural hazards due to their tendency of residing in high-risk areas and faulty shelters, having limited access to basic and emergency services, and a general lack of economic resilience.
- The option of doing nothing can be more costly than proactively identifying and managing risks. If no steps are taken to identify and manage disaster risks and climate change, resulting losses will have severe implications on the safety, quality of life, and economic performance of cities.
- Better urban management and governance is at the heart of reducing disaster and climate change risks and making cities safer.
- Cities can plan and respond better if the location and nature of risk is known, and also if risk assessment and management are mainstreamed in urban development and management programs.

Disasters and Cities

Disasters have caused major disruptions in both low- and middle-income countries, often wiping away decades of development gains in moments. Major recent disasters in developing countries include earthquakes in Haiti (early 2010), which killed more than 220,000 people, and in Indonesia (2009), which killed more than 1,000; the Nargis cyclone in Myanmar (2008), which killed more than 138,000 people; and the Sichuan earthquake in China (2008), which killed more than 87,000 people. While the economic losses from disasters tend to be greater in high-income countries (in absolute terms) due to higher value of properties and assets, low- and middle-income countries tend to face higher fatalities and disruptions to hard-earned development gains. On average, around 82,000 people are killed annually by disasters, with most fatalities concentrated in low- and middle-income countries.[1]

Urban areas suffer greater fatalities and economic losses than rural areas. Today more than half of the world's population lives in cities, with an additional 2 billion urban residents expected in the next 20 years (World Bank 2009c). Much of the population growth is expected in small and medium-sized cities in developing countries, yet 1.2 billion urban residents already live in slums, and this too is expected to grow; rural-urban migration can cause low-income settlements to double in size every 5 to 7 years (Smith and Petley 2009). Africa and Asia, which have the highest rates of urban growth globally, are also experiencing the fastest rate of increase in the incidence of natural disasters over the last three decades (UN-HABITAT 2007). Not surprisingly, many urban areas sustained heavy losses due to disasters in the last 10 years (table 1.1). Given these trends, without major changes in the management of disaster risks and urbanization, risk to city residents will increase in the future as populations grow. According to a joint World Bank–UN study, population exposed to cyclones and earthquakes will more than double by 2050, to 1.5 billion (figure 1.1 in the color section) (World Bank and UN 2010 {see note on figure 1.1}).

Urban areas concentrate disaster risk due to the aggregation of people, infrastructure and assets, urban expansion, and inadequate management. While disasters are considered external shocks that destroy development gains, disaster risk is internal to development; the United Nations International Strategy on Disaster Reduction (UNISDR 2009) notes that "disaster risk is configured over time through a complex interaction between development processes that generates conditions of hazards, exposure and vulnerability" (box 1.1). The settling of communities in high-risk areas is often a result of rapid and uncontrolled urbanization accompanied by increased competition for land, decreased vegetation cover, changes in land use, and greater variability in climate. These drivers alter population distribution, relative wealth or impoverishment, and disaster risk

TABLE 1.1
Large Disasters from 2001 to 2010 with Major Impacts on Cities

Popular name	Main countries affected	Date of event	Type of hazard	Main cities affected	Total number of deaths	Total number of affected	Total damages US$
Haiti earthquake	Haiti	January 12, 2010	Earthquake	Port-au-Prince	222,570	3,400,0000	n/a
Sichuan earthquake	China	May 12, 2008	Earthquake	Beichuan, Dujiangyan, Shifang, Mianzhu, Juyuan, Jiangyou, Mianyang, Chengdu, Qionglai, Deyang	87,476	45,976,596	85 billion
Cyclone Nargis	Myanmar	May 2, 2008	Tropical cyclone	Yangon	138,366	2,420,000	4 billion
Java earthquake	Indonesia	May 27, 2006	Earthquake	Yogyakarta	5,778	3,177,923	3.1 billion
Kashmir earthquake	Pakistan	October 8, 2005	Earthquake	Muzaffarabad	73,338	5,128,000	5.2 billion
Hurricane Katrina	United States	August 29, 2005	Tropical cyclone	New Orleans	1,833	500,000	125 billion
Mumbai floods	India	July 26, 2005	Flood	Mumbai	1,200	20,000,055	3.3 billion
South Asian tsunami	Indonesia, Sri Lanka, India, Thailand, Malaysia, Maldives, Myanmar	December 26, 2004	Earthquake and tsunami	Banda Aceh, Chennai (some damages)	226,408	2,321,700	9.2 billion

(continued next page)

TABLE 1.1 *continued*

Popular name	Main countries affected	Date of event	Type of hazard	Main cities affected	Total number of deaths	Total number of affected	Total damages US$
Bam earthquake	Iran	December 26, 2003	Earthquake	Bam	26,796	267,628	500 million
European heat wave	Italy, France, Spain, Germany, Portugal, Switzerland	Summer 2003	Extreme heat	Various	72,210	Not reported	Not reported
Dresden floods	Germany	August 11, 2002	Flood	Dresden	27	330,108	11.6 billion
Gujurat earthquake	India	January 26, 2001	Earthquake	Bhuj, Ahmedabad	20,005	6,321,821	2.6 billion

Source: EM-DAT: The OFDA / CRED International Disaster Database (www.emdat.net), Université Catholique de Louvain; and the International Federation of the Red Cross (2010).

BOX 1.1

Understanding Disaster Risk

Disasters result from a combination of hazards and the exposure of people and economic assets coupled with their respective vulnerability. Vulnerability, and therefore the disaster risk, can be reduced by improving the resilience, or the capacity to cope, of those elements exposed.

Cities are increasingly exposed to a variety of **natural and manmade hazards**, including droughts, floods, earthquakes, storms, and volcanic eruptions. The potential for a hazard to become a disaster depends on the **degree of exposure** of a population and its physical or economic assets. Urbanization, migration, population growth, and economic development all increase the concentration of people and assets in high-risk areas. The higher degree of exposure and vulnerability of both people and infrastructure within cities is a driver behind why natural hazards have greater social and economic impact in urban areas than in rural areas.

Reducing **vulnerability** requires strengthening coping capacities to minimize the degree of loss emerging from a disaster. Vulnerability can be influenced by physical attributes (for example, structural qualities of housing or infrastructure) and qualitative attributes (for example, age, health, and poverty). The coping capacity of households and communities to respond to disasters and climate variability is also unequal, with low-income urban residents having poor access to information and fewer safety nets.

Source: Adapted from UNISDR (2009).

over a short time horizon; also, when combined with inadequate urban management, these drivers will continue to exacerbate existing risks to natural hazards (box 1.2) (World Bank 2003). Coordinated and strategic action must therefore be taken in the short term to avoid creating unmanageable levels of risk to a city's built environment and population. This becomes of still greater importance when considering the impact of small-scale or recurrent disasters that impact informal settlements. Such events are rarely recorded and it has been argued that their aggregate impact in cities exceeds losses associated with low-frequency, high-impact hazards that capture news headlines (UN-HABITAT 2007).

The urban poor living in peri-urban areas and informal settlements are particularly vulnerable due to their tendency of residing in high-risk areas and faulty shelters, having limited access to basic and emergency services, and a general lack of economic resilience.

The urban poor have to make difficult choices in regard to where they reside. This decision involves tradeoffs between proximity to economic opportunities, security of tenure, provision of services, protection from extreme events, and cost. As a result, informal settlements are often located in high-risk areas. A household's capacity to cope with a disaster also varies according to income levels, house type, geographic location within the city, and the holding of insurance policies to offset incurred damages.

Climate Change and Cities

Climate change brings additional challenges to urban management and decision making for city governments, and is associated with a growing number and variety of impacts on cities, the surrounding ecosystems, and citizens' livelihoods. City governments will need to make their residents aware of the need

---

BOX 1.2

Hazard Classification

For the purpose of URA, a hazard is defined as a dangerous phenomenon, substance, human activity, or condition that may cause loss of life, injury, or other health impacts, property damage, loss of livelihoods and services, social and economic disruption, or environmental damage.

Five subgroups of natural hazards have been defined: biological, geophysical, meteorological, hydrological, and climatological (see figure below). While all subgroups present significant risk to urban areas in developing and developed countries alike, the primary focus of many international development agencies lies in geophysical, hydrological, meteorological, and climatological hazards, while agencies such as the World Health Organization (WHO) and the Centers for Disease Control (CDC) engage in the area of biological hazards.

Other hazards, such as those originating from technological or industrial accidents, infrastructure failures, or certain human activities (for example, chemical spills, explosions, and fires), are becoming more frequent in cities. The distinction between natural and manmade hazards is often subtle; technological events can sometimes trigger natural hazards and vice-versa. While many hazards are of a natural origin, manmade changes can exacerbate the frequency or intensity of the hazard.

(continued next page)

BOX 1.2 *continued*

NATURAL HAZARDS

Biological

■ **Epidemic**
  • *Viral Infectious Disease*
  • *Bacterial Infectious Disease*
  • *Parasitic infectious Disease*
  • *Fungal Infectious Disease*
  • *Prion Infectious Disease*
■ **Insect Infestation**
■ **Animal Stampede**

Geophysical

■ **Earthquake**
■ **Volcano**
■ **Mass Movement (Dry)**
  • *Rockfall*
  • *Landslide*
  • *Avalanche*
  • *Subsidence*

Hydrological

■ **Flood**
  • *General Flood*
  • *Flash Flood*
  • *Storm Surge/Coastal Flood*
■ **Mass Movement (Wet)**
  • *Rockfall*
  • *Landslide*
  • *Avalanche*
  • *Subsidence*

Meteorological

■ **Storm**
  • *Tropical cyclone*
  • *Extra-Tropical Cyclone*
  • *Local Storm*

Climatological

■ **Extreme Temperature**
  • *Heat Wave*
  • *Cold Wave*
  • *Extreme Winter Condition*
■ **Drought**
■ **Wildfire**
  • *Forest Fire*
  • *Land Fire*

Hydro-Meterological

Source: Centre for Research on the Epidemiology of Disasters (2010).

BOX 1.3

Economics of Effective Prevention

The future of disaster prevention will be shaped, in part, by growing cities. The joint World Bank–United Nations publication *Natural Hazards, UnNatural Disasters: The Economics of Effective Prevention* shows that growing urbanization will increase exposure to hazards. By 2050 the number of people exposed to storms and earthquakes in large cities could more than double to 1.5 billion, with the largest concentration of at-risk people living in Asia and the Pacific. But the report also argues that even though exposure will rise, vulnerability need not: much will depend on how cities are managed.

Natural Hazards, UnNatural Disasters focuses not only on the role institutions at all levels play in disaster prevention, but also on individuals and the private incentives or disincentives they face for prevention. Three common threads emerge in the analysis conducted in the report: the role of information, incentives, and infrastructure (or the three "I"s).

Information is key: Countries, governments and individuals have to be able to understand the risks they face by undertaking hazard modeling and mapping. But it is not sufficient to just collect risk data. It has to be made public and accessible so as to enable people to make informed decisions about prevention.

When information on hazards is made available and markets are allowed to function, prices better reflect hazard risk, guiding people's decisions on where to live and which preventive measures to take. But markets, when smothered, dampen the incentives for prevention. In Mumbai, where rent controls have been pervasive, property owners have neglected maintenance for decades, so buildings crumble in heavy rains. And it is the poor who bear the brunt of the cumulative effects of such distorted policies (skewed tax structure, inadequate city financing arrangements, and so on), which produce only a limited and unresponsive supply of affordable, legal land sites for safer housing. Like rent controls, insecure ownership reduces individuals' incentives to make long-term prevention investments. In Peru, for example, land titling is associated with an almost 70 percent increase in housing renovation within 4 years. Governments should therefore let land and housing markets work and supplement them with targeted interventions only when necessary.

When provided with the right information and correct incentives, individuals generally make good decisions for themselves. But their preventive actions also depend on the infrastructure and public services that governments provide. Poor households prefer to have easier access to jobs, even though this

(continued next page)

BOX 1.3 *continued*

may imply living in slums on riverbanks prone to flooding or on hilltops subject to mudslides. Governments could greatly expand the choices of the poor: This could include making land available in safer locations—along with adequate and reliable public transport and other services so that people remain connected to their jobs. If they have access to piped water, individuals living in low-lying areas of Jakarta will not need to draw water through bore wells causing the ground to subside.

Source: World Bank Staff.

and methods to adapt to a changing climate characterized by greater frequency and intensity of adverse natural events in an increasingly stressed environment. Moreover, the impacts of climate change and disaster risk in rural areas will influence migration patterns, which characteristically contribute to the growth of low-income urban settlements. It is estimated that 20 million to 30 million of the world's poorest people move each year from rural to urban areas (Smith and Petley 2009). Table 1.2 presents a number of potential impacts of climate change on cities (World Bank 2009a).

The unique physical, social, economic, and environmental composition of a city influences the degree of risk and vulnerability of its residents. While recognizing that the specific assessment of urban risk will differ across cities based on factors such as poverty levels, the pace of urbanization, and awareness surrounding disaster risk or climate change, a general typology including coastal cities, dryland cities, and inland and high-altitude cities may still be useful in considering the broader issue.[2]

- **Large or Megacities.** Exposure in large cities to cyclones and earthquakes is projected to rise from 680 million in 2000 to 1.5 billion in 2050 (World Bank, 2009b) (see figures 1.1 and 1.2 in the color section). The fastest exposure growth will occur in South Asian cities (3.5 percent), followed by cities in Sub-Saharan Africa. Exposure to earthquakes remains high in East Asia: 267 million in 2050, followed by Latin America and the Caribbean (150 million in 2050) and Organisation for Economic Co-operation and Development (OECD) countries.
- **Coastal cities** are made vulnerable by the low-lying land they are often built on and as such are susceptible to impacts related to climate change such as sea-level rise, flooding, and coastal erosion. Many coastal cities in the Least

TABLE 1.2
Urban Climate-Related Hazards

Climate-related hazard	Projected impact
Sea-level rise and storm surges	Sea-level rise: Erosion and saline intrusion threatens coastal ecosystems: dunes, water tables, river water flows, and wetlands. Storm surges: Threaten coastal housing and municipal infrastructure—port and trade logistics facilities, highways, power plants, water treatment plants—due to increased runoff contaminant and change in population distribution.
Extreme rain	Higher frequency and intensity of flooding, road washouts, and landslides may occur in urban areas, threatening vulnerable settlements. Heightened risk of vector-borne diseases exists.
Heat waves/heat-island effect	Very high temperatures affect cities more than rural areas given the heat-retaining built environment (buildings, paved areas) and lower air speeds. This considerably reduces nighttime cooling, and may result in higher-than-average morbidity and mortality, particularly in older persons. Possible impacts include increased energy demand for air conditioning, water contamination, increased road surface damage, increased water demand.
Water scarcity	Changes in precipitation patterns will reduce reservoir supplies and availability for urban use; runoff contamination increases.
Worsening air quality	Air pollutants from fixed and mobile sources, volatile organic compounds (VOCs) and nitrogen oxides (NOx), react to increasing temperatures with the formation of ground ozone, and surface inversion increases. It particularly affects children and older persons' health.

Source: Adapted from World Bank (2009b).

Developed Countries are found in tropical areas with hot and humid climates and low-lying land, both of which heighten their vulnerability to extreme events. Only 2 percent of the world's land is in the Low Elevation Coastal Zone (LECZ)—the area adjacent to the coast that is less than 10 meters above mean sea level—but this zone is home to 10 percent of the world's population, 60 percent of whom live in urban areas. The top 10 coastal cities in terms of exposed population are Mumbai, Guangzhou, Shanghai, Miami, Ho Chi Minh City, Kolkata, Greater New York, Osaka-Kobe, Alexandria, and New Orleans (OECD 2008).

- **Dryland cities** suffer from scarce water resources due to extended droughts and more frequent sandstorms, the effects of which can be aggravated by poor infrastructure. The effects of drought are widespread but can be particularly severe on drinking water supplies and food prices.
- **Inland and high-altitude cities** will be affected by climate change predominantly as a result of changing patterns of precipitation. In many of these cities, minor floods that affect people's lives and livelihoods take place more frequently than major disasters, but these events are seldom reported outside the local area.

Challenges of Managing Disaster and Climate Risk in Urban Areas

City management is often reactive to disasters, with little consideration given to reducing or managing risk in a comprehensive, preventive manner. In spite of the potential impacts that disasters have on the financial resources of city governments and the functionality of the city, the management of disaster risk remains ex-post, with little attention to preventing or mitigating measures. Although some emergency and disaster response capability may exist, few cities in the developing world are truly prepared to manage disasters, in part due to the day-to-day challenges that most city governments face.

In addition, city governments are often constrained by a lack of up-to-date, comprehensive, and sufficiently detailed information about hazard and exposure in urban areas, particularly low-income settlements. See annex 17 for existing international response for reducing disaster risk and adapting to climate change.

While there is a growing consensus that more investment is needed in upstream risk reduction, prevention, and climate adaptation, cities in developing countries rarely have the technical, institutional, and financial capacity to implement related programs. Those cities in developing countries that have created local units to manage disasters generally have little budget allocation or implementation power. This, coupled with centralized administration (in some urban areas), does not usually provide enough independence for the local bodies to amend laws or provide sufficient budgets for innovations in disaster risk management.

Cities can plan and respond better if the location and nature of risk is known, and also if risk assessment and management is mainstreamed in urban development and management programs. However, as previously mentioned, cities in lower- and middle-income countries rarely consider disaster vulnerability, and only a handful have initiated strategies and related programs to increase climate change resilience (box 1.4). Even if strategies exist, city management faces challenges in developing, implementing, and maintaining risk management as a result of (World Bank 2010):

- *Limited understanding of climate risks*: Many city governments lack an understanding of existing sources of risk and potential impact of climate change. The lack of standardized methodology for conducting risk assessments exacerbates this shortcoming and can contribute to haphazard development. Particular attention is also required to assess risk in areas of urban growth and informal settlements.
- *Limited institutional capacity and financial resources*: City governments have few resources to address urban growth. As such, disaster and climate change risk does not always emerge as a priority for city administration. Cities require technical and financial assistance in enhancing institutional capacities to assess and respond to disasters more effectively.
- *Absence of standard protocols for managing disaster risk and adapting to climate change*: Currently there are limited examples of cities that have standard procedures for incorporating disaster risk management and climate change adaptation in city planning.
- *Monitoring city's performance*: City managers are keen to learn best practices from other cities and want to know what will work in their own city. Currently there are limited systematic exchanges of information, best practices, and benchmarking of a city's performance for urban risk reduction.

The option of doing nothing can be more costly than proactively identifying and managing risks. If no steps are taken to identify and manage disaster risks and climate change, the resulting losses can be irreversible and have severe implications on the safety, quality of life, and economic performance of cities (box 1.3). The impact of the 2010 Chile and Haiti earthquakes illustrates this point. Although Chile's earthquake released 500 times more energy compared to that of Haiti's, the epicenter was far from concentrations of population and built assets and its depth was approximately 46 km. As a consequence, it caused limited infrastructure damage and a death toll of just 528 people.[3] In the case of Haiti, the epicenter was only 15 km southwest of the capital city Port-au-Prince and only 10 km below the Earth's surface; these factors caused economic damages and losses equivalent to 120 percent of GDP[4] and a death toll of more than 200,000 people.[5] The enormous difference in the impact of these two events highlights the importance of investing in territorial planning and building codes with the resulting resilience of infrastructure and housing. Chile has invested in an earthquake-response system and has mandated retrofitting of existing structures and earthquake-resistant designs for new structures.[6] Conversely, planning, disaster preparedness, and earthquake-resistant building codes were nonexistent or outdated in Haiti.

BOX 1.4

City Growth and Increased Urban Temperatures in Mexico City

The Mexico Valley is exposed to increases in extreme temperatures, which in conjunction with expanding urbanization has contributed to a significant heat-island effect for Mexico City. Projections reveal that the mean temperature is expected to increase by 2 to 3°C toward the end of the 21st century, and the frequency of extreme precipitation is expected to increase. Characteristically, rising temperatures are accompanied by an increase in extreme rain, consequently placing Mexico City at heightened risk of flooding and landslides, particularly in the western part of the city. Recently released data for Mexico City corroborates the linkages between urban growth, the heat-island effect, and rising regional temperatures through a notable rise in the number of heat waves per decade. See annex 3 for a detailed case study of the urban risk assessment in Mexico City.

Historical Development of Mexico City

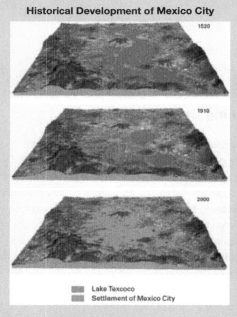

Source: Munich Re (2004).

(continued next page)

BOX 1.4 *continued*

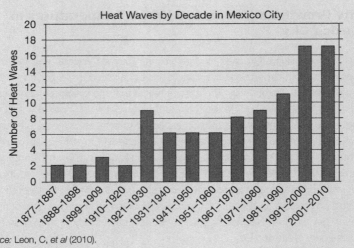

Source: Leon, C, *et al* (2010).

BOX 1.5

Understanding Urban Resilience

Resilience describes the ability of a system to withstand or accommodate stresses and shocks such as climate impacts, while still maintaining its function. At an urban scale, resilience will depend on the ability to maintain essential assets, as well as to ensure access to services and functions that support the wellbeing of citizens. This is particularly so for members of the population lacking access to financial, material, and social capital that can be used to buffer stresses.

Urban populations depend on interrelated and interdependent urban systems (infrastructure, ecosystems, institutions, and knowledge networks) that support and are supported by a city's actors or social agents (individuals, households, and private and public sectors). The resilience of a city depends on both the fragility of the urban system and the capacity of social agents to anticipate and to take action in order to adjust to changes and stresses, recognizing that their ability to act is constrained by access to resources and

(continued next page)

BOX 1.5 *continued*

supporting systems. Cities that may be considered resilient exhibit the following key characteristics:

- **Flexibility and diversity:** The ability to perform essential tasks under a wide range of conditions, and to convert assets or modify structures to introduce new ways of achieving essential goals. A resilient system has key assets and functions distributed so that they are not all affected by a given event at any one time (locational diversity) and multiple ways of meeting a given need (functional diversity).
- **Redundancy, modularity:** The capacity for contingency situations, to accommodate increasing or extreme events, unexpected demand, or surge pressures; also, multiple pathways and a variety of options for service delivery, or interacting components composed of similar parts that can replace each other if one or even many fail.
- **Safe failure:** The ability to absorb shocks and the cumulative effects of slow-onset challenges in ways that avoid catastrophic failures; or where failures in one structure or linkage are unlikely to result in cascading impacts across other systems.
- **Resourcefulness:** The capacities to visualize and act, as well as to identify problems, establish priorities, and mobilize resources. Resourcefulness is also related to the capacity to recognize and devise strategies that relate to different incentives and operational models of different groups.
- **Responsiveness and rapidity:** The capacity to organize and reorganize, as well as to establish function and sense of order in a timely manner both in advance of and following a failure.
- **Learning:** The ability to learn through formal and informal processes, as well as to internalize past experiences and failures and alter strategies based on knowledge and experience.

Achieving urban resilience requires engaging the capacities of social agents to understand and act upon the urban systems through iterative cycles of understanding vulnerability and building resilience. Both processes strengthen systems while developing and enhancing the social agents' capacities to intervene effectively in them. External agents such as practitioners, donors, or consultants may play roles as enablers or catalysts in urban contexts.

Source: Adapted from the Urban Resilience Framework developed by Arup International Development and the Institute for Social and Environmental Transition (ISET) as part of the Rockefeller Foundation-funded Asian Cities Climate Change Resilience Network (ACCCRN) project. See www.iset.org/publications or www.arup.com/internationaldevelopment and the ISET Working Paper Series *Climate Resilience in Concept and Practice*.

Notes

1. International Strategy for Disaster Reduction, 2009, based on EMDAT data. Between 1975 and 2008, 78.2 percent of mortality in significant natural disasters occurred in only 0.3 percent of recorded events.
2. Compiled by authors from International Institute for Environment and Development (2009), World Bank (20009b), and Organization of Economic Co-operation and Development (2008).
3. http://www.unesco-ipred.org/gtfbc_chile/OCHA_Situation_Report_No_4-Chile_Earthquake-20100305.pdf.
4. Compared to 2010 GDP (http://www.gfdrr.org/gfdrr/node/320).
5. Global Facility for Disaster Risk Recovery, 2010, "Haiti Earthquake PDNA: Damages, Losses, General and Sectoral Needs", gfdrr.org.
6. http://www.nytimes.com/2010/10/19/science/19quake.html?_r=2&hpw.

References

Dilley, Maxx, Robert S Chen, Uwe Deichmann, Arthur L Lerner-Lam, and Margaret Arnold. 2005. *Natural Disaster Hotspots: A Global Risk Analysis.* Washington, DC: World Bank. http://www.ldeo.columbia.edu/chrr/research/hotspots/coredata .html.

UN-HABITAT. 2007. *Enhancing Urban Safety and Security: Global Report on Human Settlements 2007.* London: Earthscan.

UNISDR. 2009. *Global Assessment Report on Disaster Risk Reduction.* Geneva: United Nations.

World Bank. 2003. *Building Safer Cities: The Future of Disaster Risk.* Washington, DC: World Bank.

———. 2009a. *Climate Change Adaptation and Disaster Preparedness in Coastal Cities of North Africa.* Washington, DC: World Bank.

———. 2009b. Climate Change Adaptation and Disaster Preparedness in Coastal Cities of North Africa. *Project Concept Note, Washington, DC: World Bank (unpublished).*

———. 2009c. *Systems of Cities: Harnessing the Potential of Urbanization for Growth and Poverty Alleviation.* Washington, DC: World Bank.

———. 2010. City Primer Application in Middle East and North Africa. Washington, DC: World Bank (unpublished).

World Bank and United Nations. 2010. *Natural Hazards, UnNatural Disasters: The Economics of Effective Prevention.*

2

Integrated Urban Risk Assessment as a Tool for City Management

Chapter Summary

- This chapter focuses on the structure of the Urban Risk Assessment—its process, uses, and challenges in initiating and mainstreaming the assessment.
- The URA is a flexible approach to assess a city's risks from disasters and climate change.
- The assessment builds upon three principal assessment pillars (institutional, hazard impact, and socioeconomic), each associated with three levels of assessment complexity (primary, secondary, and tertiary).
- A city can select the appropriate level of risk assessment based on need, resources available, capacity, and its overall goals.
  - At a primary level, the assessment requires minimal resources and can help cities identify high-risk areas and basic climate change challenges, and plan for disaster preparedness and response.
  - At a secondary level, the assessment relies on more advanced techniques requiring more financial and technical resources to develop disaster-response capacities and to plan and implement nonstructural measures to reduce risk.
  - At the tertiary level, the assessment will require greater resources to undertake detailed modeling of disasters and climate change to help cities develop superior protocols for disaster and climate risk management, including structural and nonstructural tools to reduce disaster and climate change risk.

- Assessing risk can be made an integral part of urban planning and decision making by streamlining data acquisition and management into an integrated system that can not only be updated and monitored easily, but also is accessible to all stakeholders involved in city management.
- The collection and sharing of hazard-related information will benefit emerging programs in the four phases of risk management (risk reduction, preparedness, response, and recovery) and the formulation of programs to adapt to climate change.

What Is Risk Assessment?

Risk assessment is an essential component in disaster risk management and climate change adaptation. The purpose of a risk assessment is to define the risk, answer questions about characteristics of potential hazards (such as frequency and severity), and identify vulnerabilities of communities and potential exposure to given hazards. Risk evaluation helps in prioritizing measures for risk management, giving due consideration to the probability and impact of potential events, cost-effectiveness of preventative measures, and resource availability.

Risk assessments should be undertaken at a range of scales, from the local to the global. There is great diversity in the target of assessments (people, health, buildings, or urban economy), in the sources of data (interviews, existing datasets,

Figure 2.1 Risk as a Process

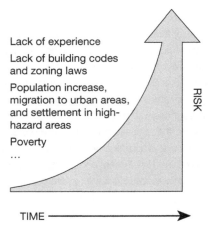

Lack of experience

Lack of building codes and zoning laws

Population increase, migration to urban areas, and settlement in high-hazard areas

Poverty

...

RISK

TIME ⟶

Source: Villagrán De León (2006).

satellite imagery, or expert judgments), and in the degree to which they are participatory or extractive in collecting data. In all cases, assessments aim to simplify complicated experiences of risk in order to assist in decision making. The complexities of undertaking a URA arise from a number of contributing factors[1]:

- *The multiple hazards to which people are simultaneously exposed.* Recent and frequently experienced hazard types may be more visible to assessors than others at any one moment.
- *The multiple sectors that are at risk.* It is difficult to aggregate vulnerability across sectors such as housing, communication networks, water and sanitation, education, health care infrastructure, power networks, etc. Each sector will have different exposure and susceptibility to risk, as well as capacities and resources for coping and recovery.
- *The multiple scales at which risk is felt and responded to.* Risk, in any one place, is an outcome of decision making and action—or inaction—at local, municipal, national, and international scales. It is challenging to include all of these scales in the analysis of impacts and capacity.
- *The multiple assets to be accounted for in measuring vulnerability and capacity.* This applies to all scales, from the individual to the city. Some assets will be contingent upon the use of others, and rarely are different types of assets commensurate.
- *The multiple stakeholders with roles to play in shaping risk.* Stakeholders' actions influence the degree to which they, and others, are placed at risk. This can be hard to pin down—for example, when such actions are part of everyday development processes.

When evaluating urban risk, it is important for city authorities to account for the dynamic character of cities. This supports the notion that risk assessments be undertaken at regular intervals so that the city governments can evaluate progress toward reducing risk and vulnerability. In countries with high population growth or high migration from rural to urban areas, planning the risk for cities involves a good understanding of the population dynamics of the country as a whole and of possible future growth. The role of adaptation to both rapid-onset hazards and those more gradual threats associated with climate change is therefore an integral part of proactive risk reduction planning for cities.

Integrated Approach to Assessing Urban Risk

The URA is a flexible approach that facilitates improved understanding of a city's risks from disasters and climate change. The URA (figure 2.2) allows for customizing how it is applied depending on available financial resources, available

Figure 2.2 Urban Risk Assessment Approach

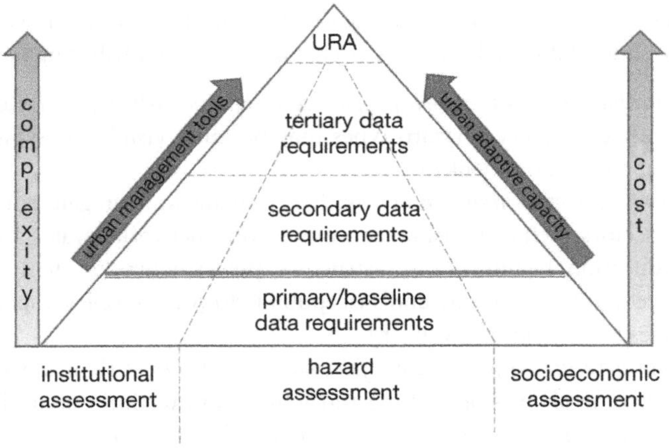

Source: Authors.

data relating to hazards and population, and institutional capacity. Through a phased approach, where each assessment level is linked to progressively more complex and detailed tasks, city managers may select the appropriate series of components from each pillar that individually and collectively enhance the understanding of risk in a given city. The approach is structured to integrate both rapid-onset hazards, such as floods or landslides, which are more typically the purview of the disaster risk management community, and slow-onset hazards, such as drought or sea-level rise typically associated with a longer-term change in climate trends. The specific components of each pillar and level of the assessment are summarized in table 2.1 and illustrated in figure 2.3.

The assessment is based upon three principal assessment pillars (institutional, hazard impact, and socioeconomic), each associated with three levels of complexity (primary, secondary, and tertiary). The framework is built around a central pillar for assessing the impact of hazards, aimed at identifying the type, intensity, and locations of potential changes and losses resulting from future hazards and climate change scenarios. Given that risk is a function of hazards, the relative vulnerability of people and economic assets, and the capacity to respond, the URA takes into account the role of institutions and the socioeconomic conditions of city residents in order to (1) understand whether agencies exist that are responsible for managing the risks arising from disasters and climate change, and (2) identify the most vulnerable populations likely to be adversely affected, as well as understanding their adaptive capacity. Each pillar is described in further detail in Chapter 3.

TABLE 2.1
Three Levels of Urban Risk Assessment

Urban risk assessment	Tasks	Link to climate change	Objectives/benefits to local government
Primary	Basic institutional mapping for disaster preparedness and response and climate change. Development of a physical base map if one does not exist or updating an existing map. Historical hazard impact assessment. Socioeconomic profile of city	Limited: General identification of climate risks based on available information from regional models.	Short term: Planning for disaster preparedness (identification of safe routes and shelters during disasters, protocols for disaster response, accessibility to emergency funds). Long term: Planning new city development to avoid hazard-prone areas.
Secondary	In-depth institutional analysis for disaster response, risk management, and climate change adaptation. Development of hazard-exposure maps and scenario-based risk models. Identification of infrastructure and populations at risk of disasters and climate change impacts. Socioeconomic assessment and poverty mapping.	Risk modeling includes downscaling of regional climate change models. Institutional assessment includes government agencies and departments with defined roles in adaptation planning.	Short term: Planning for disaster preparedness (early-warning systems, ability to estimate losses during a disaster). Improved understanding of policy and coordination requirements for city and necessary interventions for target areas. Long term: Marking yearly budget for disaster risk management, planning new development to avoid hazard-prone areas, policy/attention for target areas (land use, zoning, building codes, etc); structural measures to reduce risk, insurance, adaptation measures for institutional structure, including long-term climate change risk in retrofitting infrastructure, livelihood, and community-based programs for adaptation.

(continued next page)

TABLE 2.1 *continued*

Urban risk assessment	Tasks	Link to climate change	Objectives/benefits to local government
Tertiary	Financial capacity assessment for institutional delivery of resilience building programs.	Costs of climate change adaptation defined and prioritized.	Short term: Planning for disaster preparedness (early-warning systems, ability to simulate losses during a disaster event). Improved understanding of city's financial capacity to administer large-scale adaptation program. Municipal capacity strengthened in use of output from probabilistic risk assessment software.
	Regular assessments and streamlining of web-based application showing areas and population at risk (of individual houses and buildings).	Adaptation strategies for key affected sectors (for example, tourism and transportation) and regions of city developed.	
	Probabilistic risk modeling platform (for example, CAPRA), detailed house-level information on structural vulnerability.		Long term: Structural and nonstructural measures defined to reduce impacts of disaster risk and climate change impacts. Well-positioned for negotiating fiscal transfers for climate change.
	Household surveys of vulnerable areas.		

Figure 2.3 Levels and Pillars of Urban Risk Assessment

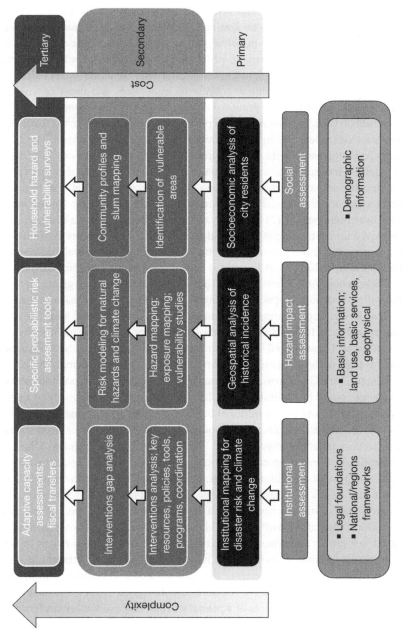

Source: Authors.

The URA allows for undertaking assessments at different levels of complexity based on a city's overall goal and resources. Each city is unique and will have different needs with regard to increasing resilience to natural hazards and climate change. Their development priorities might be different—some may emphasize improving the built environment, while others may seek to improve institutional capacity for reducing and planning for disaster risk. Generally, a city's size, available human resources, political autonomy, leadership, and financial condition will drive the priorities and potential directions for city development.

Based on the identified needs and priorities defined within a city's fiscal capacity, cities can select the most appropriate level of risk assessment. At the *primary* level, the assessment will require minimal resources and can help cities to (1) identify hazard-prone areas and basic climate change challenges; and (2) plan for disaster preparedness and response. At the *secondary* level, the assessment will require more financial and technical resources to facilitate (1) preliminary early-warning systems; (2) the ability to estimate losses during a disaster; (3) the improved understanding of policy and coordination requirements for disaster risk management; (4) the planning and implementation of structural and nonstructural tools to reduce the risk; and (5) community-based programs for resilience and adaptation. At the *tertiary* level, the assessment will require greater resources but will provide for (1) specific probabilistic tools for assessing risk assessment, to help a city develop advanced policies and programs for disaster and climate risk management, including cost-benefit analysis tools for structural and nonstructural investments; (2) advanced early-warning systems; (3) disaster-response capacity; and (4) large-scale adaptation programs. See table 2.1 for additional details.

The primary URA provides city management with an entry point to assess the challenges posed by natural hazards. It is composed of comparatively straightforward tasks that add only a minimal burden to existing functions of city governments. Cities with few financial resources and high demand or need for rapid preparation planning may consider beginning with the primary URA. This encompasses a mapping of the institutional landscape with respect to disaster risk management and climate change, a geospatial analysis of the historical incidence and trends of hazards across the city, and a broad geo-referenced demographic analysis using census data as a key input. In the long term, the assessment provides information useful to avoid hazard-prone areas when planning new city development and when developing policy for areas at high risk of disasters. Assessment of climate change risks, such as sea-level rise or drought, is limited at the primary level and therefore depends on available secondary information to situate cities within broader regional climate trends. Annex 5 presents a case study incorporating elements of a primary urban risk assessment undertaken in the city of Dakar, Senegal.

The secondary URA is intended to assist cities in targeting their financial resources and risk-reduction programs to the most vulnerable. The secondary level provides for a more refined analysis of each of the principal building blocks of the URA. Institutional strengths and weakness are evaluated and specific mandates, policies, and programs assessed for effectiveness and interagency cooperation. City-specific hazards and exposure are mapped and urban hotspots identified. Hazard risk can then be modeled, along with projected climate change impacts, and merged with maps prepared by those communities deemed at a high level of risk. Annex 6 presents a case study incorporating elements of a secondary URA undertaken in the city of Legazpi, Philippines.

The tertiary URA is designed for cities with substantial need, resources, and technical capacity to carry out assessments and deliver scaled-up programs relating to disaster risk management and climate change adaptation. It is envisioned that these components would be brought together in an Internet-based dissemination platform. Annex 7 presents a case study incorporating elements of a tertiary URA undertaken in the city of Sana'a, Yemen.

Initiating, Undertaking, and Mainstreaming Urban Risk Assessment

The URA is ideally undertaken as a part of a cyclical process of assessing risk, developing and implementing a risk management plan, and monitoring progress in risk reduction. Through its flexible and scaled approach, however, the URA can also be applied in cities without a strategic planning framework. Local governments can initiate the URA in a number of ways: (1) as a part of urban planning, such as during city planning, formation of city development strategies, or city planning exercises; (2) while preparing specific sectoral plans such as transportation, water supply and sanitation, or development of new satellite towns; or (3) as a standalone activity that is later integrated into city development strategies or master plans. Cities without a strategic planning framework can work with national or subnational governments to undertake a URA through specific departments such as those dealing with environment, climate change, water supply and sanitation, building permits, or emergency response. Ideally the URA may be initiated as a part of strategic urban planning and policy process so that it can be mainstreamed with existing urban-management tools and functions. Five steps, each described below, are suggested for carrying out a URA (see figure 2.4).

Figure 2.4 Urban Risk Assessment: Risk Reduction Planning and Monitoring

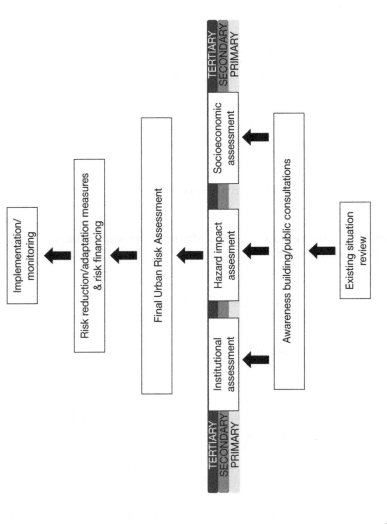

Source: Authors.

1. Reviewing the Existing Situation

a) Review existing national laws and governing framework regarding disaster and climate risk assessment and understand the requirements.
b) Form an institutional framework for undertaking the URA. This may include setting a steering committee consisting of key stakeholders and a team of technical staff that will carry out the risk assessment. Municipal staff members who are already working on land use and other city-planning aspects are most suitable to provide technical support.
c) Decide on the objectives and the level of risk assessment (refer to table 2.1). For example, a city that is exposed to multiple hazards and that would like to develop an in-depth strategy for risk reduction incorporating both structural and nonstructural elements may wish to undertake tertiary-level risk assessment. At the other extreme, a city with relatively few hazards and few financial resources may wish to start with the primary-level assessment and later move toward a higher-level assessment depending upon needs and resource availability.
d) Determine the extent of city area to be assessed. This may include focusing on only a specific area or the entire urban metropolitan region, as well as the fringes or peri-urban area.
e) Evaluate data, financial, and technical-skill requirements depending upon the level of risk assessment. Also, determine the availability, suitability, and quality of data to be collected and identify possible sources.
f) Leverage required financial and technical resources for risk assessment, as data collection and analysis can be time consuming and heavily resource dependent.

Data Acquisition and Management

Cities are undergoing fundamental changes to overall data collection and publication as their economic and political stature increases globally. However, for most of the cities in developing countries, collecting reliable and timely data is a challenging task. While the importance of sharing hazard and risk data is increasingly being recognized, there are still many obstacles to achieving this in practice. Commonly cited barriers include the absence of recognized standards and best practices related to sharing, nascent awareness and understanding of the importance and economic value of sharing data, misaligned institutional incentives precluding the sharing of data, inadequate technical expertise, and lack of simple, affordable tools.

In response to the need for reliable data for credible risk assessment and effective policy and decision making, the World Bank and the Global Facility for Disaster Reduction and Recovery (GFDRR) have launched the World Bank's Open Risk Data Initiative (OpenRDI). This recently launched initiative commits to open data to promote transparency, accountability, and improved decision making. By working with open-source software communities to build the tools necessary to share data, OpenRDI is encouraging and facilitating countries and cities to open their disaster risk data to enable more effective decision-making.[2] An example of OpenRDI is haitidata.org. It is built using the free and open-source software platform "GeoNode," and makes risk assessment data produced following the 2010 Haiti earthquake free and open for anyone to download and use. These types of emerging data-sharing platforms have a wide array of potential applications for both national and city governments and provide a ready solution to the disparate holding of important datasets for risk reduction.

The following questions are important to consider:

- Who will collect the data and how?
- When and how many times does the data need to be collected?
- Is it more cost effective to gradually build datasets from existing mechanisms, or to initiate a standalone activity?
- Where should the data be stored so that it is easy to update and is accessible to all stakeholders?

2. Building Awareness and Public Consultations

It is important that city governments recognize the value of involving the public in URA planning to strengthen its eventual implementation and monitoring and to assist in defining feasible programs for reducing risk. Engaging with community groups and nongovernmental organizations to provide necessary inputs to a URA has importance not only for the data and maps they help generate, but also for the support provided in identifying and acting on risk and vulnerability. Public consultation will support the credibility of the assessment, increase awareness of prevalent risks, and help identify potential actions that would contribute to reducing communities' vulnerability. A number of steps are suggested as part of this process:

a) **Sensitize key stakeholders to the basic concepts of disaster risk management and climate change adaptation through workshops and information sessions.** Participants of these meetings would ideally be composed of a broad range of stakeholders, including municipal staff engaged in urban planning and environmental services, disaster preparedness and response, water supply and sanitation services, civil defense, fire departments, and health services. To promote visibility and engagement on these issues, the private sector, insurance companies, university staff, and community leaders should also be included.

b) **Organize training on the linkages between urban growth, disaster risk management, and climate change adaptation.** During the training, the various components and steps of the URA can be tailored to reflect existing institutional capacity, as well as availability of pertinent information and financial resources of the city.

c) **Deliver an ongoing public information program to promote citizens' awareness of risk and the corresponding work being undertaken by the city government.** The information program may specifically target schools, colleges, hospitals, senior citizen residences, and low-income communities to assist the most vulnerable people in preparing for disasters.

3. Undertaking and Disseminating the Final Risk Assessment

The details of selecting the appropriate level of the risk assessment, inclusive of hazard impact, institutional, and socioeconomic components, are explained in Chapter 3. Once there are findings from each pillar, it is useful to disseminate the information to key stakeholders in a user-friendly way.

4. Assessing the Level of Acceptable Risk

Once the risk assessment has been completed, city governments can either ignore the risk or decide to manage it by (1) controlling processes and behaviors that generate new risks (for example, through better zoning and enforcement of building standards); (2) reducing existing risk (for example, through infrastructure strengthening; or (3) preparing for an event (for example, through contingency planning and the strengthening of civil-protection mechanisms). Risk management cannot be the responsibility of the city administration alone. Engaging civil society in the development of the URA can help engage city residents in developing plans for risk management and ensuring their buy-in. To do this, it is important to create a debate on the level of acceptable risk, as agreements on this matter will affect decision making. The public consultations undertaken in Step 1 of the URA, as well as city planning exercises, can help in understanding and defining acceptable risks.

5. Implementing and Monitoring the URA

Once the URA is developed, it may be necessary to establish legal and institutional arrangements to implement the action plan, including authorizing a body for enforcing and monitoring the action plan. After the end of each planning cycle, or after a disaster, it is useful to review the effectiveness of the action plans so that the policies or action plans can be revised. Risk indicators can be used to review progress in strengthening a city's resilience.

Challenges in Undertaking the URA

Among the challenges faced by city managers in planning and undertaking a URA is the need for various technical skills, financial resources, political support, and the extent to which the information collected actually represents reality.

Furthermore, in many cities the collection of needed data, the integrity of that data, and the capacity to use and interpret different formats of that data can be problematic. As part of the review exercise described in Step 1, the following challenges should be taken into account:

- **Specialized technical skills:** Although existing technical capacity can be used for undertaking a primary-level URA (with some training), specialized technical skills are required for components of higher-level risk assessments such as flood or seismic risk assessment.
- **Financial allocation for risk assessments:** While the primary-level URA would require minimal financial resources, the associated costs of the tertiary-level URA can be beyond a city's budget for developing urban-management tools. Specific resources will have to be identified to initiate and sustain efforts toward risk assessment and risk reduction.
- **Data collection and interpretation:** Collecting reliable, accurate, and timely data remains a daunting task in many cities. Even if the data is available, it may be with different organizations or agencies using different data formats.
- **Extent to which assessment methodologies represent the actual situation:** Community consultation-based assessment (primary-level risk assessment), while more cost effective, may not be accurate enough to plan for structural reduction of disaster risk. Available risk modeling and climate change projections also have large uncertainties associated with them.
- **Gaining and maintaining political support:** It may be difficult to gain necessary political support to initiate and mainstream the URA. Priorities may change with a change of leadership, leaders may focus more on other pressing issues and there can be vested interests in not disseminating results of a risk assessment to a city's population.

Notes

1. Adopted from UN-HABITAT (2007).
2. http://www.gfdrr.org/gfdrr/openrdi

Reference

UN-HABITAT. 2007. *Enhancing Urban Safety and Security: Global Report on Human Settlements 2007.* London: Earthscan.

3

Pillars of the Urban Risk Assessment

Chapter Summary

- This chapter focuses on the three pillars of the Urban Risk Assessment.
- The hazard impact assessment focuses on understanding hazard trends, and identifying populations and physical assets at risk of future hazards and impacts from increased climate variability.
  - At a primary level, the assessment is based on developing simple maps of hazard impacts, showing locations of historic disasters in a city with current population and assets in those areas.
  - At a secondary level, the hazard impact assessment involves estimating impacts for selected hazard scenarios based on simplified loss models.
  - At a tertiary level, the hazard impact assessment involves probabilistic risk modeling to show the potential for population and economic losses resulting from a range of hazards.
- The institutional assessment aids in developing an effective institutional policy for managing disaster and climate change risk.
  - At a primary level, institutional assessment involves mapping institutions and organizations that are explicitly responsible for addressing all the phases of disaster risk management (risk preparedness, disaster response, post-disaster reconstruction, and risk reduction and climate change adaptation) and climate

risk management. The particular focus is on those institutions that can provide the inputs to the hazard impact assessment above.

  ○ At the secondary level, the institutional assessment develops an inventory of planning instruments, including the technical capabilities of staff, the services and outputs provided from one agency to another, policies, projects, and programs.

  ○ At the tertiary level, the institutional assessment focuses on a gap assessment of current city services, management tools, policies, and programs.

• The socioeconomic assessment focuses on indentifying the geographic location and degree of urban residents' vulnerability.

  ○ At a primary level, the socioeconomic assessment identifies demographic, housing, welfare, human development, and investment variables to understand the impact of poverty, and environmental degradation on disaster and climate change risk.

  ○ At a secondary level, the socioeconomic assessment develops a comparative ranking of areas based on qualitatively codifying selected variables within areas of the city.

  ○ At the tertiary level, the socioeconomic assessment provides more refined and detailed analysis at the community level based on household surveys on issues of hazards and vulnerability.

Hazard Impact Assessment

The hazard impact assessment focuses on (1) understanding hazard trends, (2) identifying populations and physical assets at risk of hazards and climate change in a city, and (3) quantifying potential impacts of future hazards. The primary-level assessment is based on secondary data collection and stakeholder consultations to develop simple maps of hazard impacts showing where hazards have historically affected a city. At a secondary level, more detailed risk maps are developed, and scenarios of economic and social loss are defined based on impact modeling. The tertiary level involves modeling probabilistic risk through using different hazard scenarios to approximate economic loss for exposed physical assets. Annex 9 describes each module required to construct a probabilistic risk model.

The following preliminary actions form the basis of undertaking the hazard impact assessment:

(1) Defining the study area and time horizon

It is important to define the study area to set limits of the assessment. Depending upon available resources, a city may choose to assess the entire city area, or to focus on only a part of the city. The time horizon is equally important to consider. Given that increased climate variability will be accompanied by greater frequency and intensity of extreme events, city governments may consider adopting longer time horizons for the hazard impact assessment (that is, for infrastructure design, which, depending on the asset, spans 50 to 100 years), over traditional city planning time horizons (spanning 20 to 30 years).

(2) **Initiating data collection to identify hazard trends** and, when possible, estimating economic (damage to infrastructure and losses) and social (number of people affected) impacts of these disasters. The assessment should identify the areas where disaster impacts were concentrated within a city, their duration and frequency, and the resulting damages. Supporting datasets may be available from weather stations and the departments of meteorology, environment, past municipal records, and city libraries. Detailed case study analysis of past disasters is also useful, and a number of international databases such as EMDAT, DesInventar, and Munich Re's NatCat provide documentation of past events in selected cities. Regional and national databases should also be used to compile any available disaster-related information, and in parallel information collected on average annual temperature, rainfall, droughts, or heat waves. The compilation of these various datasets will assist city governments in understanding the extent to which climate change may be contributing to the incidence and frequency of hazards.

(3) **Assessing climate risk**
Tools are available to map potential climate change impacts at regional or national levels (annex 13). Although an understanding of climate risk for a city will involve downscaling global and regional circulation models, this down-scaling would also require significant improvements in modeling the physical processes to make the models appropriate for city-level investigation. Given the existing limitations in modeling at a scale applicable to cities, trends at the national and regional level will, as a minimum, provide a useful indication of potential climate change impacts. Therefore, this component of the assessment seeks to respond to the following questions:

- What is the nature and extent of current and future climate risks in the area of interest?
- What is the degree of uncertainty?
- What coping strategies are being used to deal with current climate variability?
- How sensitive and vulnerable are key sectors (such as transportation, tourism, water supply) to changes in climate variables in the study area over the assessment period?

TABLE 3.1
Characteristics of Hazards, Assessment Data Requirements, and Disaster Risk Reduction Tools

Types	Measurement/characteristics	Data required to assess hazard risk	Disaster risk reduction tools
Floods	Intensity and frequency of floods	Topography (Digital Elevation Model), drainage patterns, built-up areas, land use and landcover, historical rain gauge data	Flood plain management (including environmental land use regulations), resettlement of vulnerable populations, structural measures to reduce the risk of flooding (dam, channelization, etc.)
Cyclone and storm surge	Maximum sustained wind and radius to maximum wind at landfall, central pressure from water column, height of storm surge waves	Topography (Digital Elevation Model), drainage patterns, bathymetry, land use and landcover, historical rain gauge data	Evacuation planning, coastal zone management, development of building codes for wind and wave loading
Earthquake	Magnitude expressed on Richter scale, ground shaking measured based on damages	Information on soil, geology and liquefaction[1] potential to develop geological, seismic, and soil maps	Better physical planning (e.g., zoning according to soil stability), building codes that are seismic resistant, retrofitting infrastructure and buildings
Tsunami	Wave height, inundation run-up	Topography of coastal areas (DEM), bathymetry, location and capacity of any flood-protection infrastructure	Evacuation planning, coastal zone management

Hazard	Characteristics	Data requirements	Risk reduction measures
Drought/water scarcity	Water and food availability per capita	Surface temperatures, precipitation, reservoir capacity and actual volume stored	Reforestation, water retaining and ground water recharge practices, less water-intense agricultural practices, rain water harvesting, better water management
Sea-level rise, tidal flooding	Wave height, horizontal pressure from water column	Topography of coastal areas (Digital Elevation Model, DEM), bathymetry, tide gauge data, coastal land subsidence data	Coastal zone management
Volcano eruption, lava flow	Pyroclastic and ash fall, explosiveness of volcano, horizontal pressure of lava flow	Topography, Proximity of the volcano from people and assets	Structural measures to block lava flow, moving the population away from possible lava flow areas
Landslides, mud flows and lahars; rock and rubble fall	Failure of slopes with mass movements, horizontal pressure of mud flows, vertical or side impact of rock debris	Topography (DEM), geological data, landcover. land use	Structural measures to reduce impacts (e.g., retaining walls), zoning regulations, resettlement of vulnerable populations
Fire	High temperature and combustion	Topography, wind, land use, landcover	Building codes for fire safety, accessible routes for fire trucks

Source: Adapted from Ehrlich et al. (forthcoming).

Note:
1. Soil liquefaction describes the behavior of soils that, when loaded, suddenly suffer a transition from a solid state to a liquefied state, or having the consistency of a heavy liquid.

(4) **Conducting focus group discussions or interviews with key officials and citizen groups** to identify historical hazard trends and new risks that the city may be exposed to due to its growth pattern. Irrespective of the availability of secondary data on historical hazards and climate trends, a focus group discussion or interview with agencies involved in record keeping of weather information will be useful in understanding the impacts of past disasters, as well as the area and population affected. Information and personal accounts pertaining to the number and intensity of disasters, areas and specific population groups prone to recurrent disasters, and other contributing factors (for example, whether the event was the result of natural causes or manmade causes) should be noted. The following questions may serve as a guide to these discussions:

- What is the general trend in temperature and rainfall patterns?
- Is hazard risk or climate variability increasing at the city level?
- Are areas of urban expansion commonly exposed to hazards?

Once specific information on historic and expected future hazard trends has been compiled, the potential hazards that affect the city can be geo-referenced and used as an important input to risk mapping.

(5) **Assessing exposure of people and physical assets.** A review of current urban planning practices, land use changes, or the master plan can provide good information on settlement patterns and define which areas and populations within the city are exposed to hazards or the potential impacts of climate change. Various factors contribute to people settling in high-risk areas. These factors include existing urbanization patterns, land-use and zoning policies, in-migration of rural or poor migrants, and the availability of land for developing new settlements. The location of important physical assets such as roads, water supply and sanitation networks, drainage canals, electricity and telephone lines, and hospitals should also be included in this assessment and equally geo-referenced where possible.

(6) **Assessing vulnerability.** Building on the historical hazard analysis, it is possible to estimate the degree of physical vulnerability or the potential damage that an exposed asset or community may incur in a given event. As a starting point, city officials may consider determining which areas have a high concentration of people living below the poverty line, which buildings in the city are old or of poor quality, whether the city has an early-warning system and mechanisms in place to support its effectiveness, and the extent to which the development pattern of the city avoids hazard-prone areas.

Primary Level: Developing Simple Risk Maps

Risk maps identify specific urban areas, infrastructure, and populations at risk of disasters and climate change impacts. The following steps are suggested in their development:

i. Develop (or collect if one exists) a base map showing city boundaries, major infrastructure (roads, water supply, sanitation, sewerage, bridges, docks), land use, major community buildings (religious, markets, historic), critical infrastructure (hospitals, fire stations, police stations, government offices), and major environmental areas (coastline, wetlands, water bodies, conservation areas and brown fields).

ii. Overlay the socioeconomic profile on the base map of the city, including population density, vulnerable populations (senior citizens, poor households, women-headed households), and economic activities (commercial zones, fishing areas, farming areas, hotels, tourist facilities, cultural heritage sites).

iii. Develop a spatial hazard profile detailing the historical hazard analysis on past disasters and anticipated climate change impacts.

iv. Identify areas within the city where human actions have increased disaster risk. This activity includes identifying buildings located in hazard-prone areas (slopes, floodplains), their use (residential, commercial, industrial), and construction quality. Satellite imagery can also be reviewed to identify hazard-prone areas and buildings.

v. Overlay the city's projected growth and development maps (usually available in the master plan) to identify areas of high risk.

Identifying spatial correlation of hazards and elements exposed in these various data layers provides the city government the means to identify "hot spot" areas and, depending upon the resolution of the map, critical infrastructure and buildings. The analysis can be undertaken with the aid of paper maps, or in a Geographic Information Systems (GIS) platform, depending upon the capacity and resources of the municipality.

If GIS or paper maps are not available, community consultation involving urban planners, community groups, and key municipal service employees can be a useful alternative to define land use, environmental features (for example, river, drainage channels, wetlands), landmark buildings, infrastructure, houses, and other physical assets of the city to develop simple sketch maps. On these more basic maps, areas historically affected by hazards and socioeconomic information can still be combined to graphically depict hot-spot areas. Land-use maps are usually available from city governments, but these are often outdated in many developing cities. Once the hot-spot areas are identified, the value of the built environment can be calculated to a rough order of magnitude of possible physical losses as a result of a disaster. Similarly, the number of people affected can be defined based on population densities. See annex 5 for an example of this type of assessment in Dakar, Senegal.

Secondary Level: Developing Loss Scenarios through Simplified Impact Models

Building on the historical hazard and climate review, this level includes a detailed assessment for each type of hazard that the city is exposed to and identifies the location and characteristics of buildings and other infrastructure that may be damaged during disasters (see figure 3.1, in the color section).[1] The following steps are suggested to estimate loss and other impacts from hazards:

(i) **Undertake built-up, land-use/land-cover, building area, and building height assessment.**

If the city has information on built-up, land-use/land-cover, building area, and height assessment, the information can be used for estimating exposure characteristics of the city and can then be used in combination with appropriate vulnerability models (see next step). If such information is nonexistent or old, remote sensing and GIS can be used to assess the built-up area, number of buildings, individual building areas, and height (see table 3.2). Importantly, given that remotely sensed data is collected at a distance and is imperfect, results must be calibrated through "ground truthing," a process that supports the accuracy of image data against real features and materials found on the ground of a given location.

(ii) Define a building typology and associated vulnerability curves.

The degree of potential damage to a structure can be measured through vulnerability curves, which measure damage percentages at different levels of hazard intensity (see figure 3.2). To develop vulnerability curves, the city's building stock should first be classified using a building typology. Local engineers and architects should be consulted for defining building typologies and developing appropriate vulnerability functions.

Multiple classification systems of building types can be adapted to a given city, which will ultimately provide a general standardization of types of common construction based on existing information and opinions provided by local working groups (Cardona et al. 2010). The United States Geological Survey's Prompt Assessment of Global Earthquakes for Response (PAGER) building typology and inventory (Jaiswal and Ward 2008) (see annex 15), for example, was used for urban residential building types in Ethiopia (table 3.3). In general, building material, size, height, age, geographical

TABLE 3.2
VHR Satellite Imagery, Remote Sensing, and GIS to Develop Built-up Area Maps

Steps to develop building level built-up area map	How it is done	Comments
Step 1: Develop built-up area map The built-up area of a city consists of buildings and infrastructure (transportation, drainage, water supply, communication systems, etc.).	Urbanized area can be delineated from satellite imagery using automated computer techniques (built-up area index) using very high resolution (VHR) satellite imagery at 1:10,000 or larger scales.	Land-cover maps provide information at or smaller than a 1:25,000 scale; land-use and built-up area maps provide information at 1:10,000 or larger scale.
Step 2: Assess number of buildings Showing building footprints or building as "points" on a map	Computer algorithms can be used to develop built-up area maps. However, manual maps have less error than algorithm-generated maps. A cartographer can input points for each building seen on VHR imagery or digitize building footprints. The assessment provides an approach to quickly estimate the number of buildings in an area.	Ground verification and other sources of information are required in developing density of buildings, cost of construction per square meter, and building use.
Step 3: Assess building area and height Building area and volume are important for developing damage scenarios for any hazard.	Building footprint maps (developed in step 2) can be used to estimate density, space between buildings, area of ground floor, and proximity to roads and other visible infrastructure. The area of a building can be derived from the building footprint. The height of a building can be estimated using specialized software to process stereo imagery (two images of the same area, one slightly offset). Alternatively, a building's shadow can provide some indication of height when time of day and date of image acquisition are known, though to date this method has limited accuracy.	Use of ground surveys and old or available maps can be helpful in estimating areas and general heights of buildings in specific parts of the city.

Source: Deichmann, U. et al. (2011).

Figure 3.2 Sample Vulnerability Curves

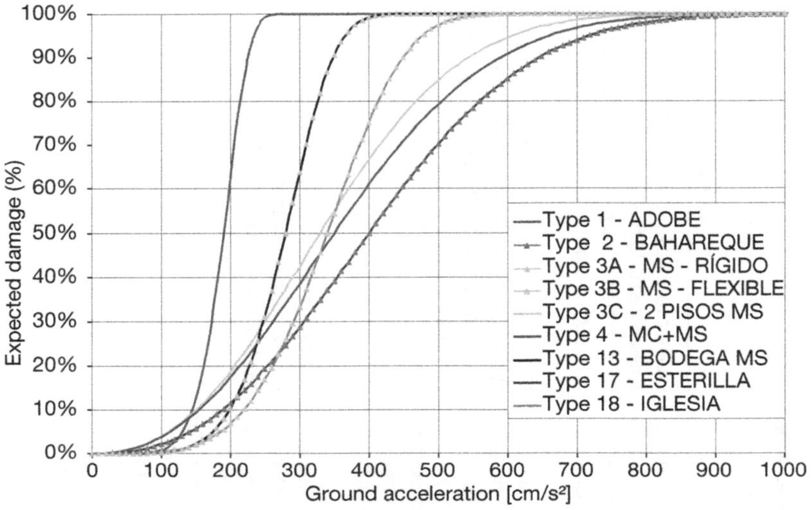

Source: Cardona et al. (2010).

TABLE 3.3
Sample Building Classification

PAGER label	Description
W2	Wood frame, heavy members, diagonals or bamboo lattice, mud infill
RS3	Local field stones with lime mortar; timber floors; timber, earth, or metal roof
RS2	Local field stones with mud mortar; timber floors; timber, earth, or metal roof
UCB	Unreinforced concrete block masonry, lime/cement mortar
C3	Non-ductile reinforced concrete frame with masonry infill walls
INF	Informal constructions (pasts of slums/squatters)
UFB	Unreinforced fired brick masonry
A	Adobe block (unbaked dried mud block) walls

Source: Jaiswal and Wald (2008).

setting, and the settlement's historical growth can provide useful indications for assigning a building's classification.[2]

With building typology defined, it is possible to calculate vulnerability curves by using distinct approaches, each of which has associated challenges and limitations. The Global Earthquake Model[3] suggests the following four possible approaches for calculating vulnerability functions:

- **Empirical:** Uses regression analysis to derive vulnerability functions from past observations of loss experienced by buildings of a particular type.

Empirical relationships have a strong degree of credibility and as such this approach provides a high standard of vulnerability functions.
- **Analytical:** Uses first principles of structural engineering to make reliable predictions of outcomes and to relate damage and loss to hazard intensity. Analytical techniques can produce valuable insight into the vulnerability of buildings where empirical data is insufficient.
- **Expert opinion:** Uses judgment of recognized experts familiar with the building type of interest to produce a vulnerability function. It is an efficient approach to estimating vulnerability, and can be valuable in the absence of empirical loss data and where insufficient resources are available for the analytical approach.
- **Empirical-national:** In this approach, vulnerability functions are developed for entire countries, or large sub- and supranational regions, without regard to building type, to best fit past loss data.

(iii) **Combine hazard, exposure, and vulnerability information to develop indicative loss and damage scenarios for potential hazards.**
Vulnerability models that relate the intensity of the hazard with the ensuing damages for specific classes for structures can be developed. The damages are reported on the y-axis and expressed on a ratio scale of 1 percent to 100 percent, where the expected loss is a percentage of the total value of the structure. A damage ratio of 100 percent means that the expected loss equals or exceeds that value of the structure. The x-axis shows the range of intensity associated with the hazard and is scaled to capture the minimum damage to the weakest structure to the highest damage to the strongest structure. Using the defined building typology and associated vulnerability curves in combination with hazard and exposure data, a simplified risk map can be developed at varying levels of detail.

The vulnerability curves for different classifications of building types can then be used to estimate total damage and losses, and based on the percentage of damage to buildings, the exposed population. An important consideration in the damage and loss assessment is the difference between valuation of formal infrastructure (houses and buildings) versus informally built construction found in low-income settlements. See the case study of Legazpi, Philippines (annex 6), for an example of this approach.

A major shortcoming in disaster risk assessments for many developing countries, however, is the unavailability of vulnerability for different housing typologies and hazard profiles. This problem is due largely to significant proportions of the building stock being informal and to damages not being recorded in a systematic manner. Field visits that record building stock and relative damages in disaster-affected areas can therefore be used to indicate vulnerability of a city's building stock.

Tertiary Level: Modeling Disaster and Climate Risk

Probabilistic risk modeling techniques are widely used by international insurance/reinsurance industry and capital markets to assess risk to asset portfolios to a range of hazards. With advances in computer modeling and GIS technologies, probabilistic risk modeling techniques can be applied to assessing a city's exposure to disaster risk in a meaningful and practical manner. Probabilistic risk models are built upon a sequence of modules that allow for quantifying potential losses (in financial terms) from a given hazard (figure 3.3).

This component of a risk assessment includes the collection and analysis of underlying hazard data to produce a probabilistic event set and to define the localized/downscaled hazard conditions (for example, elevation, soil type, bathymetry). With low-frequency events such as earthquakes, it is particularly important to engage in a robust probabilistic analysis of the hazard. This will yield a characterization of the hazard that extends beyond the limited or incomplete historical record of observed events. Probabilistic hazard models allow for quantifying the impacts of climate change on disaster occurrence. Historical event catalogues, such as the information contained in DesInventar, are still important in hazard modeling as the source of validation benchmarks. The most valuable validation data are hazard measurements or observation points from historical events that can be used to test downscaling algorithms, which are used to produce event footprints. Key outputs from a detailed hazard analysis are a probabilistic event catalogue defining the frequency and severity of possible events in addition to multiple geospatial datasets defining local site conditions impacting the event footprints.

Using the combination of existing land use datasets, topographic models, and improved analysis of land use from satellite imagery, current and future land use can be evaluated to more accurately define the hazard resulting from a natural

Figure 3.3 Probabilistic Catastrophe Risk Model

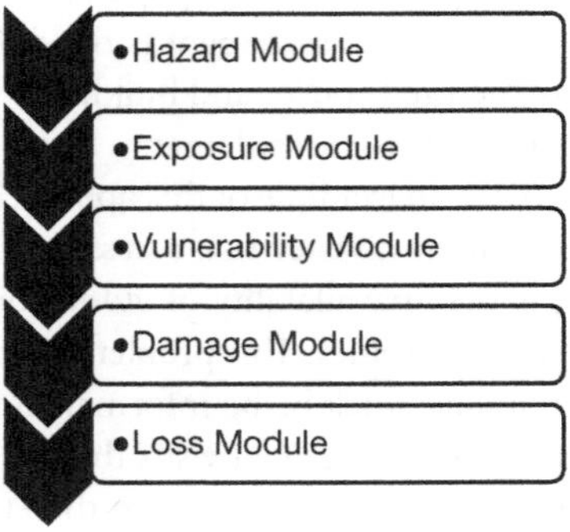

- Hazard Module
- Exposure Module
- Vulnerability Module
- Damage Module
- Loss Module

Source: Cummins and Mahul (2009).

Figure 3.4 Barcelona Physical Seismic Risk

Damage Index
ID = 0.0 - 2.5
ID = 2.5 - 7.5
ID = 7.5 - 15.0
ID = 15.0 - 30.0
ID = 30.0 - 60.0
ID = 60.0 - 100.0

Source: Barbat et al. (2010).

event. The value of this capability is being able to project future land use and examine the impacts of activities and policies in risk mitigation. Annex 9 presents a detailed discussion of each module. See the case study of Sana'a, Yemen (annex 7) for an example of probabilistic risk assessment.

Probabilistic Risk Assessment Software: Linking Remote Sensing, GIS, and Open-Source Platforms

The main objective of introducing an existing software platform for probabilistic risk assessment or creating a city-specific program is to provide city management with an analysis tool for risks that can be used to model losses from future events. Such platforms provide the user with various probabilistic risk maps for identifying vulnerable areas dependent on the severity of the hazard. The identified hazard can then be applied to assess damage to structures using vulnerability functions that quantify the expected damage to structures in response to the hazard. See box 3.1 for an overview of the Comprehensive Approach for Probabilistic Risk Assessment (CAPRA).[4]

To support the evolution of such software, and with a forward-looking view of technological advancements in this area, documentation of the source code as well as the functionality of the platform should be available. The following list captures considerations in developing software for probabilistic risk assessment:

- The platform should be suitable for distribution and future use.
- The platform should be designed as a set of modular components for incorporation in a larger risk analysis system to be developed in the future.

BOX 3.1

Comprehensive Approach for Probabilistic Risk Assessment

The CAPRA initiative started in January 2008. It is a partnership led by the Centro de Coordinación para la Prevención de los Desastres Naturales en América Central (CEPREDENAC), in cooperation with the United Nations International Strategy for Disaster and Reduction (UNISDR), the World Bank, and the Inter-American Development Bank. The CAPRA methodology applies the principles of probabilistic risk assessment to the analysis of hurricanes, earthquakes, volcanoes, floods, tsunamis, and landslides. CAPRA's platform integrates software modules related to hazard, vulnerability, and risk modeling at different levels and resolutions in accordance with the nature of hazards, the available information, and the kind of problems to be resolved.

The platform provides users with tools to analyze magnitude, distribution, and probability of potential losses due to each of the defined hazards. These metrics are projected on a Geographical Information System (CAPRA GIS) that allows for visualization and analysis. In the absence of such evaluations, governments encounter major obstacles to identify, design, and prioritize measures to reduce risk.

The hazard assessment is carried out by generating stochastic events that: (1) have different magnitudes, (2) have different frequencies of occurrence, (3) correspond to historical observed trends of recurrence of the hazard under analysis, and (4) represent the possible events with different intensity in different geographic locations.

At the core of CAPRA is the commitment to be an open and transparent platform. CAPRA promotes the use of standard data formats established under the Open Geospatial Consortium (OSG), allowing for maximum interoperability with existing systems. Also, it allows users to build their own application, using all or part of CAPRA, upon the platform, enhancing the functionality of the software.

CAPRA has strong potential for broad application in cities, as it allows for creating a dynamic database of exposure of infrastructure, buildings, and population (figure 17). It also contains a library of vulnerability functions (see Section 4.2.1) for a wide typology of structures in each of the six hazards and is capable of assessing the effect on population based on building uses.

- A simple user interface should be developed.
- Outputs should present the results in datasets that can be used in subsequent modeling.
- Open-source models should be used to the extent possible.

Tools for Screening Climate Risk

In addition to probabilistic risk modeling, tools are available to map potential climate change impacts at regional or national levels (see annex M). Although a robust understanding of climate risk for a city will involve downscaling global and regional circulation models, obtaining the required spatial resolutions for cities remains a challenge. As a starting point, taking into consideration national and regional trends in which the city is situated will provide a good indication of potential climate change impacts. These trends can derive projections for 50- to 100-year scenarios and are usually described in terms of average temperatures, intensity and duration of heat and cold waves, total seasonal and annual rainfall, extreme heavy rainfall, drought, and spatial and temporal rainfall distribution.

Planning tools can enhance the capacity of city managers or project developers to understand and integrate climate change into future planning. The most effective risk planning tools encourage users to focus on the conditions, assumptions, and uncertainties underlying the results of climate models to enable them to estimate the robustness of the information, make an informed assessment of current and future risks, and evaluate the appropriateness of response options. In particular, screening tools are generally able to provide information on some or all of the following aspects: (1) current climatic trends and projected future climate change in specific geographical areas; (2) vulnerabilities of local natural systems and communities to current or projected climate-related impacts; (3) climate-related risks on specific sectors or project activities; and (4) possible adaptation options.

Institutional Assessment

Undertaking an institutional assessment is relatively straightforward, but can require substantial data gathering. Understanding a city's institutional landscape with respect to climate change, disaster risk reduction and management, and poverty should be part of identifying climate change-related vulnerabilities and coming up with the best and most cost-effective approaches to reducing them. This will strengthen a city's understanding of how climate change affects service

delivery and ultimately support streamlining risk management across municipal
agencies. The following steps are suggested as part of the institutional assessment:

Primary-Level Institutional Assessment: Institutional Mapping

(i) **Identify which institutions and organizations are explicitly responsible for addressing climate change and natural hazards, and those that
have a more indirect involvement.** Given that disaster risk management
and climate change adaptation cut across most sectors, institutional mapping that takes into account both function and interaction of government
and nongovernment entities is advisable (table 3.4). Considering that no
city is a territorial, isolated unit, it is relevant to consider the national and
regional contexts the city is linked to. In order for a city to understand
its institutional landscape, it is important to take into account the existing
administrative and political arrangements in which the local government
is situated. This requires a closer look to the planning instruments that are
in place, including policies, programs, plans, and strategies, and is further
elaborated in the secondary level of the urban risk assessment.

This component of the assessment therefore specifically seeks to respond to
the following questions:

- Which agencies are involved in any field of disaster risk management or
climate change adaptation?

TABLE 3.4
Suggested Institutions for Mapping

Institution type	Indicative function
National offices and ministries	Responsible for emergency management, disaster risk manage-ment, and urban development
State offices	Responsible for emergency management and "green" develop-ment, industrial parks, parks and recreation, historic conservation offices, and finance departments
City offices	Responsible for climate change and disaster risk management. These departments and office may be for sustainability, works and engineering, housing, water and sanitation, emergency manage-ment, transportation, energy, and finance. Departments of health and education should also be included for their role in supporting resilience and structural integrity of schools and hospitals.
Private sector	Chambers of commerce and industrial boards
Civil society organizations	International nongovernmental organizations, and academic and technical support institutions

Source: Authors.

- How are they involved? What is their function?
- How are the agencies or institutions active in the different fields of disaster risk management and climate change related to each other?
- What policies, laws, projects, and tools are available to these agencies or institutions?
- Which agency can play a lead role in coordinating all the other agencies involved? Does it have sufficient financial, technical, and human resources to undertake such a job? Does it have a legal backing?

(ii) **Undertake an institutional mapping exercise** that includes all major government agencies within the city and delineate specific responsibilities before, during, and after a disaster. A similar exercise can also be undertaken for climate risk assessments. A sample template for mapping relevant institutions and agencies related to disaster risk management is presented in table 3.5. Under the secondary-level URA, the institutional analysis is further elaborated with a more in-depth investigation of policies, programs, and internal structures of concerned agencies to assess effectiveness of coordination across agencies.

Secondary-Level Institutional Assessment: Interventions Analysis

(iii) **Create an inventory of relevant planning instruments, including existing policies, programs, plans, and projects.** This step focuses on the planning documents developed and implemented by the identified institutions and organizations. The exercise will include taking stock of both present and proposed government policies and plans that might directly impact disaster risk. This is important to assessing current city management tools, such as master planning, building regulations and codes, policies for sectors prone to disasters (cultural heritage conservation, water security, drainage, health care facilities, and transportation systems), and plans related to adapting to climate change. Local government budgets should be identified at this stage, in addition to those budgets already committed to disaster risk management or climate change that can be used for strengthening the city's resilience to disasters and climate change.

Rapid Institutional Assessment of City Management Resources and Tools

The World Bank developed the Climate Resilient Cities Primer (2008), which proposes questions to understand a city's institutional landscape and linkages with the planning instruments. These questions assist in identifying and understanding factors that influence a city's adaptive capacity (table 3.6). According to

TABLE 3.5
Sample Institutional Mapping of Disaster Risk Management Functions

Risk assessment	Risk reduction		
	Technical[1]	Early-warning and response[2]	Public awareness[3]
Municipality • Identifying flood-prone areas	**Municipality** • Master plan • Land use/zoning • Building codes • Storm water drainage • Internal roads • Culverts and drainage planning • Implementation and maintenance	**Department of Meteorology and Environment** • Rainfall and flood forecast	**Civil Defense** • Early warning to citizens • Flood awareness
Geological survey • Mapping flood-affected areas;, hydrological modeling	**Ministry of Municipal Affairs** • Approves master plan and budget	**Ministry of Water** • Flood forecast	**Ministry of Social Affairs** • Possible role in preparing citizens for floods
Department of Meteorology and Environment • Mapping land use/land cover • Mapping environmentally sensitive areas	**Ministry of Transportation** • Design and construction of flood-protection structures • Dams • Major roads	**Civil Defense** • Early warning to residents • Fire brigades • Ambulance • Emergency relief • Post-flood compensation	**Ministry of Education** • Possible role in flood-awareness programs in schools and colleges

Universities
- Hydrological modeling
- Identifying flood-affected areas

Water company
- Water treatment
- Water supply
- Waste water treatment
- Sewerage

Red Cross or Crescent
- Fire brigades
- Emergency response

Municipality
- Emergency response
- Restoring infrastructure

NGOs
- Coordinating humanitarian efforts

Local NGOs
- Helping residents after floods

Community organizations
- Community leaders and organizations helping citizens after floods

Note:
1. Agencies involved in land-use and urban planning, environmental management, maintenance and protection of critical infrastructure and facilities, partnership, and networking.
2. Agencies involved in forecasting, dissemination of warnings, preparedness measures, disaster reaction capacities, and post-disaster recovery.
3. Agencies or institutions involved in public-awareness programs and knowledge development, including education, training, research, and information on disaster management.

TABLE 3.6
Rapid Institutional Assessment Questionnaire

A. Governance structure and disaster risk management in the city	
Appointed head of government (Y or N)	
	a. Term of assignment (Years)
Elected head of government (Y or N)	
	a. Term of elected officials (Years)
Local government office structure: Does it have. . .	
	a. Disaster risk management department? (Y or N)
	b. Environment, sustainability, or climate change department? (Y or N)
	c. Are (a) and (b) in the same department? (Y or N)
Other government office structure: Does it have. . .	
	a. Disaster risk management department? (Y or N)
	b. Environment, sustainability, or climate change department? (Y or N)
	c. Are (a) and (b) in the same department? (Y or N)
Responsibilities for disaster risk management and climate change management	
Responsibilities clearly specified? (Y or N)	
Responsibility for climate change management established? (Y or N)	
Responsibility for disaster risk management established? (Y or N)	
Authority to contract for services? (Y or N)	
Existence, capacity, and effectiveness of a city's emergency and disaster response plan	
Does a disaster response system exist in the city? (Y or N)	
Is the response system comprehensive and equipped for all natural hazards specified? (Y or N)	
Is the disaster response system regularly practiced? (Y or N)	
Is the disaster response system regularly updated? (Y or N)	

Source: World Bank (2008a).

the primer, factors include, among others, (1) the local institutional policy and regulatory capacity related to disaster risk management; and (2) climate change through issues relating to land use, building controls, economic strength and diversification, financial resources, infrastructure standards, provision of municipal services, availability of data, and technical expertise in analyzing trends related to hazards. Three question categories that allow for a rapid institutional assessment of city management resources and tools are presented in table 3.6.

Tertiary Level Institutional Assessment: Interventions
Gap Analysis

(iv) **Undertake a gap analysis that identifies shortcomings in current city management tools, and policies programs, and that provides preliminary recommendations to mainstream risk reduction.** A city may then consider ranking appropriate agencies to assess their capacity, in terms of personnel and financial management, to administer new resilience-building programs if discrete adaptation funding were made available through the National Adaptation Programs of Action. Such an assessment better positions city governments to engage national decision-making bodies in discussions of effective resource allocation for climate change or to explore possibilities of receiving fiscal transfers for risk financing.

Socioeconomic Assessment

The socioeconomic assessment focuses on (1) identifying demographic, housing, welfare, human development, and investment variables, and (2) developing comparative ranking of specific areas based on a simple qualitative codification. City managers may consider demographic and housing variables that will contribute to a more robust risk assessment (figure 3.5). Many of these factors, such as housing characteristics, are important inputs for the hazard impact assessment

Figure 3.5 Socioeconomic Considerations for Understanding Risk

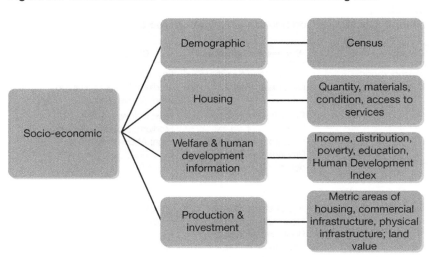

Source: International Development Research Centre (2008).

component of the URA. Collection of housing data should be closely coordinated with the analyses of building vulnerability.

Primary-Level Social Assessment: Analysis of Socioeconomic Data

For the demographic analysis, the assessment can rely on existing data captured through national censuses and household survey information collected through nongovernmental organizations or community-based groups. Suggested demographic variables that indicate relative resilience of a given household include proportion of children and elderly, gender, disabled persons, household literacy, education levels, and proportion of economically active household members. Suggested housing variables that indicate relative strength and integrity of the building will relate to the ability of walls, floors, and roofs to withstand a given hazard, and the building's typical use, for example, type and number of occupants. A simple qualitative codification can be then be applied to aggregated information geospatially referenced to a specific area of the city to signify its comparative ranking (table 3.7).

The collection of *welfare and human development* data at the city level improves understanding of the connection and reinforcement between poverty, disasters, and environmental degradation. Its inclusion in understanding urban risk can contribute to reducing vulnerability at the household level. Because of the economic nature of much of the information, it cannot always be obtained in the desired

TABLE 3.7
Sample Qualitative Codification of Neighborhood Data

Category	Suggested indicators	Classification	Value
Neighborhood characteristics	Construction density Occupant density	Low: Below average Medium: Equal to average High: Above average	1 2 3
Household resilience	Proportion of children Proportion of elderly Proportion of disabled Proportion economically active Literacy rate Education level	Low: Below average Medium: Equal to average High: Above average	1 2 3
Housing quality	Age of structure Floor material quality Roof material quality Wall material quality	Low: Below average Medium: Equal to average High: Above average	1 2 3

Source: Adapted from International Development Research Centre (2008).

spatial detail to comply with national data policies. In the absence of detailed data, and using the Human Development Index as a guide, it is suggested that the following variables be considered: average income (per capita or household), median income per capita (which is less affected by extremes of information), life expectancy at birth, and literacy rates (as proxy for education and poverty rates).

In considering variables related to *production and investment* within a city, the built environment often constitutes a major proportion of urban investments and, as such, detailed information is often available. The number of square meters built is a useful indication of investment levels and economic activity; using estimated costs of construction per square meter, an approximate value of the built environment can be obtained (table 3.8). In addition to the data regarding the built environment, associated land values will play an important role in understanding the degree of exposure to hazards that characterize certain parts of a city.

Secondary- and Tertiary-Level Socioeconomic Assessment: Community-Based Approaches

An approach that incorporates both top-down and bottom-up methods will be more robust, and therefore useful, to city governments than either in isolation. Data collected from ground-based methods through community participation can empower local residents, build social capital, and establish a common foundation for neighborhood-level risk assessments. Participatory approaches present opportunities too, enabling communities to have greater control over information and interventions, thereby enhancing their resilience. This in turn generates a debate surrounding whether urban risk assessments should, in fact, be led through bottom-up approaches that place an emphasis on community engagement and household surveys, particularly among the poor or through top-down technological approaches.

There is strong experience in engaging in direct dialogue with the urban poor regarding risk and vulnerability and having them involved in risk mapping. Beyond creating critical spatial data about low-income urban

TABLE 3.8
Production and Investment Variables

Unit	Area (m²)	Cost/m²	Value
Dwellings			
Commercial infrastructure			
Trunk infrastructure			

Source: International Development Research Centre (2008).

areas that would assist in more inclusive city planning, an advantage of this approach is the relatively high accuracy and spatial resolution of data compared to that obtained by aerial or satellite imagery; mapping and enumerations done by federations of slum dwellers have proven to be valuable inputs to analyzing urban risk. In addition, such experiences have helped to validate the existence of the urban poor and provide information to the community and city officials (box 3.2).

BOX 3.2

Field Data Collection and Community-Based Approaches

An increasing number of community-based organizations and NGOs are making use of very high resolution (VHR) images for slum surveys. One example is the work of Shelter Associates (SA) from Pune, India. For SA, VHR images are one of the most important tools for poverty mapping at the city level. Working in close collaboration with residents of slum communities, SA uses VHR images to digitize slum boundaries and attach fact sheets containing data that has been compiled by quick surveys in slums to register key information about the households, their dwellings, and the overall site characteristics. Their Pune slum census covered over 100,000 households in over 200 slum pockets scattered throughout the city. Settlements were mapped by professional agencies using plane table methods to produce large-scale slum maps showing plot and building boundaries, while residents engaged in household surveys, gaining knowledge and skills on data collection and a better understanding of their community's problems, its opportunities, and the planning process.

The spatial and socioeconomic data is entered into a GIS database and spatially analyzed for direct use by the communities to prepare upgrading plans and to negotiate with local government authorities on policy and developmental issues. The process therefore contributes to community empowerment by enabling them to be fuller partners in settlement upgrading and in the subsequent management of their community. The same approach within the Municipal Corporation of Sangli Miraj Kupwad has led to initiating a holistic approach to improve all slum pockets. SA and communities are engaged with the local administration and elected members for drawing up an action plan for slum improvement. As a result of these community-based approaches, many slums have been mapped and plans for their improvement have been produced in a cost-effective manner.

Source: UN-HABITAT, ITC, Ceisin (2008).

It is important that city governments recognize the value of raising public awareness of climate change and the need for disaster mitigation. Engaging with community groups and nongovernmental organizations to provide necessary inputs to an urban risk assessment has importance not only for the data and maps they help generate, but also for the support provided identifying and acting on risk and vulnerability.

Community groups can make important contributions to the urban risk assessment, each with increasing levels of field work: collection of detailed information regarding the physical condition of neighborhood houses and structures, digital enumeration of slums ("heads-up digitizing"), and household surveys. As described previously, features such as building height, structure material, and roof shape can be challenging to define in densely populated urban areas from remotely sensed data. The engagement of local residents in collecting this information is therefore an important entry point for collaboration between city governments and community groups.

To facilitate such an approach, the International Space University developed a prototype of an iPhone application that could be adapted to any smart phone and used by community groups (figure 3.6). The appeal of this approach lies in recognizing the extensive reach that cellular telephones have made into slum areas

Figure 3.6 Screenshots from iPhone® Application Prototype

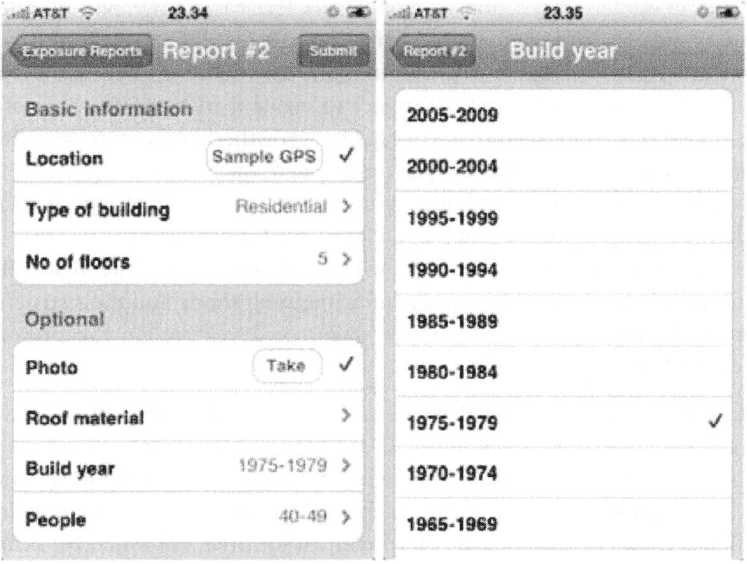

Source: International Space University (2009).

in developing countries. The application allows a user to quickly and easily generate simple reports about individual buildings that include the current position (provided by the phone's built-in Global Positioning System, or GPS), the number of floors, the building type (residential, office, store, etc.), and other optional parameters such as roof material, estimated construction year, and a picture of the building (taken with the phone's camera). These applications can now be delivered very quickly—often in the span of just a few days—thereby providing an interesting and potentially cost-effective approach for cities to consider for slum mapping.

Notably, many community residents might have access to a cell phone but not to a smart phone, and this is where the integration of SMS capabilities into a community reporting system could be valuable. This would allow for increased community participation and, although using SMS might not provide detailed reports, it would be the source of relevant information such as the current condition of important infrastructure within the community.

With the rise of freely available software and open-source platforms, the potential to streamline slum mapping and include issues of risk and vulnerability have been notably enhanced. The proliferation of handheld GPS devices and open-source technologies for mapping supports the role of communities in data gathering. Digital enumeration of slums can be undertaken using selected base maps (for example, Bing Maps) and open-source GIS programs that can be downloaded at no cost. The first step would be creating settlement profiles of informal areas, which may include slum address or location, legal status, land ownership, approximate year of establishment, housing conditions, hazards, topography, number of houses, population and population density, services, and infrastructure.

One tool useful to cities in implementing the use of such approaches is Open-StreetMap (OSM), a collaborative project to create a free editable map of the world. OSM was established to encourage the growth, development, and distribution of free geospatial data. The maps are created using data from portable GPS devices, aerial photography, and other sources such as local knowledge. Both rendered images and the vector graphics are available for download.

As part of the development of the urban risk assessment, the World Bank produced a prototype of this approach for mapping slums and their structures (figure 3.7). Although in preliminary stages of development, the prototype application features:

- Slum Sketch (hand-sketched plan), which is geo-referenced and visualized over a base map that can be removed or added.
- A set of plotted houses that, when clicked, load a form for inputting household data. Information from the household questionnaire on the incidence of hazards and perceptions of risk (presented in annex 14) would be included in addition to details about the structure or house. Other community

Figure 3.7 Digital Slum Mapping: World Bank Prototype

Source: Authors.

features such as manholes, electricity and telephone lines, water stands, and community toilets could be included and, in collaboration with the appropriate city departments, GIS base layers (for example, streets, waterways, topography and hydrology) could be included to give the maps additional context.
• A multimedia option for viewing a video clip or picture of the settlement or household.

The process described above for digital slum enumeration could be done in parallel or in sequence to more detailed data collection (both quantitative and qualitative) at the household level on both historical exposure and perceptions of risk. Through focus group discussions and individual and household surveys on the historical incidence of small localized disasters and local adaptation measures, this more time-intensive step should assist residents of informal areas in communicating and negotiating with city government for necessary investments to improve living conditions and reduce vulnerability and risk.

In considering community stakeholders in undertaking an urban risk assessment, it should be recognized that residents of low-income areas of many cities have endured the threat of eviction or destruction of their homes given that they are frequently located on public lands. On the one hand, the use of new technologies to map slums and associated collection of household information may be met with suspicion, and might actually act as a barrier to their participation and support. Yet on the other, the pace of new technology use in city management points to a need for communities to have a central role in settlement mapping that will increase the authenticity of collected data.

Notes

1. This level is derived from Deichmann, U. et al. (2011).
2. See Deichmann, U. et al. (2011), for full discussion.
3. http://www.globalquakemodel.org/risk-global-components/vulnerability-estimation/ activities.
4. www.ecapra.org.

References

Barbat, Alex H., Carreño, Martha L., Pujades, Lluis G., Lantada, Nieves, Cardona, Omar D. and Marulanda, Mabel C. (2010). Seismic vulnerability and risk evaluation methods for urban areas: A review with application to a pilot area, *Structure and Infrastructure Engineering*, (pages 1–22, January 2009), Volume 6, Issue 1&2, February, pages 17–38, Taylor & Francis, London.

Deichmann, U., Ehrlich, D., C. Small, and G. Zeug, . 2011. *Using High Resolution Satellite Information for Urban Risk Assessment*. European Union and World Bank.

Jaiswal, K. S., and D. J. Wald. 2008. *Creating a Global Building Inventory for Earthquake Loss Assessment and Risk Management*. U.S. Geological Survey Open-File Report 2008–1160.

UN-HABITAT, ITC, Ceisin. 2008. *Expert Group Meeting on Slum Identification and Mapping*.

World Bank. 2009. *Preparing to Manage Natural Hazards and Climate Change Risks in Dakar, Senegal*. Washington, DC: World Bank.

4

Conclusion: From Risk Assessment to Action Planning and Implementation

Chapter Summary

- This chapter highlights the importance of carrying out an Urban Risk Assessment as input to developing adaptation and risk-reduction plans in cities.
- Pilots of the URA in four cities point to key lessons learned about the importance of ensuring that findings are integrated into risk-reduction planning.
- The information collected and used for a URA is useful in many municipal functions, such as urban planning and policy, new building and infrastructure approvals, building codes and zoning, infrastructure and building upgrades, and environmental planning.
- Plans for climate change adaptation and disaster risk reduction are most effective when mainstreamed into urban planning and management efforts.

Introduction

URAs provide a foundation for building long-term sustainable risk reduction plans that address a city's vulnerabilities to natural hazards. These assessments are structured to improve the knowledge base and increase the capacity to deal with short- and long-term hazards that any given urban environment may face. The key to making a URA successful is the transition from completing the assessment to creating and implementing a risk-reduction plan, using the knowledge gained and the catalytic nature of the assessment. The action plan will ideally address the key risks raised in the URA, while at the same time begin the process of mainstreaming risk reduction in municipal planning and service delivery. Completion of a URA, defining the action plan and mainstreaming risk-reduction measures, should not be considered as three discrete elements but rather as a process toward a common end.

In the context of the Mayor's Task Force on Climate Change, Disaster Risk and the Urban Poor, URAs have been carried out in Dar es Salaam, Jakarta, Mexico City, and São Paulo in 2010–2011 (World Bank 2011). These risk assessments have identified key issues for the cities, and compiled data related to climate change, disaster risk, and vulnerable groups for the first time. Annexes A through D summarize the highlights identified in each of the risk assessments. In each case, action planning has been initiated based on the risk assessment and selected follow-up activities are under way.

The experience from these cases point to several lessons, in particular related to carrying out a risk assessment. In all four cities, the process itself has been equally important as the results. The main lessons include:

   i. High-level support from the mayors and heads of key agencies was essential in giving priority and support to the work. Identifying focal points within the lead agencies was key to ensuring accountability and getting the work done.
  ii. The analysis carried out through the risk assessments has highlighted the close linkages in the agendas for disaster risk reduction and climate change adaptation, particularly in the context of the urban poor, and supports integrating the two fields in urban planning and decision making.
 iii. In all of the cities, an interagency working group was set up to carry out the risk assessments. This included agencies working on urban development, service provision, poverty reduction, disaster management, and climate change. In some cases, this was the first time these agencies worked together, which has identified needed synergies for initiating adaptation planning. However, it is unclear that these interagency working groups will be sustained without a more formal working arrangement.
  iv. In some of the cities there was a disconnect between knowledge at the institutional and community level. This was addressed by involving city officials in site visits to poor neighborhoods, and in two cases involving stakeholders in the workshops. Communicating in a language that all stakeholders understood was fundamentally important. In that regard, producing materials in a simple format and local language was important for communicating results. In Jakarta and Mexico City, short films have been produced for broader dissemination of key messages.

v. Across the four cities, accessing data, maps, and climate projections was problematic. Information was scattered across many different agencies, departments, organizations, and research institutions, and to complicate the process further, some agencies were reluctant to share data. Enormous effort went into collecting the information that was made available. To benefit from and sustain this effort, setting up a permanent institutional "home" to maintain and update this interagency information in each city would be valuable.

vi. The risk assessments were perceived as a useful framework for understanding climate change, disaster risk, and impacts on residents. The multidimensional approach to assessing hazard impact, socioeconomic vulnerability, and institutional capacity brought together key issues in a holistic manner. However, this was only the first step. Stakeholder workshops held in all of the cities were useful in discussing key issues, but follow-up will be needed to integrate these findings into planning for adaptation and interagency risk reduction.

Developing Action Plans: Lessons from Vietnam and New York City

The ability to use a URA to create an action plan is critical to risk reduction, and its value will ultimately be judged through actions on the ground. Developing action plans is an in-depth process involving many stakeholders and can be a complex task. While a full detailed discussion of the steps involved is beyond the scope of this document, the summary included here points to key references.

Vietnam illustrates where the national government in cooperation with the World Bank has created standard procedures that local officials can use to develop action plans. The approach, the Local Resilience Action Plan (LRAP), is being carried out in the cities of Hanoi, Dong Hoi, and Can Tho (World Bank 2010b). The LRAP is a planning document that helps a city to assess alternative adaptation and risk-reduction options, with economic assessment of the costs and benefits of each. The action plan will result in strategic short- (less than 1 year), medium- (1 to 3 years), and long-term (more than 3 years) structural and nonstructural measures to increase resilience and reduce disaster risk. Ideally such plans would then be mainstreamed into broader urban planning and management practices.

Stakeholders work to establish priorities, highlighting those actions most critical to undertake in relation to the available funding and capacity for implementation. Other factors such as financial feasibility, political and technical complexity, social issues, and distributional and equity issues are also considered. Once priorities are established and an action plan is developed, detailed plans are prepared for each project (ranked by priority), including objectives, cost parameters, and a plan of implementation. When considering implementation, the city may decide to treat risks differently in different areas of the city, with the following options: (a) eliminate or avoid, (b) transfer or share (example through insurance), (c) mitigate (through structural interventions), and (d) accept and manage the risk.

This plan of implementation ideally addresses issues such as institutional coordination, sequencing of actions, budget, communications for implementation, and monitoring and evaluation.

New York City provides an alternative example of moving from risk assessment to action planning to implementation. In 2008 Mayor Michael Bloomberg tasked the New York City Climate Change Adaptation Task Force with developing a plan to increase the resilience of the city's critical infrastructure. The task force was composed of 40 city, state, federal, and private-sector infrastructure operators and regulators with the goal of identifying climate risks to the city's critical infrastructure and develop strategies to mitigate these risks.

Once the risks analysis was completed, an extensive process of identifying, developing and prioritizing actions was carried out. The task force focused on improving current buildings, amending building design and other regulatory codes as well as the strategic placement of public facilities. It adopted a risk-based approach to climate action, and uses Flexible Adaptation Pathways to address the anticipated risks, compensating for the uncertainty of climate impacts (NYCPCC 2010). The task force was supported by a panel of technical experts, which was also convened by the mayor.

The city also launched a pilot community engagement and planning process with vulnerable communities. Five workshops were held in partnership with community-based organizations to educate residents about the risks posed by climate change and begin local resilience planning and action. The city's comprehensive sustainability plan (PlaNYC), which is the driving force behind New York City's adaptation actions, was updated in April 2011 and built upon the pilot to better inform and engage New Yorkers on climate change.

Key Policy Areas: Lessons from England, Turkey, Kenya, and Colombia

The Greater London Authority released a draft of the London Climate Change Adaptation Strategy in 2010 in response to the evolving nature of risk associated with increased climate variability. With the aim of providing a framework to identify and prioritize risks and then to deliver actions to reduce or manage them, land-use planning was placed at the center of the climate-adaptation strategy with the objective of incorporating local actors such as municipal governments, community groups, and the private sector (Greater London Authority 2010). Based on scientific projections that southeast England will experience warmer, wetter winters and hotter, drier summers, the strategy identifies three areas of risk that need to be addressed and prioritized them accordingly: flooding (high risk), drought (medium risk), and overheating (high risk). Actions proposed to address these risks included promoting land-use planning to improve the understanding and management of flood risk and developing an urban greening program to help absorb floodwater. To implement this strategy, spatial land-use planning will be critical to determine where development should not occur, where existing structures should be removed, and where development that fits the vision for a given city should be located. In making these decisions, it is important that no significant interferences with natural processes should occur.

The Istanbul Metropolitan Municipality created a Strategic Plan for Disaster Mitigation in Istanbul (SPDMI) to reduce seismic risk focusing on building codes and disaster-resistant construction. Regulations that consider the use of proper building materials, building orientation, insulation, and ventilation can improve a structure's physical resilience, enhance public health, and increase energy conservation. The SPDMI identified abundant bureaucratic obstacles in construction, and a lack of coherent building codes, which encouraged both illegal development and substandard construction. In Istanbul, some 80 percent of buildings are occupied without the correct permission, with buildings having been altered without the necessary legal documentation (Metropolitan Municipal Authority of Istanbul 2003). Compliance with building codes can be facilitated if the codes are clear, concise, and relevant and if they are governed by incentives that make them attractive to administrators, architects, builders, contractors, and homeowners.

In Kenya, most building codes in the 1980s existed from the colonial era, making them outdated in an evolving urban environment. Therefore, a house built to the minimum acceptable level according to the codes was out of reach financially for many of the urban inhabitants and new innovative building designs were not permitted. In 1990, these building codes were redefined with the participation of various stakeholders, resulting in Code 95. This code is performance-based, and permits the use of innovative and popular materials and alternative building technologies (World Bank 2010b). However, work is still required to simplify approvals and establish incentives.

The island city of Tumaco, Colombia, is one of the country's most impoverished and vulnerable urban areas. The city is exposed to risks of sea-level rise, earthquakes and tsunamis, and ensuing liquefaction from poor soil composition. The city can be accessed by only two bridges at opposing ends of the island, but in recognition of the potential need to evacuate the city, investments were made in widening the shortest bridge to accommodate greater pedestrian and

Figure 4.1 Tumaco, Colombia

Source: Google Earth.

vehicular mobility, and evacuation simulations are run periodically. The case of Tumaco demonstrates that urban planning, or its lack, can play an important role in deciding what is built, as well as where and how, and influencing the relative degree of risk faced by urban residents.

Institutions and Governance

As with carrying out a URA, planning for risk reduction covers a range of areas, including spatial development and land management, environmental management, economic development, municipal service provision, waste management, and infrastructure development. Institutions and governance therefore play a role in the ability to manage the transition from completing the URA and creating an action plan to implementing the plan.

No two cities are exactly alike, nor will any two URAs be the same. The transition following the URA will vary from city to city depending largely on the institutions and governance of the particular city. The role of other stakeholders, such as utilities, the private sector, the urban poor, and NGOs, also has to be considered. It is the interplay between all of these actors within the political and legal framework of the city that creates the environment in which the action plan for disaster reduction will be developed. It is important to take an approach with the aim of the "development of a single governance framework for risk reduction would seem to offer opportunities for more effective policy implementation and for avoiding duplication and lack of coordination" (UNISDR 2009).

There are also instiutional and governnance issues at the international level in planning for adaptation. Given the scope of needs related to climate change, new funding such as the Green Fund are under discussion within United Nations Framework Convention on Climate Change (UNFCCC) negotiations. How best to allocate this potential funding is not yet defined. At national levels, similar to Nationally Appropriate Mitigation Actions, countries are encouraged to develop National Adaptation Programmes of Action. These NAPAs prioritize potential adaptation actions across a country.

A similar intiative at a city level may be warranted. If so, a common framework to aggregate and compare adaptation actions would be needed. These local NAPAs can be predicated on a URA as outlined in this report. Climate change is encourgaing consistency in local planning and presentationa; a credible URA meets these demands and also enables a city to monitor the impact of efforts to reduce risk.

BOX 4.1

Aspects of a Good Urban Risk Assessment

- Follows a simple hierarchy (process) and applies consistent terminology
- Combines disaster and climate risk management
- Incorporates multisector inputs from city agencies
- Is integrated within overall city functions (and regional circumstances)
- Makes use of community involvement and encourages participation from the urban poor
- Identifies urban areas historically vulnerable to hazards
- Identifies urban areas subject to new and intensifying risks
- Provides detailed inputs to preparation of local resilience action plan
- Makes use of open-source and freely available technologies
- Is structured to facilitate broad support and engagement from the insurance industry
- Results in enhanced understanding of roles and responsibilities of city agencies and communities

References

Greater London Authority. 2010. *The London Climate Change Adaptation Strategy, Draft Report*. London: Greater London Authority. http://www.london.gov.uk/climatechange/strategy.

Metropolitan Municipality of Istanbul Planning and Construction Directoriat Geotechnical and Earthquake Investigation Department. 2003. *Earthquake Masterplan for Istanbul*. http://www.ibb.gov.tr/en-US/SubSites/IstanbulEarthquake/Pages/Istanbul EarthquakeMasterPlan.aspx.

New York City Panel on Climate Change. 2010. "Climate Change Adaptation in New York City: Building a Risk Management Response." In *Annals of the New York Academy of Sciences*, vol. 1196, ed. C. Rosnezweig and W. Solecki. Wiley-Blackwell.

UNISDR. 2009. *Global Assessment Report on Disaster Risk Reduction*. Geneva: United Nations.

World Bank. 2010a. *Safer Homes, Stronger Communities: A Handbook for Reconstructing after Natural Disasters*. Chapter 10. Washington, DC: World Bank.

———. 2010b. *A Workbook for Local Resilience Action Planning in Vietnam*. Washington, DC: World Bank.

———. 2011. *Climate Change, Disaster Risk and the Urban Poor: Cities Building Resilience in a Changing World*. Washington, DC: World Bank.

Annex 1: Dar es Salaam Case Study

Overview and Key Findings

More than 70 percent of Dar es Salaam's 5 million residents live in informal, unplanned settlements that lack adequate infrastructure and services, and over half of them survive on roughly a dollar per day. With a population growth rate of about 8 percent per year, Dar es Salaam is one of the fastest-growing cities in Sub-Saharan Africa. City and municipal authorities face significant challenges with respect to providing new or even maintaining existing infrastructure and services.

The summary of this case study presents the first comprehensive overview of the intersection between climate change, disaster risk, and the urban poor in Dar es Salaam. It seeks to understand (1) what are the key aspects of the vulnerability of the urban poor in the city; (2) how climate change increases this vulnerability; and (3) which policies and programs can be developed that reduce the vulnerability of the poor, taking both current and expected future climate change into account.

The case study is a joint work among the World Bank, the Institute of Resource Assessment of the University of Dar es Salaam, Ardhi University, the Tanzania Meteorological Agency (TMA), International START Secretariat, and the Dar es Salaam City Council.

The approach used in this case study is based on the Urban Risk Assessment (URA) framework. Accordingly, it includes an assessment of the hazards, socioeconomic vulnerabilities, and institutional aspects related to climate change and disasters in Dar es Salaam.

First, the case study reviews available published information on Dar es Salaam's demographics, access to infrastructure and basic services, and climatic trends and projections. Second, it conducts a household-level socioeconomic survey on populations living in flood-risk areas. The survey is complemented by on-site observations and inspection of surroundings, as well as focus-group discussions with residents. Third, the study interviews relevant institutional representatives. Finally, a flood-modeling exercise is conducted, which maps the potential changes in rainfall regime and sea-level rise and models flooding impacts in those highly vulnerable areas covered in the socioeconomic surveys.

Key Findings of the Study

- Rapid unplanned urbanization in Dar es Salaam has led to flood risk in many informal settlements, with a wide range of associated health and other problems for residents.
- Disaster risk management has not been addressed and needs to be integrated in all aspects of urban planning in Dar es Salaam.
- The ecological and hydrological role of wetlands is not well understood or incorporated in urban development planning.
- The sustainability of infrastructure development initiatives and their maintenance is poor.

- Coordination among local stakeholders is needed.
- Industries need to be relocated away from residential areas and will require access to a waste-stabilization pond.
- Awareness-raising programs are needed at the community level for improved sanitation practices.

The Government of Dar es Salaam at Work

Despite the number of challenges that Dar es Salaam is facing, the government has been supporting key initiatives in areas such as coastal management, slum upgrading, and greenhouse gas mitigation. For instance, the Kinondoni Integrated Coastal Area Management Project (KICAMP) formulated a comprehensive plan on the management of land and water resources in coastal areas. This project resulted in banning the excavation of sands in critical areas to prevent further beach erosion along the coastal area. Households are being made aware of the value of mangroves and are involved in their protection; combined with heavy protection from KICAMP, this has led to increases in mangroves. The government has also invested recently in sea walls on highly susceptible areas to sea-level rise, storm surges, and coastal erosion such as Kunduchi beach and Bahari beach.

Another example of the government at work is the Community Infrastructural Upgrading Program (CIUP), which improves physical infrastructure such as storm-water drainage networks and strengthens the capacity of communities to better help themselves, especially those living in unplanned settlements.

On the mitigation side, the Dar es Salaam City Council has shown great leadership by closing the Mtoni solid-waste dumpsite and, in collaboration with a private company, created mechanisms for tapping and flaring the gases produced at the dump and recovering costs through clean development.

Key Constraints

Key constraints in dealing effectively with climate change, disaster risk, and the urban poor include:

DATA—The lack of high-resolution digital maps is a limitation for comprehensive risk assessment.

INFORMATION SYSTEMS—Significant increase in revenue generation is needed to ensure both increased service coverage and quality of services, particularly taking into account the additional resilience needed to reduce the risk posed by climate change for the city. Priorities in meeting the challenges include improving information systems (databases) and updating valuation rolls; optimizing the potential of property tax and simplifying the development levy; and developing vigilant collection strategies and more enhanced law-enforcement capacity.

LIMITED CAPACITY—Limited capacity hinders progress in dealing with climate change, natural disasters, and urban poverty reduction. For instance, at the community level, it is important to build capacity on the link between unsanitary waste-disposal practices, stagnant water, unclean drinking water, and disease. At the same time, environmental committees and community-based organizations need to be trained about organized waste collection and its link to reduced vector/insect breeding and disease.

At the local level, research capacity needs to be built to better understand the likely impacts of climate change in the long term for the poor of Dar es Salaam. In the city planning departments, it is important to build a common understanding of the long-term sectoral impacts of climate change for Dar es Salaam.

At the national level, the capacity of the Tanzania Meteorological Agency needs to be improved in weather and climate monitoring, including in more accurately predicting severe weather and extreme climatic events, and in analyzing and interpreting data. Improvements are also needed in disseminating alerts and early warnings.

Finally, links need to be forged and enhanced between climate experts and journalists to ensure effective dissemination of information on climate change.

Main Information Gaps Identified

This case study has been a first step in taking stock of what has already been done in terms of comprehensive risk assessment of informal settlements in Dar es Salaam. An important finding is that laws related to Urban/Town Planning and Settlement need to be reviewed to ensure they deal adequately with vulnerability and risk. It is also important to determine how existing environmental and pro-poor policies and laws can be better enforced.

The case study recommends conducting an in-depth analysis of cost-effective adaptation in light of changing socioeconomic and climatic trends in the city. Furthermore, sectoral case studies with an emphasis on the urban poor should be conducted in order to examine future needs, for a 20- to 30-year timeframe, on drainage, water supply, waste management, housing, and health planning, among others. Such case studies should involve teams of local institutions as well as relevant international institutions with advanced technical expertise.

Looking Forward

The case study suggests that the best starting point for reducing vulnerability to climate change in the future is to reduce present vulnerability, such as by reducing threats to health by improving city drainage and environmental sanitation. The case study also captures key areas for further collaborative work moving forward:

- Support for public agencies to improve waste collection, drainage, water, and sanitation programs. Although all municipal agencies are required to comply with and implement the National Environmental Policy and the National Environmental Act, often they lack the funding needed to meet the responsibilities entailed, or the supervision capabilities to counter actions that contravene city laws and bylaws.
- Integrate disaster risk management in urban planning. Guidelines for disaster risk reduction should be mainstreamed in the preparation of schemes for general planning, detailed planning, detailed urban renewal, and regularization.
- Support public health programs. Cost-effective mass-treatment programs need to be implemented for Neglected Tropical Diseases (NTDs) and more efforts also need to be put into integrated approaches to control malaria, rather than relying solely on the distribution of nets treated with insecticide. Improvements to drainage systems and their regular maintenance will go a long way toward reducing flooding and consequent ponding and stagnation of water, thereby reducing breeding sites.
- Support Clean Development Mechanism (CDM) activities. Dar es Salaam should seek further CDM support in expanding and scaling up the City Council's existing plans to manage solid waste.
- Support existing successful urban upgrading programs. These have great potential, as they involve communities in identifying problems and solutions

and cover a wide array of physical and institutional measures to improve urban areas.

- Encourage a long-term planning horizon. Adaptation planning for Dar es Salaam's poor residents should address their present urgent needs and those to come, given expected future impacts of climate change.

Case Study Summary

City Profile

Figure A1.1 Administrative Map of Dar es Salaam

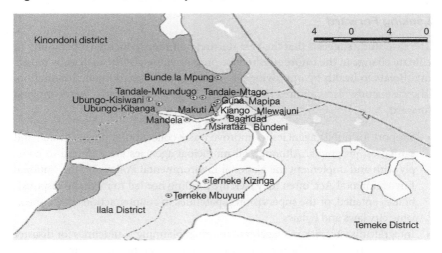

Dar es Salaam is located in the eastern part of the Tanzanian mainland at 6°51'S latitude and 39°18'E longitude. With an area of 1,350 square kilometers (km²), it occupies 0.19 percent of the Tanzanian mainland, stretching about 100 km between the Mpiji River to the north and beyond the Mzinga River in the south. The Indian Ocean borders it to the east. The beach and shoreline comprise sand dunes and tidal swamps. Coastal plains composed of limestone extend 10 km to the west of the city, 2 to 8 km to the north, and 5 to 8 km to the south. Inland, alluvial plains comprise a series of steep-sided U-shaped valleys. The upland plateau comprises the dissected Pugu Hills, 100 m to 200 m in altitude. Dominated by limestones, sandy clays, coarse sands, and mixed alluvial deposits, the soils of the Dar es Salaam region are not particularly fertile (Dongus, 2000). The city is divided into three ecological zones, namely the upland zone consisting of hilly areas to the west and north of the city, the middle plateau, and the lowlands, which include the Msimbazi Valley, Jangwani, Mtoni, Africana, and Ununio areas.

TABLE A1.1
Dar es Salaam

Total city population in 2002	2.5 million
	Estimated 5 million in 2020
Population growth (% annual)	4.39 (city mayor's statistics, 2006)
	8 (World Bank 2002)
Land area (km²)	1,590
Population density (per hectare)	1,500
Country's per capita GDP (US$)	1,300 (2007)
Date of last Urban Master Plan	2010

Built Environment and Basic Service Provision

An estimated 70 percent of Dar es Salaam's population lives in poor, unplanned settlements (World Bank 2002). Residents are usually too poor to pay for services or infrastructure and authorities too resource-constrained to maintain these; thus, health and environmental conditions are generally extremely poor. About half the residents of Dar es Salaam's informal settlements live on an average income of US$1 per day and in constrained circumstances. Many are migrants from other parts of Tanzania in search of better opportunities.

Access to clean water and sanitation are major problems for Dar es Salaam's poor, and contribute to widespread illness, including cholera, malaria, lymphatic filariasis, and diarrhea, particularly during floods, which could be more severe or frequent in the future due to climate change.

Up to about 75 percent of the residents of Dar es Salaam's informal housing settlements are unemployed or under-employed (World Bank 2002), with the main source of income for the latter group being through informal activities and micro-enterprise. Employment in Dar es Salaam as a whole declined from 64 percent to 42 percent between 1992 and 2000, and self-employment rose from 29 percent to 43 percent. Poverty for those in self-employment rose from 29 percent to 38 percent over the same period (World Bank 2002).

The city's road network totals about 1,950 km, of which 1,120 km (less than 60 percent) is paved, and is inadequate to satisfy its population density, spatial expansion, and transportation needs. Dar es Salaam hosts about 52 percent of Tanzania's vehicles, and has a traffic density growth rate of over 6.3 percent per year (JICA 1995; Kanyama et al. 2004).

The city's planning agencies have been unable to keep pace with the rapid expansion of the city, largely fueled by migrant growth. Most of the city's population lives in unplanned settlements—many in abject poverty—which are characterized by substandard infrastructure and lack of basic municipal and other services. These communities face transportation constraints, insecure housing, problems accessing clean water, unhygienic sanitation, and lack of awareness on hygienic sanitary practices. Climatic factors, such as heavy rainfall, work in conjunction with this situation to impose additional hardship and increase disease.

Pillar 1—Institutional Assessment

Agencies in Disaster Risk Management and Climate Change Adaptation
Dar es Salaam is managed by the Dar es Salaam City Council and the Municipal Councils of Temeke, Kinondoni, and Ilala. The three municipal authorities are under the Ministry of Regional Administration and local government. Each has individual sets of technical and administrative departments.

The Dar es Salaam City Council (DCC) has a coordinating role and attends to issues that cut across all three municipalities. Its functions are to:

- Coordinate the functions of the three municipal authorities regarding infrastructure.
- Prepare a coherent citywide framework for enhancing sustainable development.
- Promote cooperation between the City Council and the three municipal or local authorities.
- Deal with all matters where there is interdependency among the city's local authorities.
- Support and facilitate the overall functioning and performance of the local authorities.
- Maintain peace, provide security and emergency, fire, and rescue services, ambulance and police.
- Promote major functions relating to protocol and ceremonies.

The municipal councils are responsible for providing basic social services, which include primary education and partly secondary education (especially where the community is involved), primary health care, waste management and cleanliness, district roads, water supply, and monitoring of trade and development, especially informal sector development and management, cooperatives, agriculture and livestock development, forestry, fisheries, recreational parks, and urban planning.

The Tanzania Meteorological Agency (TMA) issues flood warnings for Dar es Salaam. It provides warnings and advisories on extreme rainfall and flooding based on daily weather monitoring. Cloud evolution is monitored through observations and by using satellite pictures. The evolution and pathway of tropical cyclones along the Western Indian Ocean are also monitored on a real-time basis. Warnings and advisories are disseminated to the public as needed, through various stakeholders such as the mass media and the disaster-management department at the prime minister's office. Flood warnings and advisories are given up to a day in advance (24-hour forecast) or at seasonal timescales (up to two months in advance).

Relevant Policies and Legislation

- At national level: National Human Settlements Development policy (2000), National Environmental Policy (1997), Ratification of the UN Framework Convention on Climate Change (UNFCCC) (1996).
- At local level: The Sustainable Dar es Salaam Project and the Strategic Urban Development Plan (SUDP) started in 1992, Community Infrastructural Upgrading Programme (CIUP) started in 2001, and African Urban Risk Analysis Network (AURAN) Project Phases I and II started in 2004.

Ongoing Programs in Disaster Risk Management and Climate Change

- *Rehabilitation of storm water drainage and sewerage system:* City authorities undertook improvements in the city center. However, a new wave of investment has led to construction of new structures in former empty spaces, including the construction of multiple-use buildings that have increased demands for water supply and enlarged high-capacity sewage pipes. The tonnage of solid and liquid waste generated has increased, demanding efficient solid- and liquid-waste management and monitoring services. On occasion, wide and deep storm water drains are appropriated by private homeowners, fenced in as part of their property, and sealed up, which causes waste back-up among poorer neighbors. Laws need to be better enforced and drainage line capacity reassessed. It is important that when this occurs, planners consider the fact that capacity needs are likely to change over the lifetime of the drainage system; the system needs to plan for changing rainfall regimes over the planning horizon, for example, up to 2050.
- *Property formalization in Dar es Salaam:* The government is implementing a project to identify all properties in informal settlements in Dar es Salaam and at the same time issuing land/property licenses or right of occupancy to curb further densification of those areas and to improve security of tenure, which could be used as collateral for economic empowerment (URT 2004 in: Kyessi and Kyessi 2007). This formalization process will be a foundation for the regularization of the slums that will ultimately allow provision of infrastructure including drainage channels for storm water, piped water supply, refuse collection using municipal and private vehicles, sanitation (pit and septic tank

emptying services), secure tenure (loans), improved housing conditions, and reduced overcrowding in unplanned settlements.

- *National Adaptation Programme of Action (NAPA):* Tanzania is party to the UN Framework Convention on Climate Change (UNFCCC) and the Kyoto Protocol and has prepared a National Adaptation Programme of Action (NAPA 2007). The capacity for investing in adaptation activities (protecting vulnerable populations, infrastructure, and economies) is still low due to financial constraints (NAPA 2007). However, NAPA will help in integrating adaptation issues in the development process, guiding development to address urgent and immediate needs for adapting to adverse impacts of climate change. Among other objectives, NAPA aims at improving public awareness on the impacts of climate change and on potential adaptation measures that can be adopted. In Dar es Salaam, activities have included planting trees along the beach, roadsides, near houses, and in open spaces.
- *Management of coastal areas:* Dar es Salaam is a coastal city and climate change is expected to exacerbate vulnerability of poor coastal communities through sea-level rise, possibly more intense coastal storms, and increased rainfall variability. Coastal management projects involve beach conservation, including conservation of mangroves and coral reefs, as well as Marine Park protection. Poverty alleviation, such as facilitation of seaweed farming, is also often included. Some of the city's coastal management projects are noted below. In particular, the Kinondoni Integrated Coastal Area Management Project (KICAMP) aims to formulate a comprehensive plan focused on the use of land and water resources in coastal areas. The project has banned the excavation of sands in Kunduchi-Mtongani as a way to prevent further beach erosion along the coastal area. Households are being made aware of the value of mangroves and involved in their protection, and, combined with heavy protection from KICAMP, this has led to an increase in mangroves. Other civil-society organizations involved in conservation, awareness raising, and environmental management included Roots and Shoots, World Vision, URASU (Uchoraji na Ramani na Sanaa Shirikishi Dhidi ya Ukimwi), and the International Organization on Migration, which helped to form environmental management societies in schools, markets, and dispensaries. Schools had already planted trees and botanical gardens in their compounds. Msasani Bonde la Mpunga is also involved in coastal conservation through a partnership with the World Wildlife Fund (WWF), the Wildlife Society for Nature Conservation, the private sector (running tourist hotels and sea boats), the International Union for Conservation of Nature (IUCN), and Tanzania Marine Park authorities.
- *Sustainable coastal communities and ecosystems:* This USAID-funded project (implemented by Rhode Island and Hawaii-Hilo universities) builds adaptive capacity and resilience among vulnerable coastal communities. The program

has introduced "raft culture" techniques, where seaweed is grown in deeper water where it is less vulnerable to fluctuations in temperature and salinity, enabling beneficiaries to earn a living throughout the year.

• *Construction of adaptive structures in Dar es Salaam:* A comprehensive beach conservation program has been designed that includes the following components: (1) sea walls have been constructed along the front of the Aga Khan Hospital to prevent further erosion of Sea View Road; (2) sea walls and groins have been constructed along some beaches, which benefits hotels by reducing beach erosion and property damage from waves, and also helps fishing community settlements that live near the sea; and (3) land reclamation is taking place along coastal areas, for example, by covering quarry pits with soil and trees and building houses on these reclaimed areas. The Kunduchi-Salasala quarry area is an example.

• *Other:* The country has strengthened multilateral relations at the international level in order to enhance the ability to cope with climate change and variability for sustainable livelihoods. For example, Tanzania and the Kingdom of Norway have agreed to partner to combat adverse impacts of climate change. Under this program, Tanzanian scholars are trained on climate change issues (planning and forecasting), and, as short courses on climate change tend to be publicized through newspapers and on television, awareness is raised among the public on climate change impacts, adaptation measures, and mitigation.

Leading Agencies
Currently, there is not a leading agency coordinating the disaster risk management activities at the local level. There is a lack of coordination horizontally among departments and vertically with national policies.

Pro-Poor Services and Infrastructure Local Expenditure
Dar es Salaam's municipal agencies provide infrastructure and socioeconomic services such as health, water, education, solid-waste management, cooperative and community development, roads, development of natural resources, trade and agriculture and livestock, and information and communication technology development. Despite efforts to improve social services for city dwellers, increased migration and unemployment have made services poor and unaffordable. Rapid urbanization in Dar es Salaam is resulting in growing numbers of the population living in unplanned, densely settled squatter areas with little or no access to social services. Despite purported improvements in fiscal position and revenue collection, improved record-keeping, and enhanced accountability, the Dar es Salaam City Council (including its municipalities) still faces considerable challenges in spending on pro-poor services and on improving infrastructure in unplanned and underserved areas.

Significant increase in revenue generation is needed to ensure both increased
service coverage and quality of services, particularly taking into account the
additional resilience needed to reduce the risk posed by climate change for
the city. Priorities in meeting the challenges include improving information
systems (databases) and updating valuation rolls; optimizing the potential
of property tax and simplifying the development levy; and developing vigilant collection strategies and more enhanced law enforcement capacity (City
Council, undated Brief DSM V2: 6).

Pillar 2—Hazards Assessment

Past Natural Disasters
Dar es Salaam is already highly vulnerable to climatic variability, which is
expected to increase as climate continues to change. The aspect of most frequent
concern to Dar es Salaam currently is heavy rainfall. In combination with poor
drainage, illegal construction, and other infrastructure problems, heavy rainfall results in flooding that causes major losses and disruptions. For the mul-
titudes of the city's population living in informal settlements, poor sanitation
contributes to an additional threat: disease. Diseases commonly occurring in
these congested, unsanitary settlements during floods include malaria, cholera,
dysentery, and diarrhea. Some other factors that contribute to flooding in these
settlements include flat topography, lack of storm-water drainage, blockage of
natural drainage systems, building in hazardous areas, and unregulated housing
and infrastructure development. Livelihood activities are also adversely affected
by both heavy rainfall and drought.

TABLE A1.2
Natural Hazards

	Yes /No	Date of last major event
Earthquake	N	
Wind storm	N	
River flow	N	2010
Floods, inundations, and waterlogs	Y	
Tsunami	N	
Drought	Y	2006
Volcano	N	
Landslide	Y	
Storm surge	N	
Extreme temperature	Y	

TABLE A1.3
Effects and Losses

Hazard	Effects	Losses
Floods	Drainage channels are blocked by refuse throughout the year as well as by structures that hinder the flow of wastewater, causing houses to be flooded by unhygienic, sewage-based wastewater in houses. Major effects are water-borne diseases.	Not available
Drought	Diseases: malnutrition, trachoma, dysentery, cholera, and diarrhea	The drought of 2006 damaged agricultural production, necessitated electricity cuts (and thus drops in industrial production), and cut GDP growth by 1% (ClimateWorks Foundation et al. 2009)

TABLE A1.4
Significant Floods in Dar es Salaam (1983–2006)

Year	Months	Monthly rainfall		
		Long-term mean (mm)	Actual (mm)	% of long-term mean
1983	May	197.8	405.6	205
1989	Dec.	117.8	175.6	149
1995	May	197.8	374.2	189
1997	Oct.	69.3	250.8	361
	Nov.	125.9	152	121
	Dec.	117.8	231	196
1998	Jan.	76.3	107.3	141
	Feb.	54.9	123.7	225
	Mar.	138.1	155.2	112
	Apr.	254.2	319.9	126
2002	Apr.	254.2	569.4	224
2006	Nov.	125.9	240.9	191
	Dec.	117.8	230.4	196

Source: Tanzania Meteorological Agency (2010).

Main Climate Hazards

Temperature trends over the past four to five decades show significant increase. Temperature is projected to increase.

Figure A1.2 Trend of Mean Maximum Temperature Anomalies during Warmest Months (December–February) at Dar es Salaam International Airport

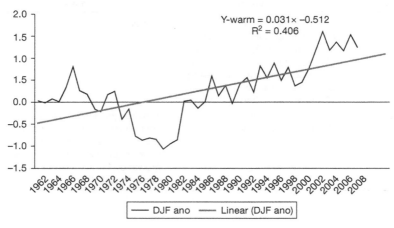

$$Y\text{-warm} = 0.031\times -0.512$$
$$R^2 = 0.406$$

Source: Tanzania Meteorological Agency (2010).

Figure A1.3 Time series of Mean Annual Rainfall in Dar es Salaam

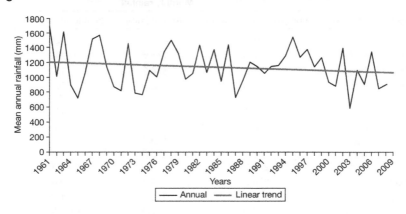

Source: Tanzania Meteorological Agency (2010).

Mean annual rainfall has declined in Dar es Salaam over the past five decades (as recorded at the Dar es Salaam Airport station).

Figure A1.4 shows mean and absolute 24-hour maximum rainfall for the period 1971–2009. Mean 24-hour maximum rainfall ranges from over 50 mm in April–May to 10 mm for July–August. The absolute 24-hour maximum rainfall for the time period studied was recorded within the past decade.

Figure A1.4 Mean and Absolute 24 Hour Maximum Rainfall for Dar es Salaam

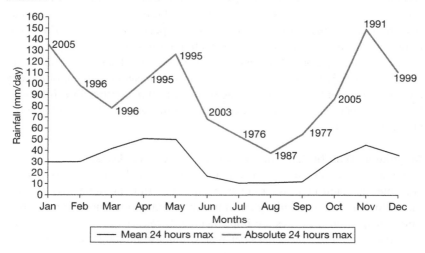

Both rainfall amount and intensity are concerns from the point of view of flooding in Dar es Salaam. Intensity has been increasing in the last 15 years, where rainfall intensity has been well above the 38 years' recorded history. This trend is expected to continue with climate change.

An important projected aspect of climate change is an increase in climatic variability, which would result in more frequent and severe floods and droughts in the city. Given that the city's poor are unable to cope adequately with current variability, their situation is likely to worsen in the future, unless steps are taken to ensure that urban development and poverty reduction specifically take into account the prospect of changing climatic conditions. Infrastructure development and urban planning, municipal services, and poverty reduction (including safety nets and health services) need not only to better integrate disaster risk management, but also to consider that the trends are changing.

Projections of Future Climate

A summary of climate baseline data and severity of dry periods for March–May (MAM) and October–December (OND) are presented in the case study. Under the Special Report on Emissions Scenarios (SRES) A2 emissions scenarios, and data representing 14 of the Global Circulation Models used to simulate the 20th century and future global climate, by mid-century, the coarser-resolution global climate models project that this site will become warmer, with more frequent heat waves. They disagree on whether this site will become wetter or drier. By 2100, mean annual temperature for Tanzania is expected to increase by 1.7°C over the northern coast, including areas around Dar es Salaam. Rainfall intensity is expected to increase. Runoff (precipitation minus evapo-transpiration), a measure of water availability, is projected to increase. The maximum amount of rain that falls in any five-day period (a surrogate for an extreme storm) is expected to increase. The maximum period between rainy days is expected to increase.

Kebede and Nicholls (2010) have analyzed Dar es Salaam's vulnerability to sea-level rise (figure A1.5). They estimate that at present 8 percent of the city currently lies in a low-elevation zone below the 10 m contour line, inhabited by over 143,000 people, with associated economic assets estimated (in 2005) at US$168 million.

Magnitude, Distribution, and Probability of Potential Losses

Although future rainfall patterns are uncertain, variability is likely to increase and intensification of heavy rainfall is expected. Thus flooding may become increasingly severe, particularly taken together with socioeconomic projections, unless adaptation measures are implemented. Increases in mean temperature, combined with fewer rainy days per year, could also prolong the length of dry

Figure A1.5 Exposed Population in Dar es Salaam in 2005, 2030, 2050, and 2070 to a 1-in-100-Year Flood under the A1B Mid-Range Sea-Level Rise Scenario, No Adaptation

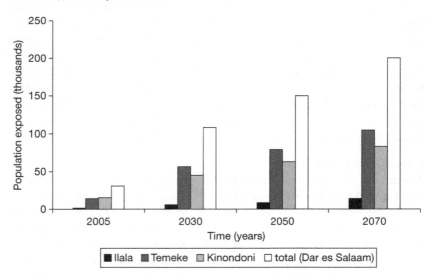

Source: Kebele and Nicholls (2010).

seasons or intensify droughts. Recent extreme climate (for example, the droughts of 2006 and 2008–2009, and the floods of 2009–2010) severely impacted sectors such as transport, energy, and health, with adverse socioeconomic implications. Projected changes in climate will have significant impacts on Tanzania's rain-fed agriculture and food production, and could thus impact urban agriculture in Dar es Salaam, a means of livelihood and subsistence for the city's poor. Warming will shorten the growing season and, together with reduced rainfall, reduce water availability. Coastal degradation and salt-water intrusion are major problems for Dar es Salaam's coastal areas today, and under projected climate change and possible sea-level rise, coastal ecosystems would be highly threatened, affecting the livelihoods and ecosystems of coastal communities. Residents of coastal wetlands that have incurred salt-water intrusion (such as Suna, Mtoni Azimio, and Msasani Bonde la Mpunga) informed the study team that they frequently need to repair their houses as salt-water intrusion is corroding the foundations and cement bricks are being eaten away.

Pillar 3—Socioeconomic Assessment

Location and Exposure of the Urban Poor

An estimated 70 percent of Dar es Salaam's population lives in poor, unplanned settlements. Life expectancy in Dar es Salaam's informal settlements is low, between 44 and 46 years, and infant mortality is high at about 97 deaths per 1,000 live births.

Residents are usually too poor to pay for services or infrastructure and authorities too resource-constrained to maintain these; thus, health and environmental conditions are generally extremely poor. Tanzania's policy toward informal settlements in Dar es Salaam has varied over past decades. In the 1960s, slum clearance was the main approach; slum sites were cleared and buildings with high construction standards were erected on cleared sites (implemented through the National Housing Corporation). This proved unsustainable, however, and was abandoned by the end of the 1960s due to high economic and social costs, and having contributed little to the net housing stock. In the 1970s and 1980s, the government's approach changed, and projects to upgrade squatter areas and to provide services (supported by the World Bank) formed the national strategy for managing the growth of informal settlements. After World Bank funding for these projects ceased, however, the government of Tanzania was unable to continue financing them, and subsequent years saw the growth and emergence of new unplanned settlements as well as deterioration of previously installed infrastructure, due to lack of maintenance.

Figure A1.6 Map of Flood Hazard Zone Overlaid on Urban Poor Settlements

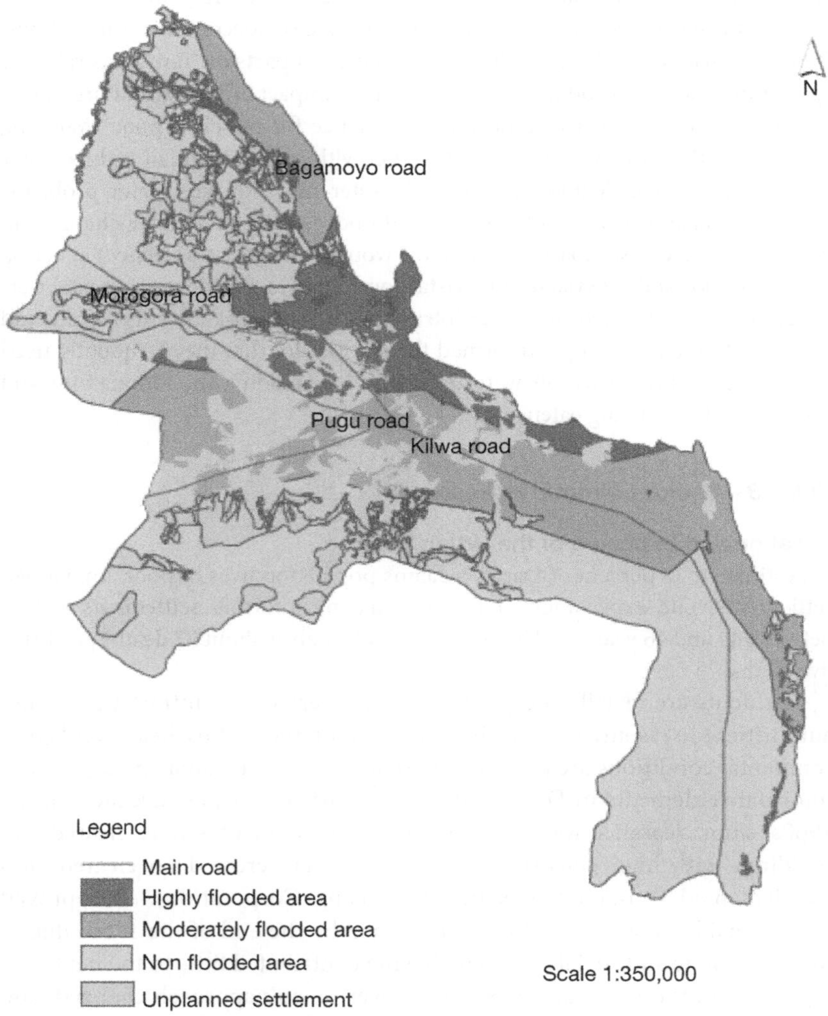
N
Bagamoyo road
Morogora road
Pugu road
Kilwa road
Legend
Main road
Highly flooded area
Moderately flooded area
Non flooded area
Unplanned settlement
Scale 1:350,000

Source: Ardhi University (2010).

Reference

World Bank. 2011. *Urban Poverty & Climate Change in Dar es Salaam, Tanzania; A Case Study, processed.*

Annex 2: Jakarta Case Study

Overview and Key Findings

This case study presents the first comprehensive overview of the intersection between climate change, disaster risk, and the urban poor in Jakarta. It discusses city progress in taking stock of policies and programs, both within the Provincial Government (Pemprov) of the Special Capital District (DKI) of Jakarta and with partners. And it discusses progress in understanding the principal hazards in the city and where they are located, as well as some understanding of undocumented citizens in Jakarta and how they are coping with the changes they experience on a day-to-day basis. As part of this effort, there is a longer document assessing risk and a short film that provide the basis for moving toward a comprehensive climate action plan for the city. The Bahasa version of the report will be a useful awareness-raising tool to build capacity among government agencies and other stakeholders on how climate change and natural disasters are and will affect Jakarta.

The World Bank, in close consultation with the Pemprov DKI and other stakeholders and partners, has prepared a case study of Jakarta. Key DKI government agencies, such as the departments responsible for the environment (Badan Pengelola Linkungan Hidup Daerah, BPLHD), planning (Badan Perencanaan Pembangunan Daerah, BAPPEDA), and spatial planning (Biro Tata Ruang) discussed existing city strategies and policies related to climate change. Pemprov DKI also hosted a stakeholder consultation workshop in December 2010, to review and strengthen the findings of this case study through conversations with different city officials and NGOs.

The approach used in this case study is based on the Urban Risk Assessment (URA) framework. Accordingly, it includes an assessment of the hazards, socioeconomic vulnerabilities, and institutional aspects related to climate change and disasters in Jakarta. With a focus on the urban poor, this study considers how poor communities are affected by climate change and natural hazards, examines approaches that have been taken to address these challenges, and identifies priorities and options for further action in Jakarta. This study draws on other reports and resources on disasters and climate change in Jakarta, as well as on interviews and discussions with government officials, local NGOs, and community leaders.

Key Findings of the Study

- Strong and sustained growth in Jakarta's population and economy have resulted in a vast increase in the urbanized area, and concomitant change in land use.
- Jakarta's rapid growth and urbanization have given rise to large-scale infrastructure problems that are mostly well documented and understood by the DKI government and the public.
- Jakarta is now highly vulnerable to the impacts of climate change. The greatest climate- and disaster-related risk facing Jakarta is flooding, which imposes very high human and economic costs on the city.
- Jakarta's poor are productive and integral members of the city's economy, and are also the most vulnerable to flood-related risks.

- The urban poor have important roles to play in addressing Jakarta's vulnerability to climate change and disasters.
- The government of DKI Jakarta has started acting on climate change, but much remains to be done to mainstream climate change across all sectors for the long term.

The Government of Jakarta at Work

DKI is making a concerted effort to develop its climate change strategy and to think more broadly and inclusively about different levels of capacity building and interventions. At the kelurahan level, government officials are starting to take active roles in understanding how climate change is affecting them and what steps they can prioritize in their own actions and local budgets. This is occurring mainly through capacity-building programs of NGOs. The government is also learning how to articulate these issues in terms of spatial interventions. Initially, the main focus of DKI on climate change was about reducing greenhouse gas emissions. The government is now thinking more broadly about adaptation measures like urban greening that address both climate change aspects.

Areas for Improvement

Currently the approach of integrating projects and programs that increase resilience, improve spatial planning, and decrease poverty in one systematized application is new for the DKI government. Both conceptually and in terms of policy creation and social services, the real links between climate change vulnerability and resilience and the urban poor remain weak. The location and required resettlement of the extremely poor communities is a delicate and complicated issue for DKI to manage, but one that is seeing increasing urgency and pressure. Ideas for the development of good climate change projects, ideally those that incorporate mitigation and adaptation, are slow to emerge from inside the DKI government.

Key Constraints

Key constraints in dealing effectively with climate change, disaster risk, and the urban poor include:

DATA—Poor availability and sharing of data for decision-making, from existing studies and new data, is one of the biggest challenges. From the experience of working through the MTF study with DKI Jakarta, data was either extremely scarce, inconsistent, or simply very difficult to access as some agencies were reluctant to release information. Partners of DKI, like other multi- and bilateral organizations, as well as NGOs and private-sector consultants, create their own data sets, but much of this information is not shared or coordinated.

INFRASTRUCTURE AND INVESTMENTS—The macro-infrastructure upgrades that will be required for Jakarta to be considered climate resilient are certainly massive and long term. These upgrades include a huge dike and polder-system called the Jakarta Coastal Sea Defense coupled with land reclamation and improved pumping capacity. This is still in the design stages. The Jatiluruh reservoir just outside of Jakarta's boundaries is the source of much of Jakarta's water. Plans have been under development for some time to expand the capacity of the pipes to increase water supply to Jakarta, and therefore ease the causes of subsidence, but the plans are not yet under way.

COMMUNICATION AND COMMUNITY ENGAGEMENT—The shorter-term micro-level capacity-building exercises and community-led actions are uneven, with some communities better organized than others. Framing the future of Jakarta using the terms "resilience" and "climate change" are new for the government and communities. There is a significant learning curve in terms of thoroughly understanding, then communicating, how climate change affects Jakarta.

Main Information Gaps Identified

In general there is a lack of data. Some of the data available (such as land tenure) may not have been scrutinized and analyzed through the fresh lens of climate change. Updated data gaps include: maps of poverty in the city; subsidence maps and images; socioeconomic and housing data on the very poor; good qualitative definitions of slums and urban settlements; information on land tenure; up-to-date census data; census data on the very poor; immigration and emigration rates; plans for resettlement of vulnerable areas; financing and long-term plans for sea-wall construction; and concrete action plans for working to halt subsidence.

Looking Forward

A few basic principles can guide the way forward for addressing climate change, disaster risk, and urban poverty in Jakarta.

- Climate change adaptation should be not so much an additional challenge to be layered onto existing policies and planning priorities, but rather an opportunity for the DKI government and key partners to gather their focus and priorities for the future.
- Given limited resources, the initial focus should be on addressing existing shortfalls in infrastructure investment and basic services, particularly in drainage, piped water, housing, and transportation.
- Policies and investments should be based on improved information, including quantitative data and an understanding of community actions and adaptive capacities.
- Enhanced collaboration—with the administrations of neighboring provinces, as well as with the local communities as active participants and partners—is crucial to the success of long-term action.
- Capacity building should be emphasized at every level. The shorter-term micro-level capacity building and community-led actions are uneven, some communities being better organized than others. Framing the future

of Jakarta using the terms "resilience" and "climate change" are new for the government and communities. There is a significant learning curve in terms of first thoroughly understanding, and then communicating, how climate change affects Jakarta.

Case Study Summary

Figure A2.1 Administrative Map of Jakarta

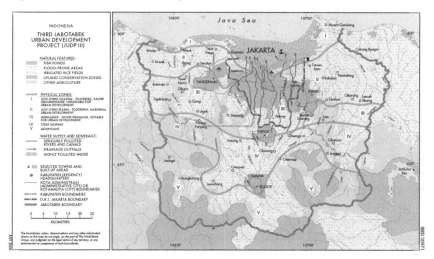

City Profile

Jakarta is located on the north coast of the island of Java in the Indonesian archipel-ago in Southeast Asia. It is the country's largest city and its political and economic hub. The city's built environment is characterized by numerous skyscrapers, con-centrated in the central business district but also built ad hoc throughout the city, especially in the past 20 years. The rest of Jakarta generally comprises low-lying, densely populated neighborhoods, which are highly diverse in terms of income levels and uses, and many of these neighborhoods are home to varied informal economic activities. The population of Jakarta is considered wealthy relative to neighboring provinces and other islands, and indeed its GDP per capita is more than four times the national average. See figure A2.1.

Jakarta is located in a deltaic plain crisscrossed by 13 natural rivers and more than 1,400 km of man-made waterways. About 40 percent of the city, mainly the area farthest north near the Java Sea, is below sea level. Jakarta is prone to flood-ing from water draining through the city from the hills in the south, and also from coastal tidal flooding.

TABLE A2.1
Jakarta Profile

Total city population in 2010	9.6 million
Population growth (% annual)	2.60
Land area (km²)	651
Population density (per km²)	14,465
Country's per capita GDP (US$)	2,329
% of country's population	4
Total number of households	2,325,973
GDP (US$)	10,222
% of country's GDP	20
Total budget (US$)	3.1 billion
Date of last Urban Master Plan	2010

The successful provision and management of services by the provincial government is lagging in most sectors. In spite of a booming economy, much private-sector property development, Jakarta's spatial planning and infrastructure, as well as service provision—transportation, green space, affordable housing, clean water, health care, and education—have not kept pace with demand.

Traffic congestion is a major problem facing the city, with only incremental efforts to relieve congestion through the development of public transportation, most prominently, the TransJakarta Busway. The increasing number of vehicles on the streets of Jakarta is outpacing the development of new roads. Total gridlock in the city is projected to occur as early as 2016 under the transportation Business As Usual scenario.

Lack of piped water is driving large multi-use developments and small residential communities alike to drill wells to access groundwater. This extraction of groundwater is causing areas of Jakarta to sink rapidly, particularly in the north of the city. Along with sea-level rise, land subsidence is one of the greatest challenges facing Jakarta.

The provision of housing for the poor and lower-middle classes continues to be inadequate relative to demand. With consistent in-migration of people into the city, estimated at 250,000 annually, housing is in constant demand, but costs are escalating. Skyrocketing land prices and rampant private-sector development that is under-regulated has resulted in a booming real-estate market that excludes the poor. Large informal settlements have grown over many years along waterways, natural rivers, and reservoirs, contributing to the pollution and clogging of these areas.

There is currently no citywide solid-waste management plan for Jakarta. Waste collection in the city is largely contracted out to private companies, with wealthier areas paying more, and consequently receiving better and more consistent service. In many areas, waste is collected and picked over by a highly efficient but informal waste picker and recycling community.

Pillar 1—Institutional Assessment

Agencies in Disaster Risk Management and Climate Change Adaptation

The key agencies in Jakarta responsible for coordinated efforts on climate change adaptation and disaster risk management are Kantor Asisten Pembangunan dan Lingkungan Hidup (Asbang), Assistant to Secretary for Development and Environment Office; Badan Pengelola Linkungan Hidup Daerah (BPLHD), the environmental agency; Badan Perencanaan Pembangunan Daerah (BAPPEDA), the planning and development agency; Badan Penanggulangan Bencana Daerah (BPBD), the provincial disaster management agency; Satuan Tugas Koordinasi dan Pelaksana (SATKORLAK), the national disaster risk management board; and Biro Tata Ruang, the bureau of spatial planning.

- Assistant to Secretary for Development and Environment Office as a point of coordination for development and environment. Under this office, there are two bureaus that are Spatial Plan (Tata Ruang) and Infrastructure (Sarana dan Prasarana). Biro Tata Ruang is responsible for coordinating the development and management of short-, medium-, and long-term spatial plans for the city. Within the plans are specific laws and articles articulating the incorporation of climate change adaptation and mitigation, as well as the need for disaster risk management. Biro Prasarana dan Sarana is responsible for monitoring the city development. However, the implementation and enforcement of these laws and articles is through BAPPEDA and the Department of Public Works.

- BPLHD is the environmental agency and the key governmental contact for many of the NGOs and other organizations working at the community level. They are involved in programs to abate greenhouse gas emissions in Jakarta, including overseeing the development of a greenhouse gas emissions baseline, to be completed in 2011. BLPHD also manages community-level adaptation initiatives and studies in partnership with NGOs and donor organizations.

- BAPPEDA is the development and management body for Jakarta. It manages large infrastructure projects such as sea-wall construction in north Jakarta, as well as the building of floodgates along the rivers and major infrastructure projects like the East and West Flood Canals. The agency manages, finances, and monitors the flood infrastructure carried out by Dinas Pekerjaan Umum (DPU), the public-works agency.

- BPBD was established as the citywide agency for disaster risk management only at the end of 2010. Until then, disaster response was handled by SATKORLAK, which is a national association based largely in the fire department and acted as more of a committee since it was not anchored in a particular agency or formalized into government structure. The formal empowerment and role of BPBD has yet to be fully developed, integrated, and made widely public.

Relevant Policies and Legislation

Climate change is integrated to a limited extent in the medium- and long-term city spatial plans, but they relate for the most part to areas of the city experiencing the greatest harm from flooding or other problems. The official language in the plans acknowledges the need for strategies related to climate change as well as plans for disaster mitigation and response, but does not go into specific detail. (See table A2.2 for policies related to climate change in the RTRW 2030 Spatial Plan.)

Adaptation plans to cope with extreme weather and sea-level rise are piece-meal within the plans and agencies. More generally, the governor of Jakarta has made public commitments in the international arena to reducing the city's green-house gas emissions.

The plans and policies of BPBD are not yet known, although a citywide strategy for disaster prevention and response will most likely be developed and managed by this agency. The National Action Plan for Disaster Risk Reduction

TABLE A2.2
Policies Relating to Climate Change in RTRW Spatial Plan 2030

	The Capital Region of Jakarta, like other major cities in the world, is facing global challenges, particularly global warming and climate change, which require action on climate change. Both adaptation and mitigation actions need to be included in spatial planning;[1]
Article 5	(5) To realize the integration and control of space utilization as referred to in Article 4, letter e, set the policy as follows: a. implement nature conservation reserves, nature conservation area, area protection, water resources, and development of green space for urban ecological balance in Jakarta; b. improve the quantity and quality of green space as an effort to improve the quality of Jakarta city life; c. reduce greenhouse gas emissions in an effort to anticipate global warming and climate change; and d. establish and maintain areas that have strategic value of the influential on environmental aspects.
Article 5	(8) In order to achieve disaster risk reduction as referred to in Article 4 letter h, set the policy as follows: a. develop infrastructure and facilities for natural disaster risk reduction; b. develop the infrastructure and non-natural disaster risk reduction; and c. promote adaptation and mitigation to prepare for the threat of global warming and climate change and increased risk of another disaster.

(continued next page)

TABLE A2.2 *continued*

Article 10	(3) Strategies to implement the policy referred to in Article 5 paragraph (5) c, include: a. implement the carrying capacity of natural resources and environmental capacity for sustainable development; b. apply the concept of environmentally friendly building and the concept of sustainable urban design; c. improve the quality and quantity of green space; d. increase alternative energy e. based waste management technology; f. improve wastewater treatment; g. reduce the use of ozone depleting substances; h. restore the function of mangrove forest; i. improve public facilities, mass transit, and j. improve the control of mobile source emissions and stationary sources.
Article 13	(1) Strategies to implement the policy referred to in Article 5 paragraph (8) letter a, including: a. develop infrastructure and facilities for flood control; b. improve and enhance the drainage system; c. develop a path, region, and disaster evacuation space; and d. build a sea dike in order to anticipate rising seawater.
Article 13	(3) Strategies to implement the policy referred to in Article 5 paragraph (8) c, include: a. direct utilization of disaster areas for cultivation activities that have a high adaptability; b. reducing disaster risk through redesign through the application of technology and engineering in disaster areas; c. mengembangankan North Coast region (northern) as an effort to anticipate changes in climate; d. improve the provision of open space for the anticipated blue intensity rainfall; e. create life side by side with water; and f. Laws refine areas of the building and the environment appropriate hazard threat.
Article 57	(1) The development of energy systems and networks referred to in Article 45 letter d is intended to merjamin supply reliability and continuity of supply of energy for household needs, services, trade, industrial, and transportation with respect to conservation and energy diversification factor. (2) energy conservation factors referred to in paragraph (1) attention to aspects of mitigation of climate change and global warming. (3) Development of energy systems and networks referred to in paragraph (1), include: a. electrical system; b. infrastructure systems of fuel gas and c. infrastructure systems of fuel oil.

Source: RTRW 2030, Biro Tata Ruang.

(NAP-DRR) lists actions for Jakarta specifically, but the actions have been developed by different sectors and ministries. The budget numbers included are the requests by the implementing party and have not been allocated or approved.

Ongoing Programs in Disaster Risk Management and Climate Change

An important step taken by the DKI government was to establish the provincial disaster risk management agency, BPBD. Currently, there is no comprehensive program of disaster risk management or response plan for the city of Jakarta. There are large-scale infrastructure projects, such as the Jakarta Coastal Defense that protects coastal neighborhoods from tidal surges, and the East and West Flood

Canals. The Jakarta Coastal Defense has been presented to the Jakarta government as a feasibility study. The East and West Flood Canals are the largest and most ambitious projects for Jakarta in terms of flood management, but the intricate and smaller secondary and tertiary systems are still under-managed and inadequate.

Many of the alert systems work at the community level and are largely self-organized. These are generally warnings from upstream floodgates that water is getting high; the warnings are sent via SMS text message to neighborhood heads so they can warn their communities. It is unknown how many of these small and informal networks are actually in place. It appears that they evolved out of local necessity. Many of the resources for the smaller, community-level projects and programs come from local and international NGOs. Small government agencies at the neighborhood level (RT and RW) are allocated budgets for some infrastructural interventions, but they are not consistent across the city and in many cases kelurahan-level budgets are not entirely spent every fiscal year due in part to complicated and lengthy approval mechanisms by the provincial government, or a lack of capacity at the local level to carry out physical interventions. This is a national trend and not specific to Jakarta.

Policy Shortcomings

Formalization, publication, and awareness-raising are still sorely lacking in the areas of climate change and disaster risk management in Jakarta, both inside many government agencies and in the public realm. In many ways the Jakarta government is only beginning to comprehensively measure and understand the city's key vulnerabilities—as well as its strengths and resources—to become climate-resilient and to anticipate potential disasters. There is also a lack of coordination between the agencies described above, and very little enforcement of well-meaning laws to create a safer and more secure built environment. BNPB (Badan Nasional Penanggulangan Bencana) was developed as the national coordinating and monitoring agency in 2008, with an operating budget for disaster response of about IDR 4 trillion (US$464 million). However, more is currently needed for upgrades and implementation as reported in the National Action Plan for Disaster Risk Reduction (NAP-DRR). (See complete case study for list of items submitted for financing by various agencies for Jakarta.)

Lead Agency for Disaster Risk Management

Until recently, a national ad hoc agency (SATKORLAK) anchored in the fire department and was responsible for disaster response, but was doing little anticipatory planning. Jakarta did not have a dedicated working group or agency. At the end of 2010, BPBD was established for the province of Jakarta. As it is a new agency, the role it will play in developing disaster mitigation plans or allocating funding for the city's kota or kelurahan remains unclear.

Mainstreaming Risk Reduction

In order to mainstream risk reduction, the government is incorporating those activities and projects into the long-term spatial plans, the most recent of which is Jakarta's plan for 2010–2030. NGOs and other donor organizations are playing important roles currently to aid communities and community-level governments to educate and prepare individual citizens, families, and community leaders to prepare for damaging events such as floods from extreme rainfall or from rises in tides. However, these actions are piecemeal across the city and it is mostly poor communities that are targeted by these organizations.

Expenditure on Pro-Poor Programs and Climate Adaptation

The 2011 city budget for Jakarta is slightly more than US$3 billion. Indonesia has a countrywide program to alleviate poverty (Program Nasional Pemberdayaan Masyarakat (PNPM)—Mandiri or the National Program for Community Empowerment2) that has had success in other urban areas, but has not adequately reached extremely poor parts of Jakarta. Many of the activities to reduce poverty are disbursed throughout various services and departments.

TABLE A2.3
Total Annual Budget of Departments Carrying out Pro-Poor Services

Agency/department	Annual budget, 2010
Community empowerment	$4,757,965
Health	$198,596,454
Family planning and prosperity	$4,810,028
Social services	$5,243,572

TABLE A2.4
Larger-Scale Initiatives Related to Infrastructure

Infrastructure investments per year DKI	Annual budget, 2009	Annual budget, 2010
Flood control		
East flood canal	$93,132,994	$60,350,180
Drainage and river dredging	$10,803,427	$11,424,314
Dam, polder, and catchment area development	$620,887	$40,605,985
Pollution containment		
Open green space development	$15,909,599	$77,238,296
Climate change adaptation		
Sea wall	$2,235,192	$5,587,980

TABLE A2.5
Institutional Mapping of Disaster Risk Management Functions

Risk assessment	Technical (planning, management, maintenance)	Risk reduction early warning and response	Public awareness
DNPI Climate change technical studies and coordination of mitigation activities	BNPD National disaster risk reduction plans and policies and NAP-DRR (2010)	RT and RW Localized early-warning systems for floods via SMS	BPLHD Climate change events and programs like car-free days
BPBD Disaster risk management and reduction plans, management, and training	BPBD Local disaster management and response plan for Jakarta (to come)	DKI Department of Public Works (PU) Coordination of early-warning system with other provinces (water management)	DNPI Conferences and publications
BAPPENAS Inter-agency coordination for infrastructure plans	BAPPEDA Infrastructure and planning projects; maintenance with PU and other agencies	SATKORLAK Emergency response	BIRO TATA RUANG Publication of 20-year spatial plan available to public
P2B Risk mapping for earthquakes			

Pillar 2—Hazards Assessment

Past Natural Disasters

The largest floods in Jakarta's history took place in 2002 and 2007. Jakarta's floods are notorious, and the resulting stalling of traffic, lost productivity, and property damage costs the city more than US$400 million per year. By 2002, more than a quarter of Jakarta's area was affected. The most disastrous flood to date, in February 2007, cost 57 lives, displaced more than 422,300 people, and destroyed 1,500 homes, damaging countless others. Total losses to property and infrastructure were estimated at US$695 million.[3] However, flooding of that magnitude is relatively infrequent and is not necessarily the principal issue for Jakarta; flooding occurs regularly throughout the year, stalling traffic, damaging houses, and gravely attenuating the flow of business at all levels of society. Even with just a moderate amount of rain, vehicular mobility in the city is critically impaired, often for hours.

The NAP-DRR cites parts of Jakarta as vulnerable to three hazards. However, for DKI Jakarta, the analysis does not go beyond the level of the kota, so it is hard

TABLE A2.6
Natural Hazards

	Yes/No	Date of last major event
Earthquake	Y	September 2009 and periodic
Wind storm	N	
River flow	Y	Regularly, extreme during rainy season
Floods, inundations, and waterlogs	Y	October 2010
Tsunami	N	
Drought	N	
Volcano	N	
Landslide	N	
Storm surge	Y	January 2008 and recurring
Extreme temperature	Y	Increasing on a yearly basis

TABLE A2.7
Jakarta's Kota in National Ranking of Kabupaten or Regencies at High Risk for Various Disasters

Earthquake (out of 151 listed)		Drought (out of 182 listed)		Flood (out of 174 listed)	
80	West Jakarta	8	North Jakarta	2	North Jakarta
95	North Jakarta	9	East Jakarta	3	West Jakarta
122	East Jakarta	10	Central Jakarta		
137	South Jakarta	11	West Jakarta		
		37	South Jakarta		

to know how the risk affects different areas of the municipalities and their diverse populations.

Main Climate Hazards

The main hazards for Jakarta relate to water management and flood control. Extreme weather causes overloading of the existing drainage system, while sea-level rise coupled with land subsidence is making Jakarta increasingly vulnerable to tidal floods due to its coastal location. Jakarta has also experienced earthquakes (although minor, but as recently as 2009) and should be prepared for other unprecedented geological events and tsunamis.

TABLE A2.8
Main Climate Hazards

Hazard	Effects	Losses
Earthquake	Until now small, with very little physical damage.	Until now, no great material or life loss from earthquakes.
River flow	Disruption of business, damage t o property, power outages, groundwater pollution, and distribution of solid waste through high and fast water flow.	Property damage, business damage, tainting of ground water, loss of life, and spread of disease and refuse.
Floods, inundations	Depending on severity can affect traffic circulation, business activity, damage to property, power outages, displacement, and spread of disease.	Loss of property and businesses, spread of illness and loss of life, and loss of access to clean water.
Storm surge	Locally known as rob, extreme tidal floods from the sea have become more serious in the past few years in the coastal areas of the city. Sea water intrusion into aquifers.	Seawater intrusion into drinking water, damage to property including boats, and halt of industry and mobility.
Extreme temperature	As a result of both urbanization and loss of green space, increases in ground temperature and resulting instances of dengue.	Loss of life due to dengue, usually within very poor communities.

Areas at High Risk of Disasters and Climate Impacts

Given the sea-level rise and subsidence that have been modeled for North Jakarta, some industrial and residential areas and ports will be submerged in the next 100 years. Most of Jakarta's remaining industries are located in the north, as are its historic and active ports, which are key for Java's fishing economy. The airport and other major roads, as well as Kota Tua, the 17th century remnants of the first Dutch settlement, will also be affected. See figure A2.2 in the color section.

Other Sources of Information on Potential Impacts of Disasters

- Jakarta Coastal Defense Strategy (JCDS): Recommendation and study by an international consortium to build a 60 km sea defense along the coast to prevent damage from both land subsidence and sea-level rise. The consortium is funded by the city of Rotterdam and is still only at the stage of a feasibility study.[4]
- Jakarta Urgent Flood Mitigation Project (JUFMP): A study and dredging plan by the World Bank and DKI Jakarta, which included the "Jakarta Flood Hazard

Mapping Framework," which does not include cost analysis but provides the infrastructure framework required. The complete financial study is available at DKI and the World Bank.[5]

- The Jakarta Building Control and Monitoring Office (Penataan dan Pengawasan Bangunan: P2B): The office is developing a risk map for Jakarta within micro-zones of 150 m² each, which analyzes buildings and soil conditions within each. This initiative relates specifically to earthquakes and building quality. The map is not yet complete.[6]

Pillar 3—Socioeconomic Assessment

Population Exposure to Hazards

All of Jakarta is considered at high risk to disaster, since very few areas of the city are immune to recurrent floods. However, the most vulnerable areas of the city are along the coast, since they are susceptible to the effects not only of tidal flooding from the sea, but also of floods from the rivers and canals that are discharged into the Jakarta Bay. These communities in the northern areas are also experiencing the greatest land subsidence. The poorest people in Jakarta are generally those squatting on empty land along riverbanks and canals. It is estimated that they comprise about 3.5 percent of the urban population. See figures A2.3 and A2.4 in the color section.

Location of the Urban Poor

The level of exposure of very poor communities in Jakarta to both climate and natural hazards is extremely high. This is due in part to many of the poorest communities have settled illegally in areas close to sources of water: along major drainage and water management areas and along the coast. This renders them

TABLE A2.9
Social Assessment

City population below poverty line (%)	3.60
Social inequality (Gini index) in 2002 (UN Habitat)	0.32
Unemployment (% of total labor force)	11.05
Areal size of informal settlements as a percent of city area	Unknown
City population living in slums (%)	5
Human Development Index (2009)	77.36
Predominant housing material	For the very poor, assorted salvaged materials; for self-builders, concrete blocks and brick.

vulnerable to flooding from increased rain, as well as extreme hydrological events and tidal anomalies and floods from the sea.

Characteristics of Informal Settlements

The poorest communities in Jakarta live in self-constructed settlements, usually on land without formal legal title, and working in informal jobs. In some instances, illegal and undocumented land leasing and landlord-tenant contracting is practiced. Jakarta has a long history of these informal settlements. In many of these areas, some individuals and families have lived in what could be considered as "slums" for decades, so well-established social networks and cultural identities of place in Jakarta run extremely deep. While the numbers for Jakarta may be slightly lower, and remain hard to accurately measure, up to 68 percent of Indonesians across the country make their living through informal means (ILO 2010). In most areas of Jakarta, the residents of informal settlements work as maids, janitors, satpams (security guards), and parking attendants, and also run small local businesses such as food stalls and small tokos (retail kiosks). In coastal settlements, the fishermen are key to providing larger companies with supplies of fish to sell across the city.

Examples of Good Practice

Jakarta has yet to develop a comprehensive plan to address extreme poverty in the city, especially in terms of involuntary relocation, housing provision, and economic development of very poor communities. Indonesia has policies to alleviate poverty like conditional cash transfers and other mechanisms, but many of these policies are not designed for the issues and challenges of a megacity. Many of the very poor subsist on jobs and small businesses that are part of Jakarta's vast informal economy. Integrating climate change adaptation and education into plans for social services and community awareness is new for the Jakarta government. It has only been in 2011 that DKI Jakarta has been engaging with local NGOs and other organizations and funders to develop and understand community resilience specifically toward risk management related to climate change. PNPM (Program Nasional Pemberdayaan Masyarakat) is a 10-year government program to reduce poverty funded in part by the World Bank, a program that will incorporate disaster risk reduction activities into their established community empowerment and capacity building; the addition US$15 million, funded over 5 years, is through a grant from the Global Facility for Disaster Reduction and Recovery, starting in 2011. However, only one or two of Jakarta's kelurahan may be eligible for this program.

Constraints and Opportunities

Very little quantified, centralized information is available about the most vulnerable communities in Jakarta, the urban poor and informal settlements. However, the highly visible climate-vulnerable locations of these communities allow for easy identification of specific locations for interventions in spatial planning and social programming (like in North Jakarta and along many of the rivers). The creation and organization of data about the urban poor in Jakarta, and specifically about their livelihoods and economic contribution to Jakarta, is key. Another asset in terms of community information dissemination and preparedness is the already-fairly decentralized local government structures of the RW and RT, with budget and administrative allocation down to a minute level in the city. With this strong system already in place, it is relatively simple to scale up or replicate good community-level programs across the city.

GHG Emissions Inventory

A GHG emissions inventory for Jakarta is currently under development in partnership with BPLHD, DNPI, and the NGO group Swisscontact.

Notes

1. Articles found in the RTRW 2030 relating to climate change.
2. For more information, see www.pnpm-mandiri.org.
3. *Why Are There Floods In Jakarta? Flood Control by the Government of the Province of Jakarta*, PT Mirah Sakethi, 2010.
4. http://www.beritajakarta.com/2008/en/newsview.aspx?idwil=0&id=17983.
5. http://web.worldbank.org/external/projects/main?pagePK=64283627&piPK=73230& theSitePK=40941&menuPK=228424&Projectid=P111034.
6. http://www.thejakartaglobe.com/opinion/editorial-mapping-out-path-to-a-quake-ready-jakarta/432586.

Reference

World Bank. 2011. *Jakarta: Urban Challenges in a Changing Climate*. Jakarta: World Bank.

Annex 3: Mexico City Case Study

Overview and Key Findings

The Mexico City case study under the Mayor's Task Force brings together new and existing knowledge for dealing with climate change, disaster risk, and the urban poor. Results from this case study are contributing to the definition of the Mexico City Climate Change Adaptation Program to be implemented in 2012. The objectives of the Mexico City case study were to (1) establish the historic pattern and trends of hydro meteorological events in the Metropolitan Area of Mexico City (MAMC) and assess its spatial distribution and socioeconomic impacts; (2) model climate change impacts in the MAMC; (3) develop indicators of risk and vulnerability; and (4) present institutional and policy recommendations to respond to the challenges posed by climate change, natural disasters, and urban poverty.

The case study was prepared in collaboration between the World Bank and the government of Mexico City. As part of this effort, a complete document in Spanish, "Pobreza Urbana y Cambio Climático para la Ciudad de Mexico," and a short film are available for wider dissemination.

The approach used in this case study is based on the Urban Risk Assessment (URA) framework. Accordingly, it includes an assessment of the hazards, socioeconomic vulnerabilities, and institutional aspects related to climate change and disasters in Mexico City. This case study provides valuable geo-referenced information regarding location of increased risk to landslides as a result of extreme rain, and identifies areas where increased heat-island effect is expected.

Institutionally, this case study has served to identify shortcomings in the current operational framework for climate change and disaster risk management, respectively.

Key Findings of the Study

In dealing with climate change, disaster risk, and the urban poor, the key challenge for Mexico City is to define actions that will facilitate the streamlining of adaptation measures within a context of limited institutional coordination and cooperation across the 50 geopolitical and administrative units that make up the Metropolitan Area.

The Vulnerability of the Poor to Climate Change and Natural Hazards
Vulnerable groups in terms of population include about 7 million people (or 42 percent of population of the Mexico City Metropolitan Area) and about 1.5 million dwellings. Most of the vulnerable population in high-risk zones lives in locations with slopes over 15 degrees (about 1 million people). This places them at risk of landslides as a result of extreme precipitation. The total population that lives in high-risk zones represents about 40 percent of the vulnerable population.

The Government of Mexico City at Work
The government of Mexico City has taken an active role in initiating climate change programs and the city is the first in Latin America to launch a local climate change strategy. The Mexico City Climate Action Program (MCCAP) consists of two complementary objectives: mitigation and adaptation.

Furthermore, the government has established the distinguished Virtual Center on Climate Change for Mexico City (CVCCCM). The CVCCCM contributes to increased and improved knowledge on the impact of climate change in the metropolitan area, and contributes the formulation and implementation of public policies. The CVCCCM operates in partnership with the Institute of Science and Technology of the Federal District and in conjunction with the Centre for Atmospheric Sciences of the National Autonomous University of Mexico (UNAM).

Mexico City has shown significant leadership in bringing together the climate change and disaster risk agendas, and has established the Inter-institutional Climate Change Commission of Mexico City, which is in charge of coordinating and evaluating the Mexico City Climate Change Action Program. Although it is premature to confirm or refute whether the measures proposed in this program will be mainstreamed into urban management practices, the wide participation and the higher-level commitment suggest solid first steps.

Key Constraints

Key constraints in dealing effectively with climate change, disaster risk, and the urban poor include:

INSTITUTIONAL COORDINATION—Despite significant progress in establishing an interinstitutional commission, the main challenge continues to be coordination˙ and cooperation. Even though the program is designed to cut across institutional boundaries, limited ownership by the participants might hinder its success.

COMMON DATA PLATFORMS—Currently multiple agencies are taking actions but with limited communication or information exchange among concerned agencies. Furthermore, each agency has its own information platform, which hinders data sharing. This signals a strong need to develop a single common interface that all government agencies can use for data storage and use.

LIMITED BUDGET ALLOCATION—Although the execution of the MCCAP has an estimated cost of approximately US$5 billion, most of which is budgeted for mitigation, there has been limited transfer of money. The only instrument that could specifically provide resources for the action plan is the Environmental Public Fund, while the remaining identified actions would have to be financed through each respective agency's annual budgets.

Looking Forward

A few basic principles can guide the way forward for addressing climate change, disaster risk, and urban poverty in Mexico:

- The consolidation of an institutional framework able to drive the medium- and long-term challenges posed by climate change and natural disasters is instrumental for protecting the most vulnerable. This framework must specify clearly each agency's role while fostering synergies and collaboration.
- A common language (for example, technical terms and concepts), as well as a common strategic direction for assessing challenges and progress toward adaptation and resilience, is critical for mainstreaming this agenda in metropolitan governance.
- The strategies for climate action plans should explicitly include reducing and mitigating the impacts of meteorological events to the most vulnerable.
- Community-based social prevention is an important component of disaster prevention
- Further work is necessary to unlock barriers in the development of the early-warning system.

Case Study Summary

City Profile

Figure A3.1 Administrative Map of Mexico City Metropolitan Area

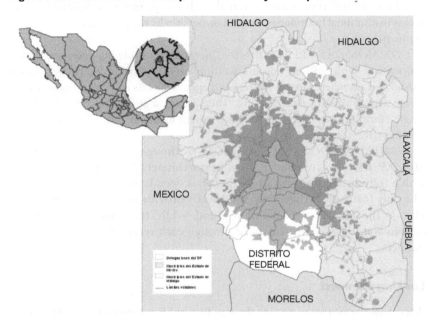

The Mexico City Metropolitan Area (MCMA) is one of the largest urban agglomerations in the world. Located in a closed basin of 9,600 km², the MCMA spreads over a surface of 4,250 km² at 2,240 meters above sea level. The MCMA has a metropolitan population estimated at 21.2 million, concentrates 18 percent of the country's population, and generates 35 percent of Mexico's gross domestic product on a surface equivalent to less than 0.3 percent of the national territory. Approximately 8.8 million people, or 42 percent of the metropolitan population, live in the city proper (Mexico City or the Federal District). The MCMA comprises the 16 boroughs of Mexico City and 34 municipalities of the State of Mexico, for a total of 50 geopolitical and administrative units that must coordinate among themselves in terms of urban planning, public services, and overall city management.

The MCMA has been growing constantly since the 1930s both physically and demographically. The pace of geographic and population growth, however, has been distinct. Physical and demographic growth reached its peak in the 1960s, and until the 1990s the physical expansion (urban sprawl) formed a continuous urbanized area with gross population density decreasing over time, and spatially increasing with distance from the historical city center. Since 1990 growth has been characterized by leapfrog expansion, and urban spatial continuity was broken. Current land use now bears limited contiguity to previously urbanized areas. For example, in 2000 the neighboring municipalities located in the State of Mexico represented 52 percent of the population and grew at an annual rate of 2.4 percent on average, while the 16 boroughs of Mexico City had a population growth rate of 0.3 percent annually.

The MCMA is characterized by seismic risk and with no natural drainage for runoff from the surrounding mountains; it is also vulnerable to flooding, particularly in the western part. The metropolitan area is affected by severe storms, heat waves, and droughts. The size of the population in the MCMA complicates the possible impacts of these events, as the infrastructure and public services are stretched thin. As a national economic engine, Mexico City's geophysical characteristics and presence of risk of multiple natural hazards underscores the need for the city to implement activities and programs that will increase its physical and social resilience. To take a recent example, the economic impact of the 2009 A (H1N1) influenza epidemic amounted to 0.4 percent of GDP (40 billion pesos).

The Built Environment and Basic Service Provision
Mexico City was the first city in Latin America to introduce a strategy for local climate action that has been designed to reduce overall greenhouse gas emissions

TABLE A3.1
Mexico City Profile

Total city population in 2010 federal district	8.8 million (INEGI 2010)
Total metropolitan area population in 2010	21.2 million
Population growth (% annual)	3.05 (CONAPO 2010)
Land area, federal district (km²)	1,485
Land area, metropolitan area (km²)	4,250
Population density (per km²)	5,958
Country's per capita GDP (US$)	9,243 (2010 estimate)
Country's population (federal district) (%)	7.87
Total number of households	2,388,534 (INEGI 2010)
Dwelling density (per hectare)	23.9 (SEDESEOL)
Avg. household income US$ (2008)	53,295
GDP per capita US$ (2008)	14,382
Country's GDP (%)	21.8
Total budget (US$)	11.7 billion
Date of last Urban Master Plan	n/a

by 7 million metric tons from its inception by Mayor Marcelo Ebrard in 2008–2012. The climate action program is part of a 15-year plan in which Mexico City is investing US$1 billion a year (approximately 9 percent of the yearly budget). The Green Plan (Plan Verde) has seven pillars: (1) land conservation, (2) public spaces, (3) air pollution, (4) waste management and recycling, (5) water supply and sanitation, (6) transportation, and (7) mobility.

Mexico City has the largest metro system in Latin America, which currently comprises 200 km of subway lines. It is currently being expanded with a twelfth metro line stretching 25 km, due to be finished in 2012—with an investment of US$2 billion. The Metro, which does not extend outside the limits of the Federal District, is complemented by a suburban rail system and an extensive network of bus routes. Mexico City's first Bus Rapid Transit line, the Metrobus system, began operation in June 2005. The city has begun construction of a third line for Metrobus that will run from the city's northwest to the central-south, extending over 16 km with 31 stations.

Water access is a complex problem for Mexico City, which has a supply network of some 13,000 km of primary and secondary pipelines. Beyond issues of expanding coverage and continuity of water services, the city rests on heavily saturated clay that has been collapsing and causing areas of the city to sink and subsequently endure more frequent flooding due to over-extraction of groundwater. Forecasts to 2015 estimate that rates of water consumption will increase by 20 percent compared to 2000 levels, with urban demand reaching 62 m³ per second. Mexico City's climate action program therefore includes measures to invest in water infrastructure, for example, the rehabilitation of the city's sewerage system as part of a program of hydraulic works.

Regarding land conservation, 59 percent of the total land area of Mexico City is designated a conservation area, with the city's remaining forested areas located in the southern boroughs. These areas are under threat from illegal development, logging, and fires, which impact regional rain patterns. At present the city's generation of garbage is increasing at a rate of 5 percent a year and the current insufficient rates of its collection have created "clandestine" fields. Bordo Poniente, one of the world's largest landfill sites, receives 12,500 tons of waste every day. In response, Mexico City has initiated a recycling program and is encouraging its citizens to separate trash.

Pillar 1—Institutional Assessment

Given the institutional and political complexities of the Mexico City Metropolitan Area, the Mexico City Climate Action Program (MCCAP) 2008–2012 requires a high level of coordination among multiple agencies and civil society. The MCCAP was developed as part of both the Green Plan and the Environmental Agenda of

Mexico City. The Green Plan extends to 15 years, laying out strategies and actions of sustainable development for Mexico City. The Environmental Agenda of Mexico City is a 5-year plan that defines the city's environmental policy. At the same time, both the Green Plan and the Environmental Agenda are part of one of the pillars of Mexico City's Development Program.

The main objectives of the MCCAP are twofold: (1) reduce carbon dioxide emissions by 7 million tons (or equivalent) in the period 2008–2012 and (2) develop a Climate Change Adaptation Program for the Federal District and begin its implementation by 2012. To achieve these objectives, the government uses various policy instruments, including direct investment from Mexico City, regulation, economic incentives, voluntary carbon markets, and education and information campaigns.

The Inter-institutional Climate Change Commission of Mexico City is in charge of coordinating and evaluating the MCCAP. This commission includes representatives from all the administrative units of the Federal District. In addition, three deputies from the district's Legislative Assembly are invited to attend each session. Among its specific responsibilities are to design, encourage, and coordinate policies to mitigate climate change effects in Mexico City; to evaluate, approve, and disseminate related projects; to develop financial strategies that generate revenue; and to coordinate actions and policies with other programs linked to the MCCAP. To facilitate coordination and provide support to the MCCAP, the Legislative Assembly of Mexico City is working on a proposal for a climate change law (not yet entered into force as of March 2011).

Although the execution of the MCCAP has an estimated cost of approximately US$5 billion, most of which is budgeted for mitigation, there has been little transfer of money. The only instrument that could specifically provide resources for the MCCAP is the Environmental Public Fund, while the remaining identified actions would have to be financed through each agency's annual budgets.

The main challenge of the MCCAP is the lack of institutional coordination and cooperation. Even though the program was designed to cut across institutional boundaries, there is lack of ownership and it is mostly considered a program of the secretary of environment. Currently multiple agencies are taking actions but with limited communication or information exchange among concerned agencies. Further exacerbating the open exchange of data is that each agency has its own information platform. This signals a strong need to develop a single common interface that all government agencies can use for data storage and use.

Climate Change Adaptation and Disaster Response

The MCCAP's program of adaptation consists of short- and long-term actions that aim to reduce risks to the population and economy of Mexico City by taking the potential impacts of climate change into account. The lines of action regarding adaptation are: (1) identifying key threats and performing a vulnerability analysis, (2) mainstreaming adaptation to enhance existing capabilities in Mexico City's government, and (3) implementing adaptation.

There are multiple agencies involved in responding to extreme hydro-meteorological events, including: The Water System of Mexico City, the Civil Protection Agency, the Public Safety Agency, the Health Department, the Social Development Agency, the Social Assistance Institute, and the Urban Development and Housing Agency. Their main tasks follow.

TABLE A3.2
Institutional Responsibilities Relating to Climate and Disasters

Institution	Headed by/level	Major function
Water system of Mexico City	Secretary of environment	Responsible for public services related to water supply, drainage, sewerage, and water treatment. They also coordinate and operate the "Storm Unit" during high-precipitation emergencies in 90 previously identified high-risk locations, with the participation of the Civil Protection Agency, the Public Safety Agency, and the Fire Department.
Civil Protection Agency	Secretary of interior	Responsible for coordinating prevention and response to natural disasters, mainly floods and earthquakes, using a "Risk Atlas" that has more than 100 maps depicting multiple hazards. In terms of flooding, they have identified critical locations based on past events, but these are not necessarily the same maps used by the Water System of Mexico City. Importantly, this agency has focused mainly on prevention, response, and capacity building for seismic disasters. They defined and are implementing the Crisis and Immediate Response Action Plan.
Public Safety Agency	Operates in coordination with the water system of Mexico City and the Civil Protection Agency	Intervenes when natural disasters occur.
Health Department	In emergencies, coordinates with the Civil Protection Agency	Responsible for periodic monitoring of epidemic prevention and response (including AH1N1 and dengue). In addition to medical attention, it organizes vaccination campaigns.
Social Development Agency		Provides support and responds to emergencies related to heat and cold waves and floods. In addition to operating public dining locations, the agency establishes shelters with food and provides psychological assistance.

(continued next page)

Institution	Headed by/level	Major function
Social Assistance Institute		Responsible for general social assistance (including psychological support) for the Federal District, but also during emergencies. Through one of its programs, it operates a hotline to support homeless people. It also supports families affected by disasters and operates 11 centers for social assistance.
Urban Development and Housing Agency		Responsible for medium- and long-term prevention of disasters through urban planning. It is involved in issues related to irregular terrains in high-risk locations. It has plans to develop an information system for Mexico City that will include geographic and urban development indicators.

Ongoing Programs and Projects Related to Disaster Risk Management or Climate Change Adaptation

Programs for climate change adaptation focus on early-warning systems and medium-term response:

- Programs on early-warning systems and upstream prevention include the implementation of a hydro-meteorological monitoring and forecasting system for Mexico Valley, an epidemiological monitoring system, and a remote identification and monitoring system for fires. In addition, initiatives are in place for management of hillside risk, the protection of native vegetation to reduce erosion, and the establishment of processes to help vulnerable populations.
- Regarding medium-term response, Mexico City is running projects on water and land conservation, land management for agricultural rural areas, reforestation with more resilient species, and green roofing in urban areas. Below are the goals and key results of the main projects to adapt to climate change in the context of the Climate Action Program for Mexico City.
- For emergency response in case of landslides or flooding, the most relevant agencies are the Department of Civil Protection, Fire and Health, complemented by Brigades of the Ministry of Social Development, to provide shelter, hot food, and psychological help to those affected, as well as the Ministry of Public Security to control access and prevent vandalism. As a permanent activity, there are homeless shelters and soup kitchens and attention to patients with severe respiratory or dehydration.

TABLE A3.3
Status of Main Projects to Adapt to Climate Change

Program/responsible agency	Goals	Results
Urban Hillsides Program—Environmental Agency	By 2012, identify 33 hillsides and develop and disseminate their management programs	As of 2009, nine hillsides identified and seven programs developed
Dengue Monitoring—Health Department	Determine mortality rate due to dengue	Annual studies made to identify the presence of the virus, risky areas mapped, and household surveys made
Monitoring and prevention of health effects due to extreme weather—Health Department	Avoid mortality and mitigate risks and health effects of exposure to extreme temperatures	Information campaigns conducted, serum kits distributed, and chlorine in water closely monitored
Epidemiological and health monitoring of climate change—Health Department	Monitor chlorine in water, water supply systems, sanitary monitoring of food production and distribution, among others	In 2010, over 36,000 water samples and 125 food samples taken for analysis. Over 1,900 visits to establishments to evaluate sanitary conditions
Support to vulnerable populations during winter season—Social Assistance Institute	Provide support and social assistance to vulnerable people	In 2010, over 200,000 warm dinners and 15,000 blankets distributed. Also, over 6,000 medical consultations provided, among other services
Risk Atlas of Mexico City—Civil Protection Agency	Develop an integrated information system shared by all administrative units	Efforts ongoing
Preventive program for hydro-meteorological risks—Civil Protection Agency	Prevention, mitigation, and response to emergencies due to hydro-meteorological events	260 informational reports disseminated, often daily during the week
Storm Unit Program—Water System of Mexico City	Response to negative effects of precipitation during the rainy season	Between 2008 and 2010, over 6,000 cases were attended and resolved
Reduction of extreme precipitation impacts in "El Arenal"—Government Secretariat	Mitigate negative impact of extreme precipitation in 14 areas	Food, drinks, blankets, and cleaning products distributed. Equipment installed to speed up the drainage, and sewers cleaned
Sustainable housing in the Federal District—Housing Institute of the Federal District	Incorporate green technologies into new housing	Solar water heaters, energy efficiency lamps, and water treatment by re-utilization, among others, incorporated in over 5,000 new dwellings

Source: Leon et al. (2010).

Shortcomings in Current Disaster Risk Management or Climate Change Adaptation Management

Disaster risk in Mexico City is handled in a primarily reactive manner and limited preventative measures have been implemented. Implementation of the early-warning system, envisioned as one of the priority adaptation measures included in the MCCAP, has been delayed due to administrative issues that urgently need to be resolved. In addition, there is an evident need to improve the sharing of information among the relevant government agencies, taking as an example the Risk Atlas (elaborated by the secretary of civil protection), to which not all agencies have access.

Leading Activities to Coordinate Agency Risk Management

The secretary of civil protection is in charge of risk management in Mexico City, although many other agencies are also involved.

Pillar 2—Hazards Assessment

Natural Disaster History

The Mexico Valley is exposed to increases in extreme temperatures, which with expanding urbanization has contributed to a significant heat-island effect for Mexico City. Projections reveal that the mean temperature is expected to increase by 2–3°C toward the end of the 21st century, and extreme precipitation is also expected to increase. Characteristically rising temperatures are accompanied by an increase in extreme rain, consequently placing Mexico City at heightened risk of flooding and landslides, particularly in the western part of the city.

TABLE A3.4
Natural Hazards

	Yes /No	Date of last major event
Earthquake	Y	1985
Wind storm	Y	2010
River flow	N	
Floods, inundations, and waterlogs	Y	2010
Tsunami	N	
Drought	Y	2011
Volcano	N	
Landslide	Y	
Storm surge	N	
Extreme temperature	Y	

Current Trends and Projections

TEMPERATURE—The temperature in the Mexico Valley reflects its geography, where warmer temperatures are concentrated in the lower elevations and cooler temperatures in the elevated areas. Nevertheless, with time, the temperature in the Mexico Valley has changed due to urbanization, constituting one of the clearest examples of a heat-island effect in the world. The highest values are observed in the northeast, where the average maximum reaches 30°C. The area with main maximum temperatures over 24°C increased considerably between 2000 and 2007, and the minimum temperature increased by 2°C and 3°C in the north and northeast, respectively, in the same period. While temperature increase in the western part of Mexico City has been lower, the frequency and duration of heat waves in the area are increasing. For example, the number of heat waves of three or more days with 30°C or higher increased from 2 in 1877–1887 to 16 in 1991–2000 in the west of the Federal District (Jáuregui 2000). Simulation exercises for temperature in January show that temperature in the northeast, which is the region that has grown fastest, increased 2°C. Although this temperature rise may in part be the effect of urbanization, some atmospheric conditions may also have had an impact, and this order of magnitude is in line with those expected this century by models simulating global warming.

To further understand temperature increases associated with urbanization, an analysis was undertaken of temperature trends in areas with rapid urbanization against those in regions that are close to highly vegetated areas. For Mexico City, the trend in the minimum temperature in regions with rapid urbanization between 1963 and 2000 is an increase of about 0.7°C per decade, while for regions close to vegetated areas the associated increase was about 0.1°C per decade.

Another way to evaluate the effects of extreme events is to analyze the 90th percentile of the maximum temperature using a projection from the Earth Simulator. For 2015–2039, the northeast region will have temperatures around 30°C for at least 10 percent of the year, as shown in figure A3.3, in the color section.

Figure A3.3 90th Percentile of Maximum Temperature, in Celcius, in 1979–2003 (left) and 2015–2039 (right)

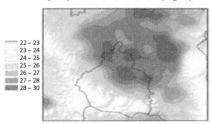 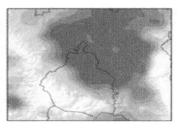

22 – 23
23 – 24
24 – 25
25 – 26
26 – 27
27 – 28
28 – 30

Source: Leon et al. (2010).

PRECIPITATION—Precipitation projections for Mexico City seem to be consistent with the general projection made by the Intergovernmental Panel on Climate Change (IPCC) in 2007, which states that precipitation will increase in regions with high precipitation and decrease in regions with low precipitation. Particularly, the intensity and quantity of extreme precipitation is expected to increase in the west of the city, and decrease in the east. In the Mexico Valley the highest precipitation occurs between mid-May and early October, with the western region receiving the most precipitation in August. On average, annual precipitation is between 700 and 900 mm (±30 percent). The highest intensity usually occurs during the afternoon and early evening. The western region presents upward trends for daily precipitation and episodes over 20 mm/hour over the past 100 years. During September and October, more than 30 mm/hour of rain may occur, which, based on a review of landslides, is the critical threshold for landslides of saturated land. Projected increases in extreme precipitation in terms of the intensity and duration are shown in figure A3.4. In the west of Mexico City, these increases constitute a significant hazard for vulnerable populations located on hillsides. Additionally, projected increases in extreme precipitation add to the risk of flooding in the west of Mexico City and the southern areas of the Federal District.

Figure A3.4 95th Percentile of Precipitation (mm/day) in 1979–2003 (left) and 2015–2039 (right)

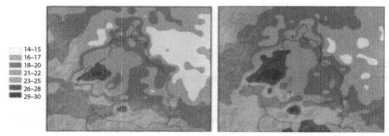

Source: Leon et al. (2010).

WATER RUNOFF—Climate change projections indicate that with increasing temperature, evapotranspiration increases at the expense of infiltration and runoff. For many urban areas, including the MCMA, changes in land use also affect this ratio, whereby as urbanization increases, less water is naturally absorbed into the ground and more runoff occurs. Assuming 100 mm of rainfall and using information about land and vegetation types, the approximate amount of water runoff was calculated for Mexico Valley.[1] The findings show a noticeable increase in runoff in 2000 when compared with 1980. The increased precipitation and resulting runoff increases flood risk in the city, particularly given the existing drainage system.

Pillar 3—Socioeconomic Assessment

Location of the Urban Poor

Vulnerable groups were identified and mapped in terms of population and housing characteristics by doing a cluster analysis with data from the 2000 official census.[2] In terms of population, vulnerable groups include areas with high concentration of people over 18 years without secondary education, people that moved in the past 5 years, and people with low income. As shown in figure A3.5, this group includes about 7 million people (or 42 percent of the population of the Mexico City Metropolitan Area) and about 1.5 million dwellings.

In terms of housing, vulnerable groups are concentrated in areas characterized by use of precarious construction materials in walls and ceilings, those without access to basic services, and where formal property ownership and rights are limited. This group includes about 5 million people (or 30 percent of the population) and about 1 million dwellings. The location of these groups is shown in table A3.6. The most vulnerable in terms of both population and housing represent about 27 percent of the population and are located in the peripheral area of the MCMA, mostly to the north and east[3] (see figure A3.5, in the color section).

TABLE A3.5
Vulnerability Matrix in Terms of Population and Housing

		Population	
		Low vulnerability	**High vulnerability**
Housing	**Low vulnerability**	2,609 PSUs* 9,516,901 people 2,329,416 dwellings 54.8% of population	514 PSUs 2,639,058 people 584,547 dwellings 15.2% of population
	High vulnerability	164 PSUs 577,583 people 128,831 dwellings 3.3% of population	1,354 PSUs 4,635,298 people 964,144 dwellings 26.7% of population

*Primary sampling units.

Source: Leon et al. (2010).

TABLE A3.6
Social Assessment

City population below poverty line (%)	59.4
Social inequality (Gini index) in 2002 (UN Habitat)	0.43 (2008) CIA factbook
Unemployment (% of total labor force)	6.3
Areal size of informal settlements as a percent of city area	n/a
City population living in slums (%)	22
Children completing primary and secondary education: survival rate	57.4 (Mexico City)
Human Development Index (2009)	75
Predominant housing material	For the very poor, assorted salvaged materials; for self-builders, concrete blocks and brick

Exposure of the Urban Poor

The information on vulnerable groups was overlaid with information on extreme precipitation and temperature, and locations with steep slopes. Maps similar to that above were created to observe the location of these groups with respect to high-risk zones: current and future extreme precipitation and vulnerable housing; vulnerable population and housing located in zones with high risk of extreme precipitation; vulnerable population and housing located in zones with slopes over 15 degrees; vulnerable population and housing located in zones with risk of heat waves; and vulnerable population and housing located in zones with risk of extreme precipitation and slopes over 15 degrees.

Table A3.7 shows the distribution of population and housing for each event. Most of the vulnerable population in high-risk zones lives in locations with slopes over 15 degrees (about 1 million people). The total population that lives in high-risk zones represents about 40 percent of the vulnerable population and about 41 percent of the vulnerable dwellings. Importantly, about 60 percent of the vulnerable population and dwellings are not located in high-risk zones.

TABLE A3.7
Distribution of Vulnerable Groups Located in High-Risk Zones

Event	PSUs[1]	%	Population	%	Housing	%
I. Extreme precipitation	48	3.55	179,019	3.86	38,909	4.06
II. Slopes over 15 degrees	288	21.27	1,004,586	21.67	208,546	21.63
III. Heat waves	117	8.64	367,450	7.93	76,771	7.96
I + II	59	4.36	251,118	5.42	53,455	5.54
I + III	1	0.07	39	0.00	10	0
II + III	23	1.70	62,449	1.35	13,175	1.37
I + II + III	0	0.00	0	0.00	0	0.00
Vulnerable in high-risk zones	536	39.59	1,864,661	40.23	390,866	40.54
Total vulnerable	1354	100	4,635,298	100	964,144	100

Source: Leon et al. (2010).
PSU refer to primary sampling units defined in the context of the 2000 census.

Economic Costs of Climate Change—Another important aspect of the socioeconomic assessment was the analysis of the economic costs of climate change in terms of GDP for the Federal District. This analysis incorporated four scenarios. The base scenario, named A2, does not include climate change impacts and assumes 1.99 percent of annual GDP growth, 1.81 percent of annual GDP per capita growth, and 18 percent of population growth for 2100. The other three scenarios correspond to different goals on reduction of greenhouse gas emissions considered in international negotiations (that is, 550, 450, and 350 parts per million, or ppm). The analysis incorporated three discount rates (0 percent, 1 percent, and 4 percent); however, based on the literature on the costs of climate change, the authors recommend using 0 percent to draw conclusions. Table A3.8 shows costs for each scenario in terms of GDP reduction and additional number of poor people by 2100 for the Federal District, using a 0 percent discount rate. Shown is the average value, as well as the 95 percent confidence interval in parentheses.

TABLE A3.8
Costs in Terms of GDP and Additional Poor

Scenario	GDP reduction by 2100, no. of times	Additional number of poor people by 2100, in thousands
A2	19.10 (5.22, 45.79)	441 (98, 1281)
550 ppm	17.35 (4.52, 43.04)	392 (81, 1176)
450 ppm	10.77 (3.15, 24.38)	213 (51, 560)
350 ppm	6.50 (2.03, 13.70)	104 (26, 249)

Source: Leon et al. (2010).

Under the status quo scenario (A2), it is expected that the GDP will be reduced 19 times on average. These results are not too different from those under the 550 ppm scenario. However, if the 350 ppm scenario is realized, the benefits could reach 32 times the current GDP (in terms of avoided losses). Also under the A2 scenario, the number of poor is projected to increase to over 1 million (or about 10 percent of population in 2100), although the average increase is expected to be 450,000. The analysis also pointed out that economic losses are not distributed equally among administrative units. Those that will lose the most are those that are currently worse off. In other terms, if the temperature increases by 2°C, Mexico City could lose up to 7 percent of its GDP and get 150,000 additional poor annually.

Notes

1. Runoff calculation was undertaken using the curve number method, developed by the USDA Natural Resources Conservation Service.

2. The census data are coded, for all variables, in primary sampling units (PSUs) or territorial units, called by the Mexican official census institution basic geo-statistic areas (AGEBs, Areas Geoestadísticas Básicas).
3. In addition to those living in low-income neighborhoods, Mexico City also has a sizable homeless population, which is particularly vulnerable to extreme events. Importantly, this segment of the population is not accounted for in the city's calculations of urban poverty, as such information relates to those who possess a dwelling.

Reference

Leon, C., V. Magaña, B. Graizbord, R. González, A. Damian, and F. Estrada. 2010. "Pobreza Urbana y Cambio Climático para La Ciudad de México." Unpublished, Mayor's Task Force Study, Mexico City.

Annex 4: São Paulo Case Study

Overview and Key Findings

In São Paulo, the largest city in Latin America, almost 11.5 million people live in 1.5 km^2. More than 40 percent of the population lives in peripheral areas that concentrate a vast proportion of the city's poor and socially vulnerable citizens. São Paulo is already experiencing some consequences of a changing climate: more frequent heavy rains, higher temperatures, and decreased air humidity. An estimated 900,000 houses in the peripheral areas are considered at risk—some located in slopes and floodable areas—and will be the most affected by climate change.

In this context, this case study presents the first comprehensive revision of policies and programs at the intersection of climate change, disaster risk, and the urban poor in São Paulo. The case study has been prepared by the World Bank, in close consultation with the São Paulo Housing Secretariat and the Green and Environment Secretariat. These two secretariats have contributed with their expertise in working with slums and informal settlements, as well as working in disaster risk management and climate change adaptation.

The approach used in this case study is based on the Urban Risk Assessment (URA) framework. Accordingly, it includes an assessment of the hazards, socioeconomic vulnerabilities, and institutional aspects related to climate change and disaster risk management in São Paulo. Extensive data collection and stakeholder consultation was carried out as part of this study. In particular, two highly vulnerable communities in São Paulo were consulted and analyzed more in depth.

With a focus on the urban poor, this study considers how poor communities are affected by climate change and natural hazards, examines approaches that have been taken to address these challenges, and identifies priorities and options for further action in São Paulo. This study draws on other existing reports and resources on disaster risk management and climate change, as well as on interviews and discussions with key stakeholders.

Key Findings of the Study

Independent studies predict that in the absence of significant policy changes, by the end of the century urban occupation in São Paulo will be twice the current one and 11 percent of the future occupied areas could be located in areas at risk for landslide. This will increase the risks of floods and landslides, impacting disproportionally the poorest.

Although this scenario will occur only in the absence of significant changes in the spatial distribution and socioeconomic characteristics of the city, it does highlight the importance of dealing with climate change and disaster risk with a focus on the urban poor.

The Mayor's Task Force in the city of São Paulo found that:

- The vulnerable groups who occupy areas at risk will have difficulty coping with unpredictable and extreme weather. Slum dwellers (currently more than 890,000 households) lack the resources necessary to adapt rapidly to the changing circumstances.
- Slums face the most hazardous conditions; more than 5 percent of slum areas are highly or very highly exposed to landslides and are highly prone to be affected by destructive events in the next 12 months.
- While the location of certain settlements in areas of flood plain or wetlands does not necessarily indicate flood hazards, it is an indirect estimate of areas potentially more exposed to such events. The incidence of precarious and informal settlements in these areas shows how intensive their occupation has been. About 20 percent of the slums and informal urbanized centers are located in flood plains. About 13 percent of the allotments and informal settlements are located in flood plains and flood hazard areas.
- In the slums, virtually all families live in poverty or extreme poverty. In addition, a great number of the basic services that the people depend upon suffer negative impacts with the severe weather. For instance, the public transportation system in São Paulo is not fully equipped to handle floods and overflows.
- The sanitation system has some deficits (6 percent of houses do not have proper sewage collection and 25 percent of the effluent is not treated).

- Energy service is irregular and the systems suffer with the storms, which lead to electricity shortage in houses and streets, creating an unsafe feeling among the inhabitants.

The Government of São Paulo at Work

The city of São Paulo has been a pioneer in monitoring greenhouse gases at the city level. As part of the C40 group, São Paulo has committed to prepare a GHG emissions inventory, adopt a future reduction target on GHG emissions, create a local action plan in a participatory process, implement climate policies and measures, and monitor and verify results.

In 2005 São Paulo launched its first inventory. Furthermore, in 2007, the City Assembly passed a law that required new houses and buildings assembled with more than four bathrooms to adopt a solar-panel heating system. In 2009 the City Assembly approved the City Climate Law to ensure the city's contribution to stabilizing GHG in the atmosphere in accordance with UNFCCC principles.

The City Climate Law set a reduction target of 30 percent in GHG emissions against the baseline 2005 emission levels. Additional targets should be defined each two years. The law establishes a number of commitments for the city to follow by sector. From 2005 to 2010, the city already has cut its emissions by 20 percent, largely due to implementing biogas power plants on two large landfills.

A Special Fund for the Environment and Sustainable Development was created in 2001 with the purpose of financially supporting projects that aim to improve the sustainable use of natural resources; control, monitor, protect, and recuperate the environment; and initiate environmental education. Currently, the fund does not have budget revenue from the municipal government of São Paulo, instead its revenue coming from various resources (R\$8 million) that are directed to 15 projects from NGOs chosen through tenders; and Carbon Credits Auctions (R\$33 million + 37 million), the amount originated from CDM projects implemented at the Bandeirantes Landfill and São João Landfill. The fund has been used to support the creation of a database on GHG emissions, publication of an inventory of anthropic emissions every five years, and actions for climate change mitigation, including incentives for the private sector and research institutions.

Areas for Improvement

Some of the recommended areas for work out of the Mayor's Task Force include:

- Housing—Increase the regularization and improvement of slums and irregular allotments and remove families from risky areas.
- Health—Increase the number of people served in health services and increase its qualities.
- Transportation—Increase the coverage of bus, trains, and subway routes, improve bus stops and terminals, renovate electric bus system and cars, enable public transport, decrease traffic rates, and increase traffic safety.

- Education—Improve public system, decrease evasion rates, especially for the medium (or secondary) education; increase the number of public nurseries (insufficient to meet the growing demand).
- Water supply—Increase the water quality and protect water basins.
- Sewage—Increase system coverage and avoid illegal disposal of sewage into water courses.
- Waste management—Increase inspection of illegal dumping places, decrease waste generation, and increase recycling.
- Cleaning—Improve cleaning coverage for culverts and streets.
- Drainage—Clean and dredge the river bottoms, clean and increase the existing drainage underground channels, and build more "pools" ("piscinões") around the city.
- Looking forward—Mainstream climate change, climate variability, and disaster risk reduction in planning land use. This should strengthen the municipality's own medium-term planning, enabling them to prepare for (among other things) the hosting of Global Expo in 2020.

Looking Forward

Overall, this study highlights some of the challenges a metropolis like São Paulo is facing regarding present and future climate change and disaster risk scenarios, especially when dealing with an ever-increasing socially vulnerable population. The document also shares the lessons already learned by the city when addressing this subject. In the short and medium term in addressing climate change, disaster risk and urban poverty, key areas for reform include:

- Coordinate and integrate information databases among the different city secretariats. As of now the city faces a multiplicity of information produced and used by different agencies. The unification of information could lead to shared programs.
- Extend public disclosure of information and public participation in the design and implementation of climate projects to ensure stakeholders are involved.
- Incorporate climate change policies into city administration in order to guarantee continuity.
- Enhance mapping capacity to better inform resilience in decision making.
- Improve inequality in adaptive capacity across the city through capacity-building programs for stakeholders, practitioners, city managers, and decision makers. Structured learning resources and the exchange of experiences with other cities can be applied to increase the understanding of the linkages between climate change and disaster risk management and the urban poor in different levels.

Case Study Summary

City Profile

Figure A4.1 Administrative Map of São Paulo

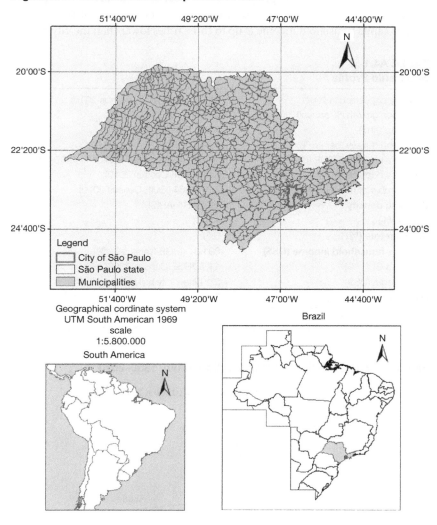

Legend
- City of São Paulo
- São Paulo state
- Municipalities

Geographical cordinate system
UTM South American 1969
scale
1:5.800.000

The population growth rate in São Paulo is decreasing (in 2010 it was only 0.76 percent compared to 1.16 percent in 1990). The difference between the numbers of people in the city between day and night could reach 2 million people. Nevertheless, the population rate in the periphery is increasing (growing from 4.9 million to 5.5 million from 1991 to 2000), representing 30 percent of the urban expansion. The periphery concentrates the majority of the poorer inhabitants (the average household income is half the average for the city and the per capita household income is up to three times lower than the city rate).

TABLE A4.1
São Paulo Profile

Total city population in 2010	11.25 million (IBGE census 2010)
Population growth (% annual)	0.75 (SEADE 2000/2010)
Land area (km²)	1,523 (IBGE census 2010)
Population density (per km²)	7,388
Country's per capita GDP (US$)	10,960 (Brazil central bank and IBGE 2010)
Country's population (%)	5.89 (IBGE Census 2010)
Total number of households	3,576,864 (IBGE Census 2010)
Dwelling density	(SEHAB/HABISP)
Slums (%)	1.6
Irregular lots (%)	6.32
Average household income (US$)	891.37 (IBGE Census 2008)
Country's GDP (%)	11.7 (IBGE Census 2008)
Total budget (US$)	3.1 billion (city hall budget 2010)
Date of last Urban Master Plan	2002

Note: IBGE: Instituto Brasileiro de Geografia e Estatística; SEHAB: Sao Paulo Municipal Housing Secretariat; SEADE: State Data Analysis System Sao Paulo; HABISP: Information and Prioritizing Intervention System

Figure A4.2 Growth Rates for City of São Paulo, 1950–2010

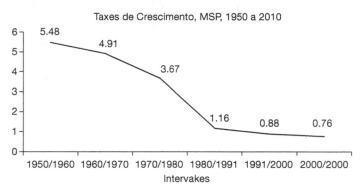

Taxes de Crescimento, MSP, 1950 a 2010

Source: HABISP.

Figure A4.3 São Paulo City Social Vulnerability Index, IPVS

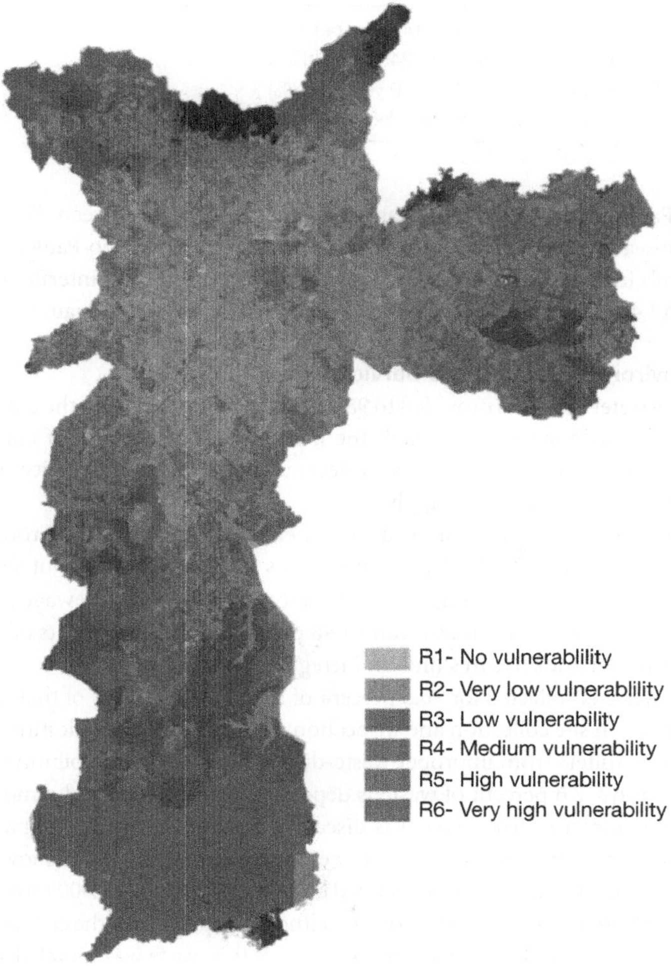

R1- No vulnerablility
R2- Very low vulnerablility
R3- Low vulnerability
R4- Medium vulnerability
R5- High vulnerability
R6- Very high vulnerability

Source: HABISP.

Life expectancy in São Paulo is 71 years. The mortality rate is 6.53 for each thousand and the child mortality rate is 15.83 for each thousand. The city has 4.89 percent illiteracy among youth above 15 years old. Almost 47 percent of the population above 25 has less than eight years of formal education (primary education lasts nine years and secondary, three additional years). The population is mainly made up of people ages 25 to 59, as shown in table A4.2.

TABLE A4. 2
Population of São Paulo

Population from 0 to 14 years old (%)	24.1
Population from 15 to 24 years old (%)	14.8
Population from 25 to 59 years old (%)	49.6
Population from 60 and more years old (%)	11.5

Source: SEADE (2009).

São Paulo is located in the Atlantic Plateau, with hills between 718 and 720 m above sea level. There is no registered seismic activity in São Paulo. Regional hills climb from large floodplains through fluvial terraces into interfluvial areas. Figure A4.4, in the color section, shows the city´s declivity and main rivers.

Built Environment and Basic Services

Adequate water supply is provided to 98.6 percent of the houses in the city (almost 65 m³ per inhabitant/year), though the increase in the number of consumers, scarcity of new water resources, and decrease in basin water quality increases concerns about future water supply.[1]

Sewage collection is reported at 87.2 percent sewage (2006). From all the domestic sewage collected, 81 percent receives proper treatment. But slums and irregular housing lots have improper sanitation conditions and sewage is thrown directly into streams and rivers. Almost 48 percent of the inhabitants of the city's water basin wetlands live in slums and irregular settlements.

Solid waste is collected for 96.5 percent of the houses. In spite of that, there are irregularities in site collection and inspection (more than 300 clandestine dumps), and the city suffers from improper waste-disposal clogging and polluting culverts and waterways: 2.6 percent of waste is deposited in containers and removed by a City Hall contractor; 0.64 percent is discarded in the land or in waterways; and another 0.16 percent is burned in yards or empty lands. City Hall data shows that, in 2010, the total amount of waste generated daily by the city was 17,000 tons—10,000 tons come from residential collection and almost 100 percent of the collected waste went to regulated landfills. Less than 1 percent of this waste was recycled.[2]

There is enough energy supply to meet city demands (99.99 percent of the houses possess energy), according to AES Eletropaulo Metropolitana S.A. (an energy utility). It is not unusual for the city to have localized blackouts, especially during heavy rains. Electricity theft is common in poor regions of the city. The industrial, residential, and commercial sectors are more or less equal in their energy consumption (17 percent of the national consumption is equivalent to 35.3 million megawatt/hours).

The city's traffic is extremely heavy, with more than 7 million vehicles. The subway system (managed by the state) is connected to the rail system (also managed by the state), through a CPTM (Train Management Agency). An average of

Figure A4.5 Greenhouse Gas Emissions from Electric Energy Use by Sector in São Paulo

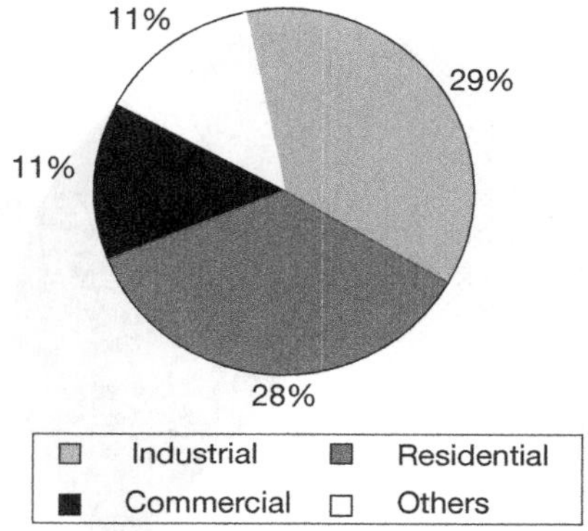

Source: São Paulo GHG's inventory.

2.1 million passengers a day are transported through 89 stations, 260.8 km, and 63.5 km of subway tracks. Approximately 15,000 buses circulate through 1,335 routes and 28 terminals. Every three years it is estimated that the number of bus trips increases by 1 million (CPTM, Metro and SPTrans 2010). The design and number of routes is considered insufficient to adequately serve the entire population. The situation is even worse for the poor, since a great number of them live in the periphery areas and work in more centralized neighborhoods where the job opportunities and wages are better. As a result, they spend hours in public transport commuting.

In 2005, the city had 34 city parks (15 million m³), which increased substantially in 2008 to 48 parks (24 million m³) and 17 linear parks.[3] The SVMA plans for 100 parks by 2012 (50 million m³), 20 linear parks, and 5 natural parks. São Paulo had, in 2009, only 21 percent of its original forest coverage.[4]

The "Agenda 2012" program was enacted into law in 2008 and prescribes the transparency of actions and priorities managed by the city. Each region of the city has its targets, which range among health, education, traffic, water quality, sewage piping, quality of parks, leisure areas, safety, and transportation.[5]

Pillar 1—Institutional Assessment

Agencies in Disaster Risk Management and Climate Change Adaptation

The Emergency Management Agency acts on the federal, state, and municipal levels. Its goal is to plan actions to prevent and minimize effects of disasters, either natural or human caused, assist people affected by them, and rehabilitate or recover the places destroyed by those events. In the city this responsibility rests with the City Public Safety Secretariat, through the City Emergency

Figure A4.6 Transport Use in São Paulo

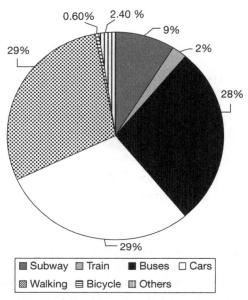

Source: Research Origin and Destination 2007.

Management Agency (COMDEC). Nonetheless, its personnel are allocated to the 31 decentralized units or "subdistricts."

The City Emergency Management Agency acts on prevention and recovery, assistance and aid, and on search and rescue, and is assisted by the Firefighter Department. At the communities located in areas of risk, there should be a Local Emergency Management Group, or NUDEC. They should be made up of volunteers trained by the National Emergency Management Agency to help during emergencies and risky situations.

The Emergency Management Center (CGE) is responsible for observing meteorological data (there are 180 monitoring stations) and for informing COMDEC. Then COMDEC alerts the subdistricts, which monitor the volume of rainfall using pluviometers installed at 31 points in the city.

The Summer Rainfall Operation is a city plan that brings together the Housing, Transport, Urban Infrastructure, Social Assistance, and Subdistricts Coordination Secretariats, led by the Emergency Management Agency, and targets disasters that occur during the summer (when heavy rainfall is common). Whenever necessary or from November through April, the city organizes initiatives to prevent disasters or to assist in emergencies, recovering the area after the flood or landslide and providing shelter for those in need.

When a heavy rainfall approaches, CGE issues an alarm to COMDEC, as well as to the traffic authorities (CET), the Health Secretariat (SMS), Green and Environment Secretariat (SVMA), and Housing Secretariat (SEHAB). Each subdistrict must then activate the process using the Emergency Management Agency agents allocated to the region, following a standard operational procedure. The initiatives include prevention (evacuating houses in at-risk areas), search and rescue of people in floods or landslides, and restoration of affected areas.

After the flood or landslide, the firefighters rescue possible victims. Water and sanitation authorities fix broken water pipes and energy agents check the electricity posts. Social assistants verify housing conditions and, if necessary, direct people to temporary shelters while SEHAB arranges for "rent allowance" or allocate housing for the needy. The City Health Secretariat, through its Health Vigilance Coordination (COVISA), trains its environmental agents to inform—both before and after the heavy rains—the vulnerable communities about endemic diseases spread by water (such as leptospirosis), their symptoms, and the need for medical treatment. The basic health units (UBS) receive folders and posters to distribute to the population on how to avoid leptospirosis and the proper treatment. COVISA also alerts each region of the city about its specific risk of leptospirosis, aiming to prepare the health professionals for the emergence and spread of the disease.

Examples of Disaster-Related Program or Relevant Decrees

The Summer Rainfall Operation is an existing plan from the city that brings together the Housing, Transport, Urban Infrastructure, Social Assistance, and Subdistricts Coordination Secretariats, led by the Emergency Management Agency.

Decree 47.534/2006 reorganizes the city system of the Emergency Management Agency. There are other laws at administrative levels that regulate the Emergency Management Agency and the operation procedures.[6]

There is no information on the maintenance and testing of the procedures. From an ordinary citizen's point of view, those alarms are neither timely nor efficient, since they require constant monitoring through the CGE´s website. In at-risk areas, this is even less likely to occur, since the rate of viewing the Internet in general in the city in 2003 was 25 percent. There is no data available on expenditures on disaster risk management or adaptation programs.

Shortcomings in Disaster Risk Management and Climate Change Adaptation Management

The interviews and research indicate that the Emergency Management Agency has a shortage of agents in the at-risk communities, for distributing and teaching the use of the plastic pluviometers (PET) and water-level rulers. CGE also needs resources to train emergency management local agents about informing the population of the risks of heavy rain. The Health Secretariat has a shortage

TABLE A4.3
Institutional Mapping of Disaster Risk Management Functions

Risk assessment	Risk reduction		
	Technical (planning, management, maintenance)	Early-warning and response	Public awareness
Civil defense	Civil defense • Agents and NUDECs	CGE • 18 meteorological stations	CGE • Website

of medical personnel and adequate facilities to assist citizens with lepstospirosis or climate-related diseases. A direct and efficient channel with the community in at-risk areas must be created to alert people in emergencies. The same needs to be done for the general population. Overall, prevention measures in at-risk communities should be strengthened.

Estimated Levels of Spending on Pro-Poor Services and Infrastructure
The City Emergency Management Agency works on disaster management activities. Interviewees noted that the agency lacks resources to carry out its projects, develop new initiatives, train and support communities based on units or groups, properly service the population in emergencies, and develop means of preventive maintenance.

At the beginning of 2011, the mayor of São Paulo and the governor of São Paulo jointly launched a US$5 million initiative to fight floods in the city. It included cleaning the Tietê River; acquisition of pumps to move water from the Pinheiros River to the Billings water reservoir; a system of underground channels to dredge the Tietê River; and the creation of the Varzeas Tietê River Linear Park (with plans to remove 5,000 families that should not be living at the edges of the river).

Pillar 2—Hazards Assessment

Past Natural Disasters
There is no publicly available systematization of climate hazards or measurement of potential impacts and losses. This is a substantial gap in information that the city needs to address.

A prominent city newspaper provides information on recent rainfall events:

• November 2009–March2010. Heavy rainfall accounted for 78 deaths and 20.000 homeless. Jardim Romano (a poor neighborhood) was flooded for more than two months.
• October 2009. Tietê and Pinheiros´s rivers overflowed and there were 86 flooding points in the city.

- February 2008. In the neighborhood of Mooca in the east of the city, the water height reached 2 meters. Firefighters were called 53 times to rescue stranded people. Train passengers were trapped in the railway cars for more than six hours (due to lack of power caused by the rain).
- November 2006. The city experienced 230 flooding points (doubling the number for the same month the previous year).
- May 2004. The heaviest rainfall in years (140 mm in a single day) caused 120 flooding points in the city; small rivers flooded. One person disappeared in a flooded area.

TABLE A4.4
Natural Hazards

	Yes/No	Date of last major event
Earthquake	N	N/A
Wind storm	N	N/A
River flow	Y	2009
Floods, inundations, and waterlogs	Y	2011
Tsunami	N	N/A
Drought	N	N/A
Volcano	N	N/A
Landslide	Y	2011
Storm surge	Y	2010
Extreme temperature	N/A	N/A

TABLE A4.5
Hazards, Effects, and Losses

Hazards	Effects	Losses
Heavy rainfall—more than 30 mm/day	Landslides Floods	Lives Houses and material, resident property, cars
	Stream overflow River overflow Leptospirosis and water-transmitted diseases	Health conditions
Extreme heavy rain—more than 100 mm/day	Landslides Floods	Lives Houses and material, resident property, cars
	Stream overflow River overflow Leptospirosis and water-transmitted diseases	Health conditions
Air dryness	Health problems (mainly respiratory)	Health conditions

Source: Institute of Research and Technology 2009.

Main Climate Hazards

According to the Institute of Research and Technology (Instituto Nacional de Pesquisas Espaciais, or INPE 2009), São Paulo is composed of a variety of surfaces with different temperatures, forming a mosaic of urban climate. There are heat islands, thermal inversion areas, pollution bubbles, and local differences in the wind patterns. Therefore, it is impossible to plan a single initiative or define a precise quantity of rain or degree of heat that could cause tragedies. Each area has its specific soil, drainage, occupation, and permeability conditions and, as a result, a different threshold to be met.

That said, INPE produced the data for figure A4.7, which shows the amount of heavy rainfall in São Paulo per decade, from 1933 to 2000, indicating an increase in the number of days of heavy rainfall—with more than 100 mm of precipitation in just one or two days.

INPE confirms that rainfall above 10 mm per day is considered heavy, but is not potentially dangerous. More than 30 mm per day of rainfall can cause serious floods, and more than 50 mm can be even riskier for the city (before the 1950s, rainfall above to 50 mm per day was nonexistent, but currently this occurs two to five times every year).

Figure A4.7 Days with Intense Rainfall per Decade

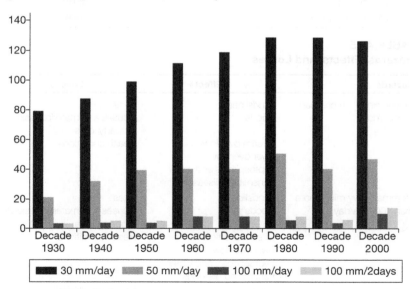

Source: IAG/USP, Analysis by INPE 2010.

Figure A4.8 Number of Flooding Points Registered by CGE in São Paulo per Year, 2004–2011

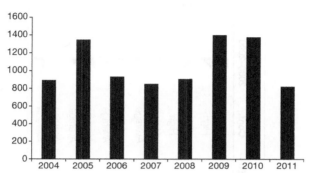

Source: CGE and Mauricio Maia blog, 2011, http://alagamentos.topical.com.br/pontos.

Summary of Climate Projections from the Regional ETA-CPTEC (Centro de Previsão de Tempo e Estudos Climáticos) Model for São Paulo

For INPE, the main climate risk scenarios for São Paulo are:

- Floods—This risk scenario is characterized by the overflow of river water onto the adjacent lowlands, when the plains along the main watercourses of the Alto Tietê Basin become flooded. Despite investments to increase flow capacity of the main waterways, floods continue to occur due to urban growth and the natural dynamics of floods and existing interventions in waterways.
- Heavy floods—Rugged conditions allow for heavy floods, that is, high water volume and speed. Flooding of this nature may destroy buildings and other urban infrastructure, cause other material damage, and endanger the lives of residents living near rivers.
- Flash floods, with high potential for drag—Public policies for channeling streams and constructing roads in valleys cause flash flooding along the streets, where surface water concentrates (which also occurs in suburban areas, without paving). This process is characterized by the power of accumulated surface water and the high destructive power of drag. These conditions expose people and housing to high risk. The greatest probability of loss of life is found in the periphery regions, and loss of goods in consolidated central neighborhoods. Rainwater runoff concentrated along watercourses or on public roads is responsible for most deaths in floods, when people are dragged by the water.
- Occasional flooding—Occasional flooding (accumulations of shallow water that rarely penetrate the interior of the buildings and affect most public roads)

TABLE A4.6
Climate Projection for Metropolitan São Paulo

	Present observed	Present simulated	2030–2040	Conf.	2050–2060	Conf.	2080–2090	Conf.
Temperature	▲	▲	▲	High	▲	High	▲	High
Warm nights	▲	▲	▲	High	▲	High	▲	High
Cold nights	▼	▼	▼	High	▼	High	▼	High
Warm days	▲	▲	▲	High	▲	High	▲	High
Cold days	▼	▼	▼	Average	▼	High	▼	High
Heat waves	Unobserved	▲	▲	Average	▲	Average	▲	High
Total rain	▲	▲	▲	High	▲	High	▲	High
Intense precipitation	▲	▲	▲	Average	▲	Average	▲	High
Precipitation > 95th	▲	▲	▲	Average	▲	Average	▲	High
Precipitation days > 10 mm	▲	▲	▲	Average	▲	Average	▲	High
Precipitation days > 20 mm	▼	▲		Average		Average		Average
Consecutives dry days	▼	▲	◣	Average	▲	Average	▲	High

Source: INPE/CEPTEC.

▼ Increase   ◣ Decrease

occur widely in various parts of the city, primarily because of deficiencies in the drainage system. Occasional floods are temporary inconveniences for pedestrians and vehicles.

- Trash thrown into water courses—Some 6,000 households throw waste directly into waterways in the metropolitan region of São Paulo. The garbage contributes to siltation and clogging of these waterways, and can be carried by runoff, captured by the river, and taken to lower slopes, where the waste is deposited. The detention reservoirs of Tietê River are located in these lower slopes and can be damaged by the debris.
- Landslides on slopes—The slope regions are generally subject to informal settlements and prone to landslides, which can cause serious accidents and deaths of residents.
- More severe rainfall—There is a clear correlation between more severe rainfall (greater than 100 mm) and more rugged terrains. The climate analysis by INPE indicates that severe rainfall will occur more in areas of the city that are at risk of landslides and flooding, increasing the vulnerability of the inhabitants.

Exposure to Hazards

The Technological Research Institute (Instituto de Pesquisas Tecnológicas, or IPT) was commissioned by the city to map the geotechnical hazardous areas in São Paulo in order to identify sector vulnerabilities to landslides and stream washouts in areas of precarious urban settlements. In this study, a hazardous area is defined as one likely to be hit by natural or human-induced conditions that cause adverse effects. People living in such zones are exposed to physical harm and are prone to material losses. Typically, in Brazilian cities, these areas correspond to low-income housing units (precarious informal settlements).

The factors found essential for analyzing hazards include the type of process expected, the likelihood of the process occurring, the vulnerability of the urban settlements, and the potential for damage.

The analysis included morphological and morphometric features of the terrain; geological materials and profile of the alteration; geological structures; evidence of geological movements; ground coverage; and conditions associated with wastewater, rainwater, and subsurface water. As a result, a hazard zone for landslides and stream washouts has been defined for vulnerable urban settlements. The methodology used to map the zone included the following activities:

- Oblique low-height helicopter aerial photography.
- Field work to examine the features and limits of hazardous terrains in previously identified hazards zones.
- Assessment of the likelihood of destructive processes.
- Assessment of potential consequences due to dwelling vulnerability.
- Estimate of hazard level per sector.

- Recommendations for hazard-control initiatives.
- Data input into a geo-referenced database, integrated with the Housing Secretariat's (SEHAB) HABISP System.

Figure 4.9 shows the hazardous areas mapped in the informal, vulnerable settlements. Slums have the highest rate of landslides and washouts. About 20 percent of the land where slums are settled is subject to geotechnical hazards. Slums in São Paulo represent roughly 76,000 households exposed to hazards. There are 407 highly hazardous areas located in 26 subdistricts.

Displayed in the figure are geotechnical hazard areas overlapping data on steepness. As expected, critical areas are closely associated with high steepness. Such areas are more likely in the peripheral zone of the city (northern, eastern, and southern suburbs). The most critical areas are precisely where the most precarious settlements

TABLE A4.7
Incidence of Hazardous Areas in Informal Settlements in São Paulo

	Urbanized centers	Settlements/allotments	Slums
Landslide risk (%) (IPT 2010)	10.43	3.90	14.79
Washout risk (%) (IPT 2010)	2.44	0.68	5.38

Source: HABISP–SEHAB; IPT 2010.

Figure A4.9 Geotechnical Hazard Areas

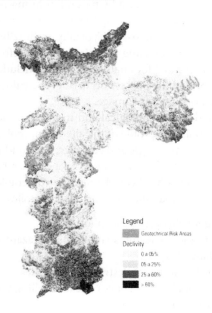

are located. Lack of access to a formal land market by the poorest families generates the conditions for these combined factors of social and environmental vulnerability.

In addition to identifying hazardous areas, the IPT also ranked them in four levels of criticality. A qualitative hazard analysis has been made on the data obtained from field observation, integrating the analysis parameters into a hazard assessment record card, with the support of aerial imagery. The degrees of hazard are shown in table A4.8.

A cross analysis of hazardous areas ranked by their critical level and informal settlements, as shown in table A4.9, concludes that slums face the most hazardous conditions. In total, more than 5 percent of slum areas are highly or very highly exposed; these areas are highly vulnerable to destructive events in the next 12 months.

TABLE A4.8
Degrees of Landslide Hazard

Class of hazard	Description of hazard
R1—low	Potentially low degree of geological and geotechnical predisposing factors (steepness, type of terrain, etc.) and of intervention in the sector for developing landslides and washouts. There is no evidence of instability in slopes and drainage banks. It is the least critical condition. If the status remains unchanged, no destructive events are expected over one year.
R2—medium	Potentially medium degree of geological and geotechnical predisposing factors (steepness, type of terrain, etc.) and of intervention in the sector for developing landslides and washouts. There is some evidence of instability (yet incipient) in slopes and drainage banks. If the status remains unchanged, there is little probability of destructive events during long, strong episodes of rain over one year.
R3—high	Potentially high degree of geological and geotechnical predisposing factors (steepness, type of terrain, etc.) and of intervention in the sector for developing landslides and washouts. There is significant evidence of instability (ground cracks, sag of embankments, etc.). If the status remains unchanged, destructive events may be expected during long, strong episodes of rain over one year.
R4—very high	Potentially very high degree of geological and geotechnical predisposing factors (steepness, type of terrain, etc.) and of intervention in the sector for developing landslides and washouts. There is strong evidence of instability, supported by numerous accounts of hazardous conditions (ground cracks, sag of embankments, , walls cracking in houses or retaining walls, tilted trees or poles, slide scars, erosion features, dwellings built near stream banks, etc.). It is the most critical condition. If the status remains unchanged, destructive events are highly probable during long, strong episodes of rain over one year.

TABLE A4.9
Cross-Referencing Data: Areas Ranked by Their Critical Level and Types of Settlements in São Paulo

	Low hazard	Medium hazard	High hazard	Very high hazard
Slums (%)	2.92	11.90	4.11	1.40
Settlements/allotments (%)	0.65	2.93	0.97	0.43
Urbanized centers (%)	4.59	7.62	0.56	0.09

Source: HABISP–SEHAB; IPT 2010.

This conclusion stresses the urgency of taking preventative measures. Furthermore, such hazards can be leveraged by prospective climate conditions, potentially increasing the degree of hazard level in areas currently ranked as low or medium risk.

It is worth stressing that IPT's map does not take into account floods and water logging. While floods are not as lethal as mudslides and landslides, they represent the most frequent hazards to which the population is exposed. These events result in great material damage and may have secondary effects on health by increasing the likelihood of spreading waterborne diseases such as leptospirosis. People living near streams or rivers—especially children and the elderly, who are the most vulnerable—are also exposed to direct risks such as drowning and physical injury in highly destructive landslides.

Pillar 3—Socioeconomic Assessment

TABLE A4.10
Social assessment

City population below poverty line (%)	5.6 in 2000. Atlas DH
Social inequality (Gini index) in 2002 (UN-Habitat)	0.543 metropolitan area (PNAD 2006)
Unemployment (%)	12.3 in 2009 (SEADE)
Areal size of informal settlements (% of city area)	7.92 in 2010 (HABISP)
City population living in slums (%)	0.48
Households without registered legal titles (%)	7.9
Children completing primary and secondary education: survival rate (%)	Abandon rate for primary, 1.3; and for secondary, 5.4
Human Development Index (2009)	0.841 in 2000 (IBGE)
Predominant housing material	Brick

Population Exposure to Hazards

The most significant climate hazards for São Paulo are floods and landslides. Flooding points have not been fully mapped by the city, only floodable points on streets; these are related to traffic problems, as shown in figure A4.10.

When dealing with landslides, the city commissioned IPT to map and rank the critical spots. A qualitative hazard analysis has been made on the data obtained from field observation, integrating the analysis parameters into a hazard-assessment report card, with the support of aerial imagery.

A map overlapping social vulnerability (mapped through the IPVS index) and climate vulnerability (using IPT and INPE data) was produced.

The following layers were included in the database to produce the map:

- Informal/precarious settlements in São Paulo (2010): Obtained from HABISP-SEHAB (Housing Secretariat) containing the official demarcation of each settlement organized by slums, urbanized slums, and informal settlements. Information about the quantity of houses, infrastructure, and average income level available.
- Geotechnical risk areas (2010): Obtained from HABISP-SEHAB, a study from the Technological Research Institute (IPT) from the state of São Paulo, the data consists of the areas mapped by the IPT using in-place verification, which presents geotechnical risk for landslides and undermining among water streams. The areas were characterized by four degrees of hazard level, varying from low risk to very high risk.
- Geotechnical chart (1999): This chart was elaborated in analogical format and contains the main geomorphologic areas of the city. The Planning Secretariat digitalized the map and the data could be integrated in the geo-referenced dataset.
- Index of social vulnerability (IPVS), per the census (2000). São Paulo State was divided into six groups of social vulnerability. Based on multivariate statistical analysis, the IPVS uses the data from the last population census, conducted in 2000. The calculation of the IPVS uses two types of information: demographic characteristics and socioeconomic condition of the families;
- Declivity map: Based on the topographic chart of the city developed by EMPLASA (Empresa Paulista de Planejamento Metropolitano), the declivity map is a raster dataset containing classes of declivity for each pixel. This dataset reveals the topography of the city, indicating those areas with high declivity and thus more inclined to landslides.
- Transportation infrastructure and public infrastructure: This data contains the localization of the public infrastructure of the city, such as schools and health clinics. Obtained from the HABISP-SEHAB and SEMPLA (São Paulo Secretaria Municipal de Planejamento), this dataset was used to infer

Figure A4.10 Main Flooding Points of Streets

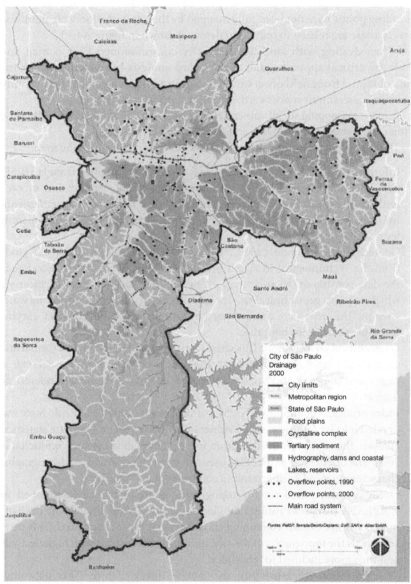

Source: SVMA, Environmental Atlas, 2000.

the existence of public infrastructure under geotechnical risk as well as analyze the proximity of this equipment to the vulnerable areas.

- HAND model: This dataset, produced by the National Spatial Research Institute, supports the work on Brazilian megacities and climate-change vulnerabilities. The data was calculated from the topographic chart of the city using spatial analysis. Based on a raster representation obtained from the declivity map, the dataset informs those areas with highest vulnerability to landslides and floods.
- Water reservoir locations (piscinões, or big pools): This data, collected from SEMPLA, corresponds to the locations of the 16 water reservoirs constructed in the city to control floods.
- Hydrograph and drainage system: This system corresponds to the watercourses of the city and the natural drainage system.
- Flooding: This layer—mapped by the Traffic Engineering Company (CET), which is responsible for traffic control in the city—contains the points where floods occurred.

The analytical approach used for the mapping task was based on spatial analysis techniques in the Geographical Information System (GIS). All the layers were compiled in an integrated geo-referenced database. The calculations were based on overlays applied over the reference layers of informal settlements, slums, and urbanized slums. It was then possible to calculate the relative incidence in terms of area of geotechnical risk of flooding. It was also possible to calculate the relative incidence of the Social Vulnerability Index in each of the reference layers.

Calculating both incidences, social vulnerability and geotechnical risk, led to comparisons between all the informal, precarious settlements in the city. The results of the geographical analysis operation were tabulated and organized by themes of vulnerability and hazards. The most vulnerable settlements were those that present the higher percentage of areas within highest geotechnical risk and social vulnerability. Finally, thematic maps were generated showing the layers included in the database, allowing visualization of the critical areas all over the city.

Location of the Urban Poor

Most precarious settlements are located in more peripheral areas of the city. Such areas concentrate environmentally vulnerable situations and are the most poorly served by basic services and urban infrastructure. The analysis indicates that there is a strong overlap between the locations of high-risk areas and the informal settlements throughout the city. Figure A4.11 shows the location of precarious housing (slums, irregular lots, and urbanized slums).

Figure A4.11 Spatial Distribution of Precarious Settlements in City

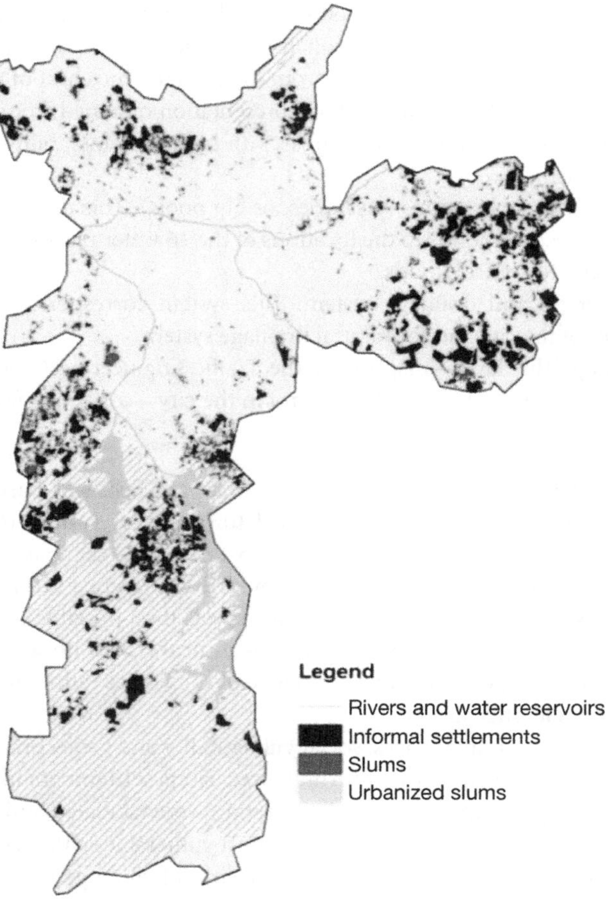

Legend
— Rivers and water reservoirs
■ Informal settlements
■ Slums
▢ Urbanized slums

Source: HABISP 2010.

Slum Characteristics

The distribution of the census in the city by groups of social vulnerability clearly discloses the socioeconomic macro-segregation pattern that places the central area. In particular, the distribution shows the southwest quarter of the city as the region with the lowest levels of social vulnerability, as opposed to the peripheral zone, where the highest levels of social vulnerability are recorded. These more critical situations can be found in the southern, northern, and eastern periphery of the city. Not by accident, most of São Paulo's precarious settlements are set up in these peripheral areas.

According to the city, in 2010 approximately 890,000 precarious dwellings were in the city. Over 85 percent of these households are located in slums and irregular settlements, spread across all regions of the city. Displayed in table A4.12 is the distribution of households per type and location in the large administrative regions of the city.

Slums record the highest proportion of children and youth up to 19 years old (41.7 percent), which is consistent with the presence of younger heads for households and a greater number of children. As for household income, most families earn less than three times the minimum wage.[7] Although many of the heads of household are employed in the formal labor market, low levels of education hinder access to better work opportunities. About two-thirds of the heads of household have not completed primary education (SEADE Foundation 2008).

These areas still lack access to urban infrastructure and services supply, as shown in table A4.13. There are significant deficits in public lighting, paving, and urban drainage in slums, urbanized centers, and allotments. Waste disposal and collection are not available to all households, often because collecting vehicles have no space to circulate. The most critical problem, however, concerns the sanitation network. The severity of this situation is mostly evident within the slums, where more than half of the households have no access to sewerage facilities, thus greatly exacerbating environmental problems and exposing inhabitants to disease and health hazards.

TABLE A4.11
Houses by Type of Precarious Settlements and Administrative Regions of City Housing Secretariat

	Wellsprings1	North1	South1	Southeast1	East1	Center1	Diffuse2	Total
Slum1	54,886	65,696	117,793	64,980	67,072	10,724	0	381,151
Informal settlement (1)	100,031	60,769	44,953	22,739	154,552	0	0	383,044
Urbanized center (1)	11,193		1,973	1,051	2,640	262	0	24,522
Tenement (cortiços) (2) (3)						11,086	69,303	80,389
Irregular housing complex (1)	669	7,403	4,657	2,533	3,056	1,659	0	20,702
Total	166,779	141,996	169,376	91,303	227,320	23,731	69,303	889,808

Source: (1) HABISP, February 2010; (2) obtained from SEADE Foundation survey; (3) the total amount of tenement houses is an estimation by the SEADE Foundation.

TABLE A4.12
Access to Urban Services and Infrastructure in Precarious Settlements in São Paulo

	Urban Infrastructure			Waste Collection			Sanitation	
	Access to public lighting	Paving	Walkways and culverts	Door-to-door collection	Curb container collection	Other	No access	With access
Households in slums (%)	68.30	67.10	55.70	64.90	20.70	14.40	52.30	47.70
Households in residence centers (%)	86.30	91.10	80.80	67.90	13.50	18.60	8.20	91.80
Households in allotments (%)	92.30	81.50	81.20	91.50	3.40	5.10	20.20	79.80
Total (%)	**81.90**	**75.70**	**70.40**	**79.50**	**11.10**	**9.50**	**33.30**	**66.70**

Source: Fundação Seade; Secretaria Municipal de Habitação, SEHAB; Pesquisa Socioeconômica em Favelas e Loteamentos no Município de São Paulo, 2007.

A poverty ranking based on the World Bank's poverty threshold criteria reveals the gravity of the situation for the families living in those settlements, as shown in table 4.14.[8] In the slums and urbanized centers, virtually all families live in poverty or extreme poverty. There is a slight improvement in housing settlements with regard to this indicator; yet about 80 percent of the families in that setting live in poverty or extreme poverty. This finding reinforces the importance of public services supply and policies for those whose ability to fulfill basic needs is extremely low, exposing them to even more critical levels of social vulnerability.

The situations of social vulnerability disclosed by the data are often associated with exposure to geotechnical and flooding resulting from occupying land

TABLE A4.13
Number of Precarious Inhabitants per Level of Poverty

	Poverty		
	Indigent	Poor	
Families in slums (%)	31.90	66.60	98.50
Families in residence centers (%)	33.60	66.40	100.00
Families in settlements (%)	26.10	53.30	79.40
Total (%)	**28.90**	**59.40**	**88.30**

Source: SEADE Foundation; SEHAB/HABISP (São Paulo City Housing Information System) São Paulo Slum and Allotments Socioeconomic Research, 2007.

unsuitable for housing. Moreover, in most cases the dwellings are self-built over long periods. Thus, low technical quality of dwellings associated with occupying areas unsuitable for housing brings about hazards, often involving imminent risk. Characteristic of these areas are steep slopes and unstable land and flood zones during rainfall periods.

Climate Smart Practices

The Várzeas do Tietê Park, a project of the state government, in partnership with São Paulo, will be 75 km, the largest linear park in the world. There are about 7,000 households that will have to be removed. The resettlement will be done in the same region, with the construction of new housing units in a partnership between the City Housing Secretariat (SEHAB), Housing and Urban Development Agency (CDHU), and Metropolitan Housing Company of São Paulo (COHAB). The park will cover São Paulo and seven other cities, benefiting an estimated 2 million people. In addition to the 7,000 households removed in São Paulo, 2,000 more will be removed in other cities. The Várzeas do Tietê Park will have a total area of approximately 10,000 hectares, with significant environmental gains, because it is considered essential for preserving the river and sanitizing the areas that affect the margins. The project should be completed in 2016. The project will restore and preserve the environmental function of wetlands, provide flood control, and create options for leisure, tourism, and culture. In the project, Via Parque will be built, a track with a 23 km extension with car and bike paths and a lot of space for walking. The Tietê River, including its tributaries, lakes, and ponds, will be restored, as well as riparian and native vegetation. Special areas for leisure, courts, arenas, cafeterias, and administrative spaces will also be built.

Key Lessons in Addressing Poverty in a Climate-Smart Way

The study points to recommended actions, which are listed below:

• Allocate personnel from the Emergency Management Agency to each vulnerable community, working as the Local Emergency Management Group, or NUDEC. The personnel should be made up of volunteers, trained by the National Emergency Management Agency, to help in emergencies and risky situations. This would allow preparation for emergencies and quicker and more effective response. The same would apply to health agents.
• Extend mapping and systematization of the city's entire flooding areas— including all housing regions—and use this data to prioritize initiatives.
• Improve measures to enable public transportation and the use of cleaner fuels.

- Implement an emergency transport plan for heavy rainfall, using buses with bi-articulated engines and special corridors for those vehicles to transit.
- Implement an efficient alert system for the entire population when there is heavy rainfall, with all government entities working rapidly with a direct channel of communication to the communities in the areas impacted by the heavy rain.
- Extend studies to analyze and enable change in the city's growth pattern and land-use patterns to concentrate housing and job opportunities in specified regions. Providing adequate facilities, such as hospitals, schools, places for leisure and sports, and other facilities, would avoid long daily commutes and decrease the traffic and greenhouse gas emissions (such as São Francisco Global, described in "Opportunities"). Another approach is to promote the occupation of other degraded places downtown (such as Nova Luz), which already have infrastructure but which are undervalued and contain dilapidated buildings.
- Promote an integrated policy to manage waste issues in the city. Not only should the policy take care of public cleaning, but also deal with waste reduction, inform the population about sustainable consumption, and enable recycling.
- Extend measures for supervision and adequate disposal of waste, as well as improve the periods between cleanings of streets and culverts.
- Extend enforcement of the Municipal Climate Law obligating buildings with high concentrations or circulation of people (such as malls, large residential condos, or commercial buildings) to install recycling centers.
- Extend procedures related to environmental inspection, and epidemiological and entomological control in selected locations, aiming at the quick discovery of biological effects caused by climate change and potential treatments.
- Extend initiatives to restore all permanent conservation areas, especially those located in floodplains, in order to avoid or minimize risks caused by extreme climate.
- Extend the law that obligates new corporate projects to maintain a permeable area in order to absorb water.
- Extend energy-efficiency measures throughout the city.
- Find funding for public projects and NGO climate safety activities.
- Extend awareness of the Municipal Climate Law to public agents, that is, the law must become part of the daily routine of planning and executing policies in all related government agencies.
- Integrate and extend climate change policy, bringing together several organizations and public players. The Climate Change Economy Committee begins this movement, but its role needs to be reinforced.

- Promote increased citizen participation and planning on climate initiatives, including organized demands for new policies. In order to do that, society needs to be informed about the issue and their role in it.
- The climate policies must be incorporated into the city's management. The policies should be implemented regardless of changes in mayors in a new election or a change of secretary in the middle of the term.

Constraints Identified by the Consulted Communities

- Lack of an efficient public transport system, which would improve accessibility to other parts of the city and reduce walking distances.
- Lack of quality and coverage of piped water and a sewer system, which currently could rupture during heavy rainfall and infiltrate houses and reach rivers and streams.
- Lack of means to prevent electricity theft through makeshift connections, resulting in a high cost of energy and posing a risk during heavy rain.
- Lack of channeled streams, which could prevent the death of people who may fall during heavy rains.
- Lack of retaining walls on hillsides at risk.
- Lack of quality of garbage collection and inspection of illegal dumps.
- Lack of adequate cleaning of streams and culverts.

Opportunities

The City Housing Secretariat—SEHAB—provides the Housing Information System—HABISP:

This information provides a comprehensive overview and update of planning and environmental conditions in the settlements of the city. The information allows people to define priorities for intervention, as well as assist in developing city policies and integrated plans with other agencies. These include: SABESP, São Paulo State Sanitation Utility; SVMA, City Green and Environment Secretariat; SME, City Education Secretariat; CDHU, Housing and Urban Development Agency; and Caixa Econômica Federal (the Federal Bank). The HABISP information system is a tool that is easy to use, as well as being interactive and readily accessible via the Internet (www.habisp.inf.br). HABISP promotes increased citizen participation—it provides an opportunity for data disclosure and is an important resource for the population, providing information about policies and plans under development.

Opportunities to promote adaptation strategies:

Existence of a comprehensive legal framework: The legal framework for the city to deal with the impact of climate change already exists. The Municipal

Climate Law sets the foundation for the necessary measures related to energy, transport, land use, health, construction, and waste management to be performed by the city, other government entities, and private players. A reduction target was established and public disclosure of the results is expected. Nevertheless, future regulation is needed on some issues, such as payment for environmental services and subnational cooperation.

Mapping of areas where landslides occur: The areas at risk for landslides are already identified and geo-referenced by the municipality, allowing the prioritization of prevention. The same is needed for all flooding areas beyond the locations already mapped. This data would be most useful if shared among secretaries for planning. If strong preventive projects are implemented, the risks will be lower and less will need to be spent on emergency action.

Existence of the beginning of a unified approach to climate issues and policies: The EcoEconomy and Climate Committee were created to unite the city entities around the subject, and also bring together state and national players, citizen organizations, and government agencies. The 2009 Decree 50.866/2009 inaugurated the committee's works. The forum aims to propose, stimulate, and follow the adoption of plans, programs, and actions that help satisfy the city policy. It also intends to support actions to mitigate greenhouse gas emissions, promote adaptation strategies, create seminars and campaigns, and promote the adoption of social and environmental criteria in the city's purchases of products and services. Members of the committee can help in identifying technology trends linked to climate change and offer feedback on eventual amendments to the Municipal Climate Law. The structure exists and meetings take place regularly; there is still need to strengthen community capacity to propose and implement projects.

São Francisco Global Urban Plan, by SEHAB: The plan creates guidelines to integrate the 50,000 inhabitants of the third-largest slum on the east side of São Paulo into the formal city, by extending social housing, the construction of a hospital, school, community center, and services center, which will also serve as a commercial center and income generator. It also includes extending the transport system and improving roadways. With paved streets and nearby trees, the ease of access to public transportation, town inhabitants will use a car less in everyday tasks. The objective is that the town will stop being a "bedroom city" and will provide the products and services essential for everyday day living in central city locations. Plans for new housing will maximize the conservation of the remaining green areas and water springs in the new town. Together with SVMA, a park will be created, at an old dump, measuring 367,000 thousand m^2.

Ecofrota Program: At the beginning of 2011 the city initiated a program that provides for the use of 20 percent biodiesel in public transport throughout the city. The initiative aims to reduce the emissions of particulate matter by 22 percent, carbon monoxide by 13 percent, and hydrocarbons by 10 percent, and reaches the annual goal of reducing fossil fuels by 15 percent, as provided in the Municipal Climate Law. This states that the entire public transportation system in the city should operate on renewable fuels by 2018. The project will identify any public transport fueled with cleaner fuels, including biodiesel, ethanol, hybrid, and electric.

City hall to renew the transport fleet: SP Trans has been renewing its bus fleet, which services the city, substituting the old vehicles with more advanced modern models. Of the 15,000 buses in the city, 9,684 (65 percent) have already been replaced, lowering the average age of the vehicles in use to four and a half years. In addition, just by adding larger buses between 2006 and 2010, the fleet capacity increased 21 percent and the number of transported passengers grew by 11 percent.

Solar systems to heat the water: The City Assembly approved Law 14459/07 requiring that from that date forward all new residential or commercial buildings should be prepared to use a solar-based system to heat the water used by its inhabitants. The new houses and buildings assembled with more than four bathrooms must adopt a solar-panel heating system. Some commercial buildings, such as private clubs, gyms, hotels and motels, schools, hospitals, clinics, and industrial laundromats also must install the solar panels. The system should meet at least 40 percent of the annual energy needs of the toilet water and water for pools that the building may require.

Sustainable Building Project: Developed by PMSP/SEHAB, this project has been initiated in a part of Heliópolis, a large slum in the southeast of the city with almost 130,000 residents. Over the last few years this area has been undergoing urbanization and improvement: houses are now made mainly of bricks instead of scarce wood.

Carbon credits: Carbon credits are being used to develop social and environmental projects in areas near the plants, such as linear parks, public squares, eco-points installation, and a center being built to hold wild animals and to house birds. For example, the Bamburral slum (570 families living next to the Bandeirante waste site) is the first slum to be urbanized with funds from carbon credits. The community urbanization provides infrastructure, stream channeling, and construction of four clusters of houses that will receive 260 families that live in at-risk areas. The construction of a deck over the creek is also planned in order to facilitate the movement of residents, as well as a linear park with areas for sports and leisure.

Linear parks: The Várzeas do Tietê Park, at 75 km, will be the largest linear park in the world. There are about 7,000 households that will have to be removed. The resettlement will be done in the same region, with the construction of new housing units in a partnership between the City Housing Secretariat (SEHAB), Housing and Urban Development Agency (CDHU), and Metropolitan Housing Company of São Paulo (COHAB). Várzeas do Tietê Park will have significant environmental gains, because it is considered essential for preserving the river and the sanitation of the areas that affect the margins, restoring and conserving the environmental function of wetlands, and providing flood control. Riparian and native vegetation will also be restored.

Operation Clean Stream: This operation is a joint initiative with the state government of São Paulo to recover and treat streams throughout the city. The first phase was initiated in 2007 and ended in 2009. More than 800,000 people benefited from cleaning 42 streams and piping 500 liters per second of sewage. The program deals with the remediation of the water and improvement of the sanitation in informal homes, benefiting 1,637 inhabitants. The program will continue with the cleanup of 40 more streams up to 2012. During operations, the city is responsible for maintaining stream margins and layers, and removing houses that may prevent the passage of the sanitation piping system.

Headwaters Program, by SEHAB: The program aims to service all vulnerable settlements located in protection areas such as Guarapiranga and Billings dams in order to restore drinkable water quality. The program partners among the three parts of the government and focuses on using the sub-basin as an integrated planning unit of government initiatives. The city's master plan allows the construction of new vertical housing projects for 4,000 people at the margins of the drinking water reservoirs of Guarapiranga and Billings (the first supplies water to 1.2 million inhabitants, and the second to 3.8 million). Billings currently has 12 km² of its water mirror occupied by informal settlements and receives 400 tons of waste every day. Guarapiranga has 1.3 million illegal residents in its margins.

Social Partnership Program: The City Housing, Social Welfare and Social Development of Public Policies in São Paulo has the objective of providing access for low-income people to the formal rental allowance market. They are subsidized by the fixed monthly amount of $300.00, with no adjustments for 30 months. Eligibility into the program requires income of 1 to 3 minimum wages, enabling access by vulnerable groups, including: the homeless in special social protection networks; families from areas expropriated by São Paulo, displaced due to floods or fires; and residents in at-risk areas. The social work is based on a development program that systematically monitors eligible families, providing social and economic development initiatives to restore social rights, especially decent housing.

Urban Carbon Footprint

According to a 2005 study,[9] the city's main source of emission comes from energy use, especially from transport (11,986 tons of carbon dioxide equivalent CO_2e).

Solid-waste disposal is the second-most important source (2,696 tons of CO_2e). Liquid effluents (7 tons of CO_2e), Land Use Change and Forestry (51 tons of CO_2e), and agricultural activities (1 ton of CO_2e) are not relevant sources in terms of city emissions (see figure A4.12).

In terms of energy, the use of fossil fuels in transport is the most critical issue for the city, since the fleet is made up of more than 7 million vehicles (growing each year) and the traffic is heavy (the average peak in traffic varies between 80 and 111 km in 2010, and the medium speed rate was of 16 km per hour in 2008).[10]

Although most recent models of cars are "flex"—using both ethanol and gasoline—most private and public fleets run on fossil fuel, especially gasoline and diesel (52 percent of the fossil fuel emissions come from gasoline, 45 percent from diesel, and 3 percent from natural gas). The law prescribed reducing the city´s greenhouse gas emissions by 30 percent, compared with 2005 emissions. Additional targets should be defined every two years.

Initiatives such as the use of more energy-efficient street and traffic lighting and the establishment of infrastructure and incentives to promote the use of low-carbon vehicles are being offered, but specialists agree that the city needs to face the problem of planning land use in order to promote shorter commutes between home and work.

Figure A4.12 São Paulo GHS Study

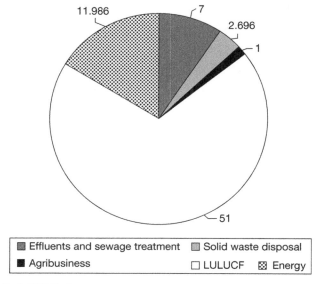

Effluents and sewage treatment Solid waste disposal
Agribusiness LULUCF Energy

Source: São Paulo GHG Study.

Notes

1. IBGE Census 2000 and City Hall website 2006.
2. City Hall website 2006.
3. Linear park is an area around an important reservoir or drinking water basin, where a structure is implemented to protect the environment and at the same time provide the nearby population with leisure or sports activities.
4. City Hall site/environment section.
5. http://www.agenda2012.com.br/oprograma.
6. http://www.prefeitura.sp.gov.br/cidade/secretarias/seguranca_urbana/defesa_civil/legislacao/pops__2009/index.php?p=7929.
7. The minimum wage established by 2011 is around US$325.00 per month.
8. As the threshold for indigency and poverty, the value of R$280.40 (updated in September 2007) was used, based on the POF (Family Budget Study) undertaken by IBGE in 1987. Indigents are considered those with total family income per capita below R$140.20 and, poverty stricken, those who earn up to R$280.40.
9. São Paulo's GHG's inventory, http://ww2.prefeitura.sp.gov.br/arquivos/secretarias/meio_ambiente/Sintesedoinventario.pdf.
10. São Paulo's GHG's inventory, available at http://ww2.prefeitura.sp.gov.br/arquivos/secretarias/meio_ambiente/Sintesedoinventario.pdf

Reference

World Bank and Diagonal Ltd. 2011. *Climate Change, Disaster Risk Management and the Urban Poor: São Paulo, processed.*

Annex 5: Case Study—Dakar, Senegal

Dakar, the political and economic capital of Senegal, has a metropolitan population of more than 1.8 million. This sprawling urban conurbation represents less than 1 percent of the national territory but shelters 25 percent of the national population. The city is exposed to various natural hazards, most prominently recurrent floods, coastal erosion, and sea-level rise. In June 2009, a pilot study on a spatial and institutional approach of disaster risk management titled *Preparing to Manage Natural Hazards and Climate Change Risks in Dakar, Senegal: A Spatial and Institutional Approach* was carried out with support from the World Bank's Spatial and Local Development Team, the Global Facility for Disaster Reduction and Recovery (GFDRR) in collaboration with the World Bank Senegal Country Office, the GeoVille Group, and the African Urban Management Institute (Wang and Montoliu-Munoz 2009). Urban hazards such as recurrent flooding and coastal erosion have been considered in the pilot study, which (1) proposes a new methodology for quickly assessing natural hazard risks at a metropolitan-regional scale using tools of spatial analysis based on geographic information system (GIS) data, and (2) applies the principles and diagnostic questionnaire of the Climate Resilient Cities (CRC) Primer to view the institutional framework for hazard risk management in the city as it relates to climate change.

Public Awareness Raising, Stakeholder Consultations, and Community Participation

Initial consultations with the municipality led to the study's launch. Results from the study were later disseminated through workshops and public consultations to increase awareness of and sensitize local agencies and communities.

Understanding the Institutional Landscape

A quick institutional assessment (based on the CRC approach) was undertaken based on interviews of local authorities, including prefects; city authorities (mayors and deputy mayors); technicians from the cities of Dakar, Guédiawaye, Pikine, and Rufisque; urban planners; land-use specialists; and financial experts. The survey analysis reviewed (1) general information on four administrative departments of the Dakar Metropolitan Area (Dakar, Guédiawaye, Pikine, and Rufisque); (2) governance structure related to disaster risk management; (3) urban planning and land-use regulations; and (4) other factors such as political and economic impacts of disasters and climate change.

The survey found that the implementation framework for disaster risk management (DRM) was ambiguous and complex at the local level, even though Senegal has been actively pursuing disaster risk reduction (DRR) strategies at the national and regional levels. For example, in the case of flooding, the local mayor's office was often responsible for disaster response. But with most local governments lacking adequate resources and technical capacity for infrastructure investments and service delivery, complex issues such as the risks of climate variability remained unaddressed. Furthermore, land-use planning, which has the ability to influence the urban-rural form, remains under the influence of the national rather than local government, rendering it comparatively ineffective.

Hazard Impact Assessment

Understanding the Historical Hazard Trend

The assessment of historical hazard impact for this study was based on reviewing information on historic disasters from secondary sources. The assessment identified flooding, coastal erosion, and drought as the most frequent and significant natural hazards affecting the Dakar metropolitan and surrounding areas.

TABLE A5.1
Natural Hazards in Dakar Metropolitan Area

Hazard types	Characteristics	Available information and source
Flooding	Recurrent and increased impacts of flooding Causes: Increased rainfall, human factors, geological setting of the city	Scientific research papers: Various UN-HABITAT: Estimated 10,000 people and US$9 million economic damage due to the next flooding ReliefWeb: Flood maps of Western Africa Dartmouth Flood Observatory: Data on past floods reported in Dakar GLIDE disaster database: Past floods reported in Dakar National and local newspapers and databases: Information about past flooding disasters
Coastal erosion	Damage from coastal erosion is a more constant risk. Cliffs retreat up to 2 meters a year. Causes: Geotechnical properties of soil and human intervention (e.g., sand extraction)	Scientific research papers: Various UNESCO Dakar Office: Historical overview of past events National and local newspapers and databases
Drought	Major hazard at continental level; can lead to increased impacts from flooding	Scientific research papers: Various
Earthquakes	Low earthquake potential	Munich RE (NATHAN database)
Tornadoes	Medium probability of tornadoes	Munich RE (NATHAN database)
Hail storms	Low hailstorm probability	Munich RE (NATHAN database)

The review of secondary data also led to identifying sea-level rise as the most pertinent climate change-related risk for the coastal city of Dakar.

Defining Study Area and Time Horizon

Based on available quantitative and qualitative data, local information, and the know-how of local experts, the Dakar Metropolitan Area was classified into three subdivisions for this study: (1) urban areas, including communes in the Department of Dakar (the city center) and four communes (Rufisque, Bargny, Diamniadio, and Sébikotane) and three joint districts (Rufisque Ouest, Rufisque Nord, and Rufisque Est) in the Department of Rufisque, which in general are areas with strong urban and industrial economic activities; (2) rural areas, including two large communes in the Department of Rufisque defined locally as Sangalkam and Yène; and (3) peri-urban areas, which lie in between these other areas, including mixed land use and relatively lower densities. Three points in time were considered for the land-use analysis of the study (1988, 1999, and 2008).

Vulnerability

In the study, spatial indicators of vulnerability were derived from hot spots of exposure, assuming that extreme concentrations of exposure will lead to locally increased vulnerability.

Hazard Exposure Maps

The spatial analysis combined results from hazard mapping with population maps, land-price data, and land-cover information in order to derive the exposure of different variables in different locations to the three selected natural hazards. The scale of the spatial analysis was regional/metropolitan, a level of detail relevant for raising awareness and engaging institutions.

Land Use and Land-Use Change

Spot 5 (2.5 m resolution) and Landsat satellite maps were used to develop base maps for 1998 and 2008 as well as to analyze land use and land-use change for two periods (1988–1999 and 1999–2008). Spatial analysis showed that land cover in the area under study had changed significantly in the past 20 years—the surface of urbanized areas had increased by more than 25 percent in that period, about 1 percent per year. Population growth between 1988 and 2008 took place largely in areas prone to a moderate or high hazard potential. In particular, peri-urban areas had the highest percentage of population growth in hazard-prone areas.

Identification of Hot Spots

Hazard maps were overlaid on GIS with maps of population growth to identify "hot spots." In communes defined as peri-urban, almost 40 percent of new population had settled in areas with significant hazard from inland flooding, coastal erosion, or sea-level rise. This rate was about twice as high as urban (19 percent) and rural communes (23 percent) in the area under study. Peri-urban open land (non-built up) was also identified as more exposed to risk (figures A5.1 and 5.2, in the color section).

Approximate Loss Scenario

A broad calculation of the exposure and vulnerability of economic assets in the area under study was inferred from the spatial analysis of land values. Using this

Figure A5.3 Population Growth (1988–2008) in Areas with Hazard Potentials

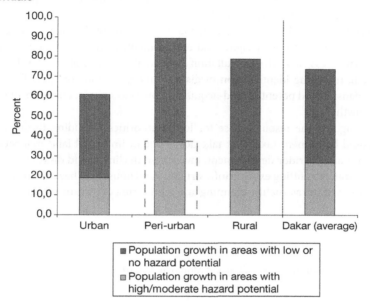

method, the study estimated that the Dakar Metropolitan Area represents a total land value of US$44 billion. Out of this total value, more than US$2 billion, or 5 percent, is exposed to a high potential for natural hazards. Given the imperfect functioning of land markets in Dakar, this is only an approximation of the exposure of economic assets to natural hazards.

Recommendations

i. Implement a general-awareness campaign targeting local public agencies and communities. The campaign should focus on the impacts of natural hazards and climate change on day-to-day lives, with attention to changing behavior.

ii. Strengthen local institutional capacity and interagency coordination by identifying a viable and well-recognized institutional champion at the metropolitan level, focusing on: (a) development of early-warning and quick-response systems, paying attention to underserved peri-urban areas; and

(b) improvement of local organization and capacity to enforce urban zoning and regulations to reduce vulnerability to natural hazards, with special focus on underserved and fast-growing peri-urban areas.

iii. Strengthen local land-use planning and management through: (a) improvement of land property rights and enforcement, with special focus on peri-urban areas; and (b) consultation around the metropolitan development plan, including identification of disaster hot spots and corridors for urban expansion and potential land-acquisition plans to support corridors of urban growth.

iv. Strengthen the resource base for local authorities, including through proposed betterment taxes that take advantage of improved land-management plans and corridor development; investment in climate and disaster-proofing through retrofitting existing infrastructure and housing in hazard-prone areas; improved infrastructure planning and monitoring of investment quality.

Note

This chapter was drawn from Wang and Montoliu-Munoz (2009).

Reference

Wang, H.G., and Montoliu-Munoz, M. 2009. *Preparing to Manage Natural Hazards and Climate Change Risks in Dakar, Senegal.* Washington, DC: World Bank.

Annex 6: Case Study—Legazpi, Philippines

The Legazpi case study illustrates how remote sensing and the geographic information system (GIS) can be applied for assessing urban risk. The methodology and the case study were developed through a collaboration of the Institute for the Protection and Security of the Citizen (IPSC), the Joint Research Centre (JRC) of the European Commission, and the World Bank with funding from the Global Facility for Disaster Risk and Recovery (GFDRR) and JRC. Institutional, social, ecological, and climate risk assessments were not undertaken.

Hazard Impact Assessment

An assessment of historical hazard impacts was undertaken using secondary sources such as the emergency events database (EM-DAT) and other information. The most devastating hazards in Legazpi are tropical cyclones (locally called typhoons), followed by floods, earthquakes, and tsunamis. Flooding is a frequent consequence of heavy rainfall caused by tropical cyclones and sea-level surges.

Exposure

Remote sensing and GIS analysis were undertaken to develop built-up, land use and land cover, building area, and height assessments, as discussed below.

Land Use

Satellite images were analyzed for land use and land cover. Analysis was restricted to an area of 1 km × 1 km. The topography for Legazpi is relatively flat and swampy, crossed by rivers and creeks. Figure A6.1, in the color section; shows a satellite image of Legazpi. The red box identifies the sample area for which the loss model was applied (taken from Deichmann et al. 2011).

The settlements of Legazpi follow the coastline of the bay. Informal settlements are built directly on a gently sloping beach followed by flat land. A small harbor is protected by a pier. In the second row behind the harbor lies another district of poorly constructed huts and houses, including a school. A small business and warehouse district extends toward the north, followed again by residential areas with houses of different size, age, and quality. The flat and swampy area in the interior is crossed by roads, along which many residential houses were recently built.

Exposure

Three types of digital information, with increasing information content, were used to quantify building stock. Figure A6.2a, in the color section; shows a pan-sharpened QuickBird satellite image at 0.6 m spatial resolution. The high resolution allows the identification and location of buildings to generate a data layer of the presence of buildings, which is encoded as a dot layer and shown in figure A6.2b. Building footprints can be outlined generating the building footprint areas encoded as polygons (figure A6.2c). Finally, the building footprints may have the building height as an attribute, thus providing building volumes (figure A6.2d). The information derived from these layers is shown in table A6.1.

Vulnerability

The classification presented in table A6.2 provides five building types used in Legazpi. The list was adapted from the global inventory of building types

TABLE A6.1
Building Stock for Settlement Sample

Building stock	Building location (no. of buildings)	Building footprint (area measure)	Estimated building volume
	2,990	254,916 m²	1,584,067 m³

TABLE A6.2
Categories of Building Type Used in Legazpi to Qualify Building Stock

Building type	Definitions	Brief description of structural characteristics of building type	Damage
1	Reinforced concrete frame with brick in-fill walls	Constructed with highest standards. Typically employed for large and tall buildings. Will include hazard-related building codes.	Sustain pressure and vibration
2	Brick traditional with reinforced concrete columns	Constructed according to engineering standards. Typically on cement pillars, with roof and pavements also in cement.	Sustain pressures and shakes
3	Brick traditional	Constructed according to traditional building standards, using local expertise and material (mortar, adobe, bricks, and wood). Largely varies among geographical areas.	Typically damaged during catastrophes
4	Assembled material (brick and corrugated iron)	Constructed with assembled material for a lack of resources, typically found in poor neighborhoods of urban centers and settlements.	Typically unstable and vulnerable to damage
5	Timber and bamboo or assembled material	Constructed from material that needs to be constantly fixed and repaired.	May be resilient to earthquakes but very vulnerable to floods

available from the World Housing Encyclopedia (WHE 2009), from disaster risk work conducted in Manila, and from experience in the field.

The enumerated building stock was classified into the five building types (table A6.2 and figure A6.3, in the color section). Information gathered during the field visits informed further classification of buildings within the area of interest. The main criteria for labeling each building were the building size (footprint) and the space between the buildings. For example, very small buildings, spaced closely with a small footprint, are deemed of low quality in poor neighborhoods (building type 4). Large buildings are classified as well constructed and likely to provide good resilience (building types 1 and 2), although this should be confirmed on a case-by-case basis.

Estimating Exposed Population

Figure A6.4a shows the districts for which population totals are available. Two district population figures were available: one provided by the World Health Organization (WHO) and based on the National Census of 2006, and the other based on an estimate from the Municipality of Legazpi for 2008. Both statistics used the same district boundaries. The two statistics are within the range of error of population estimates. For the estimation of affected people, the statistics from WHO are more suitable since they are closer in time to the satellite image from which the building stock was derived. Downscaling proceeds as follows. The first step is to compute the total population of the districts that intersect the area under study. Assuming that densities within these adjacent districts are homogeneous, the total population of the area of interest is derived from an area proportion between total population in the districts and the area of interest (table A6.3).

The next step is to compute density measures. These can be derived for the built-up area as a whole (figure A6.4b) or they can be related to the area taken up by buildings only (figure A6.4c). Results are reported in table F.4, where the area unit of measurement is a 10 m × 10 m square. The figures suggest that over the entire built-up area (which includes roads, open space between houses, etc.), there are slightly fewer than two people per 10 m grid square. If only the buildings are considered, there are approximately six people per 10 m square. This could be considered a measure of the average building space occupied by a household. Based on data collected from the field visits, these estimates seem reasonable.

Damage Scenarios

Two scenarios were developed, one for tsunamis and one for earthquakes. They include only direct damages, not indirect effects such as landslides triggered by an earthquake. The two scenarios were selected in consultation with local experts

Figure A6.4 Estimating Exposed Population

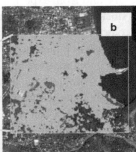

TABLE A6.3
Downscaling Population Statistics Based on Built-up Area and Building Stock

	Area (km²)	WHO (2006)	Municipality (2008)
Districts intersecting 1 km × 1 km study area	2.29	33,283	30,171
1 km × 1 km	1	14,534	13,175

TABLE A6.4
Densities for Built-up Area and Area of Building Footprints

	Area (km²)	Density over 10 × 10 m area
Built-up area in 1 km × 1 km	0.82	1.77
Building footprint area in 1 km × 1 km	0.25	5.81

as having a high probability of occurring in the Legazpi region. The impact scenarios are based on a building damage model structured within a geographical information system. The current models were developed using knowledge gathered from open sources, literature, and field visits.

Earthquake Disaster Risk

The earthquake scenario assumes an intensity of 8 on the Modified Mercalli Intensity (MMI) scale. An intensity of 8 is ranked destructive, with an average ground peak acceleration of 0.25 to 0.30 g, where g is the speed of gravitational acceleration (9.8 meters per second squared; Smith and Petley 2009). Because of the lack of vulnerability curves for Legazpi, the qualitative description of the MMI scale was translated into damage percentages used in the simulation, as shown in table A6.5.

Earthquake Losses

Applying the damage proportions in table A6.5 to the estimates of total building stock—measured as the total area covered by building footprints in each building type—yields estimates of total damages by type of building. The building stock value considered in this exercise is the cost of reconstruction. Local construction engineers provided these estimates in Philippine pesos. The values available

TABLE A6.5
Empirical Fragility Curves for Earthquake Intensity

Building type	Description	Damage description	Damage (%)
1	Reinforced concrete frame with brick in-fill walls	Slight	5
2	Brick traditional with reinforced concrete columns	Slight	10
3	Brick traditional	Considerable	30
4	Assembled material (brick and corrugated iron)	Great	80
5	Timber and bamboo or assembled material	Great	60

where then converted into U.S. dollars per surface unit. The total value of the building stock of a given building type is the product of the footprint area times the cost per unit area. The losses are then the product of the expected damage expressed as percentage for a given building type (figure A6.6).

Earthquake-Affected Population

The entire population within the area under study would be affected by the earthquake. The potential fatalities can be estimated from the collapse ratio. It was hypothesized that the buildings would collapse when damage is higher than 60 percent for either brick or concrete buildings. This occurs for building types 4 and 5, accounting for more than 60,000 m^2 of buildings. That living space would account for up to 4,800 people. This is a crude and probably worst-case estimate, since the actual number of people possibly affected by collapsing buildings will be influenced by, for instance, the time of day the earthquake occurred. During the day, many people will be outside, while losses may be highest during the night. Estimates from past earthquakes would help refine these numbers.

Tsunami Disaster Risk

The study assumed a tsunami wave height of 4 m at the shoreline, hitting the coastline at right angles (see figure 6.5 in the color section). The damaging effect of tsunamis depends on wave height and wave speed. The wave height is a function of local bathymetry, on land topography and shoaling—the increase in height due to bathymetric characteristics. The velocity and wave height determine the pressure exerted on buildings and therefore their destructive behavior. The tsunami wave diminishes as a function of distance, topography, and surface characteristics often referred to as surface roughness. Modeling precise wave impacts on built-up infrastructure requires in-depth modeling, which was beyond this case study.

Figure A6.6 Inundation Height Zones for Tsunami Wave Height of 4 m at Shoreline

TABLE A6.6
Earthquake Losses to Building Stock

Building type	Total building stock (m²)	Value (US$/m²)	Total value of building stock (US$)	Damage (%)	Total damage (m²)	Total losses (US$)
1	18,328.3	435	7,972,810	5	916.4	398,640.5
2	73,413.6	250	18,353,400	10	7,341.4	183,534.0
3	102,151.1	110	11,236,621	30	30,645.3	3,370,986.3
4	60,548.4	65	3,935,646	80	48,438.7	3,148,516.8
5	383.3	10	3,833	60	230.0	2,299.8
Overall	254,824.7		41,502,310		8,7571.8	8,755,783.4

Tsunami Physical Damage

The Legazpi case study employs an inundation model developed by the UK Tsunami Initiative (NERC 2009). For modeling potentially inundated areas, it is assumed that on flat coastlines the extent of the inundated zone depends more on surface roughness than on topography. The applied model calculates the inundation distance from the shoreline resulting from a certain tsunami wave height and assuming that the water flows inland with a distance proportional to the height of the wave at shore and to a friction factor that slows the water flow. The friction factor is measured based on "roughness coefficients" determined mainly by land use and land cover.

Roughness coefficients for land-use categories in the Legazpi region are listed in table A6.7. As this exercise is limited to a study area in a central part of the town with mixed use (residential, commercial, and business), the only land use considered is of the type "built-up."

The inundation distance from the shore and produced by a tsunami of height H_0 is calculated as follows:

$$X_{max} = 0.06 \, H_0^{4/3} / n^2,$$

where n is the surface roughness coefficient as derived from table F.7 and H_0 is the wave height at the shore. The simulated tsunami is based on a historic tsunami in Luzon and Mindoro islands with a wave height of 4 m at the shoreline. This resulted in the inundation distances shown in table F.8. This distance from the shore up to which inundation may reach inland differs by land-use types. In a 4 m scenario, the inundation of roads, for example, could extend up to 7 km from the shore due to low roughness.

The damage to the building stock is a function of the energy from wave impact and the vulnerability of the buildings expressed as fragility curves. As fragility curves for a tsunami were not available for this part of the Philippines, fragility curves reported for the July 2006 South Java tsunami were applied. This assumed that the building stock of Legazpi is similar. One factor influencing damages is the inundation height. The study distinguished three intensity levels: for an inundation height less than 1 m, between 1 and 2 m, and more than 2 m (figure A6.6). Apart from water depth, several other factors influence the degree of damage and could be incorporated based on empirical evidence from past tsunamis or suitable assumptions. These include flow velocity, the amount of debris, and whether

TABLE A6.7
Roughness Coefficient Based on Land Use

Land-use type	Roughness coefficient
Mud flats, ice, open fields without crops	0.015
Built-up areas	0.035
City center	0.100
Forests, jungles	0.070
Rivers, lakes	0.007

TABLE A6.8
Inundation Distance from Shore

Land-use type	Roughness coefficient	X_{max} (4 m scenario)
City center	0.100	38 m
Trees and forest	0.070	78 m
Built-up areas	0.035	311 m
Open fields and roads	0.015	1.7 km
Rivers and lakes	0.007	7.8 km

or not other buildings shield a house. The damage observations were translated into percentage of damage for each of the three intensity zones. Assuming the 4 m wave scenario, all buildings fall into one of the three inundation zones. Table A6.9 shows different building types and corresponding fragility values for the three intensities.

Tsunami Damages and Losses

The three intensity zones provide damages and losses shown in tables A6.10 through A6.12. Each zone has a different amount of exposed assets (the total building stock) and percentage of damage for the different building types. Table A6.10 identifies the building stock for the inundation height of less than 1 m, table A6.11 for the inundation height of 1 to 2 m, and table A6.12 for the inundation heights of more than 2 m.

Tsunami-affected Population

The population affected resides in the three intensity zones. The affected population is estimated by intersecting the inundation zones with the distribution of the population before the tsunami. The estimate shows more than 4,200 people affected by a 4 m tsunami wave within the 1 km × 1 km test area alone. Fatalities for such an event are not estimated, for two main reasons. First, there are no good estimates for mortality during similar tsunamis that might provide guidance. Second, fatalities are often due to the debris floating in the water that would require development of a hydrodynamic impact model.

TABLE A6.9
Building Types and Corresponding Damage Values per Building Type

Building types		Percentage of damage (inundation < 1 m)	Percentage of damage (inundation 1–2 m)	Percentage of damage (inundation > 2 m)
1	Reinforced concrete frame with brick in-fill walls	5	15	20
2	Brick traditional with reinforced concrete columns	10	25	60
3	Brick traditional	25	70	100
4	Assembled material	25	70	100
5	Timber and bamboo	25	70	100

TABLE A6.10
Damages for Intensity Determined by Inundation Height of Less Than 1 m

Building type	Total building stock (m²)	Value (US$/m²)	Total value (US$)	Damage (%)	Total damage (m²)	Total losses (US$)
1	2,126.9	435	925,214.6	5	106.3	46,260.7
2	9,783.7	250	2,445,915.0	10	978.4	244,591.5
3	6,517.9	110	716,964.6	25	1,629.5	179,241.2
4	6,661.9	65	433,024.2	25	1,665.5	108,256.0
5	46.1	10	460.7	25	11.5	115.2
Overall	25,136.4		4,521,579.0		4,391.2	578,464.6

TABLE A6.11
Damages for Intensity Determined by Inundation Height of 1 to 2 m

Building type	Total building stock (m²)	Value (USD/m2)	Total value (USD)	Damage (%)	Total damage (m²)	Total losses (USD)
1	2,126.9	435	925,214.6	15	319.0	138,782.2
2	16,816.6	250	4,204,142.5	25	4,204.1	1,051,035.6
3	12,765.7	110	1,404,221.5	70	8,936.0	982,955.1
4	15,867.9	65	1,031,412.9	70	11,107.5	721,989.0
5	172.0	10	1,720.3	70	120.4	1,204.2
Overall	47,749.1		7,566,711.7		24,687.1	2,895,966.1

TABLE A6.12
Damages for Intensity Determined by Inundation Height of More Than 2 m

Building type	Total building stock (m²)	Value (US$/m²)	Total value (US$)	Damage (%)	Total damage (m²)	Total losses (US$)
1	0.0	435	0	20	0	0
2	9,340.7	250	2,335,185.0	60	5,604.4	1,401,111.0
3	12,482.4	110	1,373,061.8	100	12,482.4	1,373,061.8
4	33,504.0	65	2,177,757.4	100	33,504.0	2,177,757.4
5	106.8	10	1,067.9	100	106.8	1,067.9
Overall	55,433.9		5,887,072.1		51,697.6	4,952,998.1

Note

This chapter was extracted from Deichmann et al. (2011).

References

Deichmann, U., D. Ehrlich, C. Small, and G. Zeug. 2011. *Using High Resolution Satellite Information for Urban Risk Assessment.* European Union and World Bank.

NERC. 2009. *The Tsunami Initiative. Linking Insurance and Science.* www.nerc-bas.ac.uk/tsunami-risks.

Smith, K., and D.N. Petley. 2009. *Environmental Hazards: Assessing Risk and Reducing Disaster.* 5th ed. New York, NY: Routledge.

WHE. 2009. *World Housing Encyclopedia. An Encyclopedia of Housing Construction in Seismically Active Areas of the World.*

Annex 7: Case Study—Sana'a, Yemen

Sana'a, the capital of Yemen, is situated 2,200 m above sea level. Surrounded by mountains, the city is located in the western part of the country. The Sana'a Basin is spread over 3,200 km². Administratively, the city is divided into ten districts. Sana'a has a population of more than 1.7 million (2004 census) and has experienced the highest growth rate of any capital city in the world. Over the next 15 years, the growth rate is expected to continue at 5 to 7 percent per year. The Municipality of Sana'a is currently preparing a long-term City Development Strategy (CDS) for Sustainable Development. The strategy entails evaluating flood and landslide risk. The World Bank, with support from Global Facility for Disaster Reduction and Recovery (GFDRR) and in collaboration with the Sana'a municipality, conducted the Sana'a Probabilistic Risk Assessment study.

Probabilistic Risk Assessment in Sana'a

Sana'a suffers from a severe problem with storm-water drainage due to its location. The city sits in a valley in an inter-mountainous plain that contains many wadis originating from surrounding mountains draining toward the Great Wadi of Saylah. Due to rapid expansion of the city during the last two decades, natural wadi courses have been built up and populated. The residential areas and main streets are prone to flooding, resulting in property damage and traffic problems during the annual rainy season. Also, all city storm-water drainage systems drain

TABLE A7.1
Different Tasks and Key Outputs of Sana'a Study

Task	Key output
Task 1: Historical Hazard Identification and Probabilistic Analysis	Sana'a probabilistic hazard analysis reports, software, and manuals, including the historical hazard review and analysis, probabilistic hazard analysis event characterization, probabilistic hazard modeling software subsystem, and datasets and maps in geographic information system (GIS) format with metadata files.
Task 2: Inventory of Exposure and Vulnerability	Sana'a inventory of exposure and vulnerability report and manuals, including the development and compilation of the inventory of assets and their classification and valuation.
Task 3: Probabilistic Loss Modeling and Analysis and City-Level Analysis	Sana'a probabilistic loss modeling and analysis, including the validation of loss exceedance curves (LECs) and eventual adjustment to the loss-modeling process, risk analysis, applications of catastrophic risk modeling within the context of the Sana'a City Development Strategy (CDS) and Urban Master Plan, institutional strengthening for disaster risk management (DRM), probabilistic loss-modeling software subsystem, and datasets and maps in GIS format with metadata files.
Task 4: Sana'a Natural Hazard Risk Map and Risk Analysis Software Development	Sana'a Integrated Storm Water Management (ISWM), including comprehensive analysis of hydrology and hydraulics, peak flow capacity in the Saylah system, feasibility study and capital investment plan for ISWM, proposal of Flood Early-Warning System (FEWS), operation and maintenance of ISWM, printed high-quality and full-color citywide map with components of ISWM, and datasets and maps in GIS format with metadata files.

Source: GFDRR 2010

into the main Wadi Saylah, causing major property damage and traffic disruptions as this wadi has been integrated into the city's major transport arteries. The rapid expansion of Sana'a and expectations of continuous urban population growth of 5 to 7 percent a year over the next 15 years means that the city is already encroaching onto the slopes of the surrounding mountains, increasing vulnerability to landslides and rock falling.

Recognizing the negative and avoidable impacts of recurrent flash floods in Sana'a, the city has started building a storm-water drainage system, named the Saylah Project, to protect the channel of the Great Wadi of Saylah, and to develop a flood-protection system and recharge the aquifer. A probabilistic risk assessment was undertaken in Sana'a in order to develop an Integrated Storm Water Master Plan (ISWMP) for the city—requiring detailed hydrological information—and to assess the risk of floods and landslides to the greater urban area of

Sana'a. The risk modeling will identify losses from natural disasters and develop scenarios to incorporate estimates of urban growth and build-up by 2020. The project also will integrate the findings of probabilistic risk assessment into the CDS and make recommendations for integrating the CDS and disaster risk management information for the Urban Master Plan, and for potential institutional capacity-building needs with regards to DRM.

Probabilistic Risk Assessment

The risk assessment for Sana'a has been carried out in an integrated manner by identifying all possible water-related hazards, including how they are likely to develop in the future as a consequence of urbanization or other development. The hydrology and hydraulic analysis was conducted to identify the Sana'a basin and sub-basin characteristics and determine flow in each sub-basin given a rainfall amount. These analyses provide information about the probability of a hazard's occurrence and the respective loss potential. Different probabilistic events have been modeled to quantify the risk to buildings by their occupancy types— residential, commercial, industrial, and squatters. The model produces risk maps that provide information about the expected flood frequencies and magnitudes (extent, depth, duration, and flow velocities).

Figure A7.1 Sana'a Urban Growth

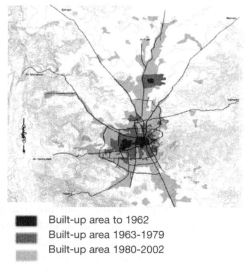

■ Built-up area to 1962
■ Built-up area 1963-1979
■ Built-up area 1980-2002

Source: GFDRR 2010

Historical Hazard Identification

Flood Hazard

The urban development of Sana'a has increased flood hazard for two reasons: (1) modifications to existing land features and (2) increased population and buildings in flood-prone areas. Modifications to land features change the runoff of watersheds, resulting in greater floods than would occur with undeveloped conditions. The primary impact of urbanization is conversion of natural ground cover to impervious surfaces, such as paved roads and building rooftops. Natural ground cover and soils provide depressional storage that absorbs initial rainfall before surface runoff occurs. Rainfall absorbed into the ground migrates slowly as subsurface flow. See figures A7.2 and A7.3, in the color section.

Landslide Hazard

A landslide is a mass of rock, earth, or debris moving down a slope. The geology of Sana'a is dominated by sand and sedimentary rock, which produces instability given the presence of pores and cracks. The abundant rains during the rainy season saturate the rocks and result in landslides. Erosion also triggers these slides. Rain, wind, temperature variations, and human activities such as mining exacerbate the dangers. Finally, and probably of greatest significance, the vulnerable natural setting is being steadily invaded by development and the infrastructure that supports it.

The following datasets were collected to model historical hazard for Sana'a:

- Meteorological data
- Hydrological data
- Mapping
- Historic flood records
- Historic landslide records
- Demographic data
- Flood vulnerability
- Economic data

Exposure and Vulnerability

An inventory of exposure and vulnerability was developed for physical assets at risk. The exposure inventory benefited from land-use and land-cover data from the IKONOS satellite (table A7.2). The inventory contained buildings (residential, commercial, industrial, and public), infrastructure (transportation roads and bridges), and networks (water, sewerage, power, and communications). The inventory also provided the number, types, and distribution of assets, as well as their valuation. The exposure inventory of buildings in Sana'a city was developed at census tract level.

TABLE A7.2
Land-Use and Land-Cover Classification

S. No	Classification	Classification definition
1.	Agriculture	Covered with cropland, fields with definite boundary and pattern
2.	Airport	Includes airstrips or helipads
3.	World Heritage site	World Heritage sites recognized by UNESCO
4.	Commercial	Multistoried commercial buildings, retailing shops, etc.
5.	Dense urban	Includes developed areas where many people reside or work Examples include apartment complexes, row houses, and commercial/industrial complexes Impervious surfaces account for 80 to 100 percent of the total cover
6.	Dense vegetation	Areas characterized by dense tree cover (natural or semi-natural woody vegetation, generally taller than 6 m); tree canopy accounts for 25 to 100 percent of the cover
7.	Industrial	Covered mainly with factories and industries manufacturing goods, involving large areas
8.	Low urban	Low density of buildings with some vegetation within the yards; vegetation is also seen along the roads; more open areas are lying between the houses
9.	Open land	Vacant or unused areas in built-up or agricultural regions
10.	Parking	Facilities for stopping vehicles for a brief time
11.	Public parks	Open spaces provided for recreational use, usually owned and maintained by a local government
12.	Residential	Includes areas covered with homes, varying from apartments to singly owned houses Well-defined pattern of houses, surrounded with trees and grass
13.	River	Linear water features like streams and rivers
14.	Roads	All types of drivable roads and streets
15.	Skyscraper	High-rise buildings (>40 m), especially apartments or buildings with facilities like parking spaces and swimming pools
16.	Sparse vegetation	Low and scattered vegetation; thin density of trees, bushes, and scrubs
17.	Squatters	Informal settlements in and around urban areas (irregular pattern)
18.	Suburban	Mostly singly owned residential areas on the outskirts of the city with low population density Impervious surfaces account for 40 to 50 percent of the total cover
19.	Urban	Includes developed areas where people of medium density reside or work Impervious surface accounts for 60 to 70 percent of total cover
20.	Water bodies	Consists of confined (small) water bodies, like lakes, reservoirs, and dams

Risk Modeling Software

The study led to the design and development of software called HazSana'a, to perform probabilistic hazard analysis and deterministic scenario analysis based on maps of flood and landslide hazards. The HazSana'a software enables users to capture and process probabilistic, deterministic, or user-supplied data on floods and landslides. This capability made it possible to produce city risk maps that identify the most endangered areas and neighborhoods.

In addition to identifying risk areas, the advantage of HazSana'a comprehensive risk assessments is in comparing the components of risk quantitatively. HazSana'a can rapidly generate many sensitivity analyses in order to weigh the pros and cons of different approaches to risk reduction as the cost is compared to the reduction in risk.

Damage and Loss

For a flood analysis, damage is estimated in percent and is weighted by the area of inundation at a given depth for a given building footprint. Direct damage to the general building stock (percent damage to structures and their contents) is estimated through vulnerability functions. Default curves to estimate structural damage for the analyses have been selected for each HazSana'a building class and associated occupancy (e.g., residential, specialized-commercial, and industrial) (figure A7.4). Losses corresponding to various flood return periods are listed in table A7.3.

Figure A7.4 Curves of Flood Vulnerability

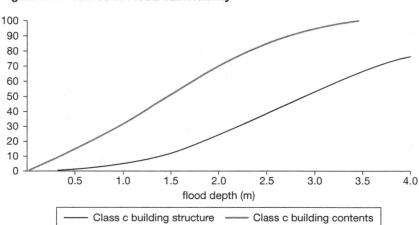

Source: GFDRR 2010

TABLE A7.3
Return Periods and Corresponding Losses for Buildings

Return period (years)	Occupancy	Building losses (million riyals)		
		Structure loss	Content loss	Total loss
10	Residential	114.505	95.676	210.18
	Commercial	26.426	66.056	92.48
	Industrial	4.123	76.192	80.31
	Squatters	2.892	5.012	7.9
	Total	*147.946*	*242.936*	*390.88*
25	Residential	537.086	370.351	907.44
	Commercial	152.308	350.326	502.63
	Industrial	14.994	275.483	290.48
	Squatters	20.732	29.677	50.41
	Total	*725.119*	*1,025.84*	*1,750.96*
50	Residential	2,255.06	1,571.61	3,826.67
	Commercial	495.401	1,171.94	1,667.34
	Industrial	52.463	896.084	948.55
	Squatters	55.02	81.061	136.08
	Total	*2,857.94*	*3,720.70*	*6,578.64*
100	Residential	3,677.57	2,423.03	6,100.60
	Commercial	838.014	1,831.25	2,669.26
	Industrial	93.957	1,439.09	1,533.05
	Squatters	106.167	142.197	248.36
	Total	*4,715.71*	*5,835.56*	*10,551.27*

Source: GFDRR 2010

Note

This chapter was extracted from GFDRR (2010).

Reference

Global Facility for Disaster Reduction and Recovery (GFDRR). 2010. *Probabilistic Risk Assessment Studies in Yemen.* Washington, DC: GFDRR.

Annex 8: Case Study—Bogota, Colombia

The Republic of Colombia has seen significant seismic and volcanic activity in recent years. The capital city of Bogota is the country's largest and most populous and has the highest concentration of risks in the country (World Bank 2006). The city is located in a moderate seismic zone, with its complex topography making it prone to landslides and flooding. Apart from these geographic factors, massive migration and urbanization have increased the city's vulnerability to disasters. A large portion of the city has grown haphazardly and many buildings violate safety regulations. Dense informal settlements have developed on highly unstable hill slopes and filled-in ravines, making them prone to landslides, while poor drainage and overflowing rivers result in frequent flooding in many parts of the city.

Holistic Risk Evaluation for Bogota

Various multidimensional risk assessment models have been developed over the years. One such model applied to evaluating risk in Bogota is the Urban Disaster Risk index (UDRi). UDRi assesses disaster risk using "hard" and "soft" variables, taking into account not only a city's physical exposure, but also indirect aggravating factors that account for the socioeconomic fragility and coping capabilities of the city's population and its institutions. In the case of Bogota, UDRi has helped identify risk-prone localities and their specific social, institutional, and organizational vulnerabilities, which is useful for effective risk management. UDRi comprises (1) a physical risk index R_F, which is defined by the convolution of hazard parameters and the physical vulnerability of exposed elements; (2) an aggravating coefficient F, obtained from fragility and resilience descriptors based on indicators related to social vulnerability; and (3) total risk R_T, obtained from the physical risk aggravated by the impact factor in each unit of analysis, that is, a comprehensive view of risk in each zone of a metropolitan area (figure A8.1).[2]

Assessing Risk for Bogota

Total risk for the entire city of Bogota is high but this risk is not distributed evenly, reflecting the large socioeconomic inequalities in Colombian society. Less affluent parts of Bogota have historically suffered more damage and destruction than more affluent areas. UDRi has helped identify the comparative risk of all 19 localities to assess seismic, flood, and landslide risk. An exposure characterization of the city has been drawn up to evaluate—building by

Figure A8.1 Descriptors of Physical Risk, Social Fragility and Lack of Resilience

F_{RF1}	Damaged area	W_{RF1}
F_{RF2}	Number of deceased	W_{RF2}
F_{RF3}	Number of injured	W_{RF3}
F_{RF4}	Rupture of water mains	W_{RF4}
F_{RF5}	Rupture of gas network	W_{RF5}
F_{RF6}	Length of fallen power lines	W_{RF6}
F_{RF7}	Affected telephone exchanges	W_{RF7}
F_{RF8}	Affected electricity substations	W_{RF8}
F_{FS1}	Slum neighborhood	W_{FS1}
F_{FS2}	Mortality rate	W_{FS2}
F_{FS3}	Delinquency rate	W_{FS3}
F_{FS4}	Social disparity index	W_{FS4}
F_{FS5}	Density of population	W_{FS5}
F_{FR1}	Hospital beds	W_{FR1}
F_{FR2}	Health human resource	W_{FR2}
F_{FR3}	Public space	W_{FR3}
F_{FR4}	Rescue manpower	W_{FR4}
F_{FR5}	Development level	W_{FR5}
F_{FR6}	Preparedness	W_{FR6}

$$R_F = \sum_{i=1}^{8} W_{RFi}\, F_{RFi}$$

Physical risk, R_F

Aggravating coefficient, F

$$F = \sum_{i=1}^{5} W_{FSi}\, F_{FSi} + \sum_{j=1}^{6} W_{FRj}\, F_{FRj}$$

Source: Cardona 2010

building—probabilistic disaster losses, taking into account Bogota's seismic microzonation. A look at the "socioeconomic layers" map (figure A8.2, in the color section), for instance, reveals that localities such as Ciudad Bolivar and Bosa that are inhabited by poorer residents are more risk prone.

Exposure and Vulnerability to Multiple Hazards

In terms of seismic risk, Candelaria has the most critical situation from the point of view of the physical risk (0.426) and total risk (0.694), because its aggravating factor (0.631) is significant, although it is not the highest in the city (see figure A8.3, in the color section). The localities with greater impacts are Usme, Ciudad Bolivar, San Cristobal, and Bosa, whereas the lowest values are those of Barrios Unidos, Teusaquillo, and Chapinero. The localities with high values of the physical risk index, in addition to Candelaria, include Usaquen (a district of middle-high socioeconomic income level, located on soft soils and with mid-size buildings), Santa Fe, Suba, and Teusaquillo; the physical risk index is less in Ciudad Kennedy and Rafael Uribe Uribe. The greater values of total risk index appear in Candelaria, Santafé, and Barrios Unidos, and the smaller values are those of Ciudad Kennedy, Fontibon, and Tunjuelito.

Other than earthquakes, landslides are a major threat to Bogota, which is surrounded by mountainous terrain belonging to the Eastern "Andean" Cordillera. During the past 30 years, Bogota has witnessed aggressive and disorganized urbanization that has pushed people to build their homes on highly unstable slopes and landfills that collapse easily, leading to heavy injuries and loss of life. The city has grown in a northerly direction along the flanks of the mountains. These areas of higher relief are composed of sedimentary rocks, which are highly fractured and covered by thick sand and gravel deposits. Natural denudation and mining for construction material and brick manufacturing have led to unstable ground. Estimates are that between 1999 and 2003, out of the total emergency calls that the Dirección de Prevención y Atención de Emergencias de Bogotá (DPAE), 36 percent related to landslides.[3]

One of the most high-risk localities in Bogota is Ciudad Bolívar, located in the southeastern mountains (see figure A8.4, in the color section). Nearly 60 percent of the area is prone to high or medium risk of landslides. People live in self-constructed shelters and building codes are not followed.[4] Poverty rates and overall social vulnerability indices are high compared with the rest of the city.

Bogota also suffers from frequent flooding. One of the key reasons is that three major rivers—Juan Amarillo, Tunjuelito, and Bogota—flow through the city. When it rains, the river basins overflow, flooding low-lying areas. Inadequate and clogged drainage has aggravated the problem, especially in the south

Figure A8.5 Flood Risk for Bogota

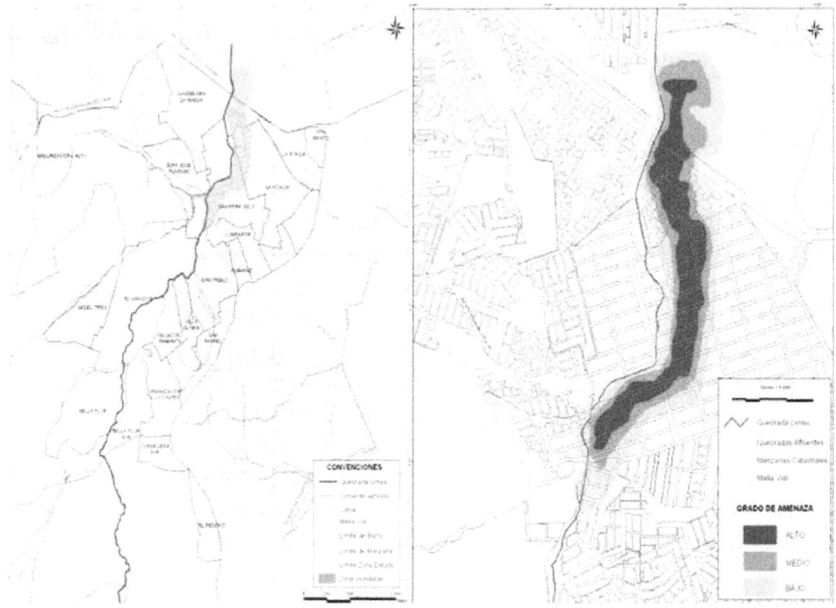

Source: Cardona 2010

and east of the city. Almost 500,000 people live in flood hazard areas (Rogelis 2007). One of the major flood-prone areas is the Tunjuelo River Basin, located in the south of Bogotá City, where 2.5 million people (or about 35 percent of the total population of the city) are concentrated (see figure A8.5, in the color section). This 388 km² drainage basin is characterized by a high degradation due to pollution and human intervention. Most settlements here are informal and occupied by low-income families.

Damage and Loss

In terms of emergency preparedness, UDRi has contributed to the development of damage scenarios. Daytime and nighttime injuries (figure A8.6, in the color section) are estimated based on occupancy and building-by-building blocks of the city. Data reveals that while all residential, commercial, and industrial buildings have 90 percent occupancy during the day, at night all residential buildings are fully occupied. In comparison, hospital buildings have 100 percent occupancy at day and night.

This development of damage scenarios has helped local authorities in Bogota to measure the potential human impact that an event can have and identify appropriate contingency and emergency plans, including:

- Health services
- Emergency units
- Security
- Debris and construction materials
- Housing
- Food
- Services (water and energy)
- Functional vulnerability (roads and emergency routes)

Comparison with Other Cities

Apart from Bogota, the multidimensional model has been applied to measure risk in three other cities: Barcelona (Spain), Manizales (Colombia), and Metro Manila (the Philippines). Table A8.1 shows that the highest value of physical risk is in Bogota, while Metro Manila has the highest aggravating coefficient. Both cities are located in zones with intermediate seismic hazard, but a high aggravating factor puts Metro Manila in a worse situation.

Action Plan for Risk Management in Bogota

Bogota has taken important steps in mitigating disaster risk over the last couple of decades. Under the World Bank-financed Bogotá Disaster Vulnerability Reduction Project, significant studies to identify risk, including hazard mapping, vulnerability assessment, and risk management, have been carried out. In fact, today Bogota has some of the world's most detailed records of risk and vulnerability. Vulnerable populations have been relocated and several mitigation efforts, such as structural reinforcement, are under way. Risk communication has also been beefed up through various media, handbooks, and community training. Following are additional related efforts:

- **Involve local communities and the private sector in disaster reduction and mitigation:** Over the past decade, administrative authorities in Bogota have made a lot of progress in improving the city's risk management and emergency preparedness. Local and private-sector involvement has, so far, been limited and should be encouraged in order to make the government disaster-reduction agenda sustainable.

Figure A8.7 Total Risk Index

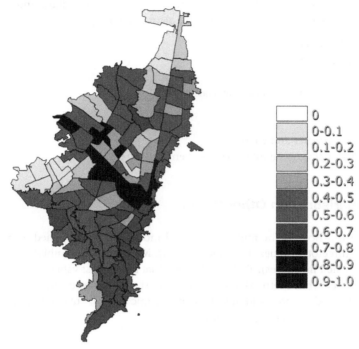

	0
	0-0.1
	0.1-0.2
	0.2-0.3
	0.3-0.4
	0.4-0.5
	0.5-0.6
	0.6-0.7
	0.7-0.8
	0.8-0.9
	0.9-1.0

Source: Cardona 2010

TABLE A8.1
Comparison of Total Risk for Bogota, Barcelona, Manizales, and Metro Manila

Index	Bogota	Barcelona	Manizales	Metro Manila
Physical risk, R_F	**0.32**	0.08	0.27	0.24
Aggravating coefficient, F	0.55	0.42	0.56	**0.59**
UDRi = Total risk, R_T	0.50	0.11	0.44	0.38

Source: Cardona 2010

- **Relocate vulnerable populations:** Since 1995, Bogota has implemented a massive resettlement program, reducing the number of informal settlements. The city of Bogota's Resettlement Program for families living in high-risk zones incorporates three components: (1) relocation, (2) improved livelihoods, and (3) environmental rehabilitation to avoid new occupation of the evacuated area. In 1997, more than 9,000 families were identified as living in high-risk areas, with 82 percent of them resettled as of 2008. However, many families remain vulnerable and illegal settlements in hazardous areas continue to grow.

- **Identify appropriate ways to transfer risk:** In Colombia, private and public assets are traditionally not insured. A national strategy is needed that encourages risk transfer that benefits the poor. It is important to identify all risks in order to quantify the universe of exposure hazards in the country. With these findings, the government can encourage states to protect vulnerable areas and handle post-disaster reconstruction by designing appropriate means to transfer risk and finance schemes such as microinsurance (Arnold 2008).
- **Build capacity to address disaster risk:** As part of the World Bank's Natural Disaster Vulnerability Reduction Project, the Colombian government has made good inroads in decentralizing capacity for disaster risk management. However, the program still needs to reach more than half of the municipalities in the country.
- **Enforce building codes:** In 1997, the Colombian Parliament passed Law 400, which established seismic-resistant building standards for new construction. Since then, Colombia has revised its building codes, but enforcement remains weak and needs to be revised. Stricter implementation and monitoring is necessary to make the built environment safer.
- **Improve emergency preparedness for critical events like earthquakes:** In terms of emergency response, rehabilitation, and recovery, Bogota has made a lot of progress—especially when the city has to deal with frequent events such as landslides and floods. However, the city still has a long way to go in order to be reasonably prepared for critical events, such as a severe earthquake.

Notes

1. This case study is drawn largely from Carreno et al. (2009) and Carreño, Cardona, and Barbat (2005).
2. For more details, see Instiuto de Estudios Ambientales (2005).
3. Fires accounted for DPAE's largest number of emergency calls (37 percent), according to (Pacific Disaster Centre 2006).
4. http://emi.pdc.org/soundpractices/Bogota/SP6-resettlement-high-risk.pdf.

References

Arnold, M. 2008. "The Role of Risk Transfer and Insurance in Disaster Risk Reduction and Climate Change Adaption." Policy Brief for the Commission on Climate Change and Development.

Cardona, O.D. 2010, "Application and Robustness of the Holistic Approach for Disaster Risk Assessment of Urban Centers." Presentation to the World Bank, June 2010.

Carreño, M.L., O.D. Cardona, and A.H. Barbat. 2005. "Seismic Risk Evaluation for an Urban Centre." In *Proceedings of the International Conference: 250th Anniversary of the 1755 Lisbon Earthquake*. Lisbon.

Carreño, M.L., et al. 2009. "Holistic Evaluation of Risk in the Framework of the Urban Sustainability." In *II Congreso Internacional de Medida y Modelización de la Sostenibilidad*. Barcelona: CIMNE.

Instiuto de Estudios Ambientales. 2005. *Indicators of Disaster Risk and Risk Management – Main Technical Report*. National University of Colombia/Manizales, Institute of Environmental Studies/IDEA. Washington, DC: Inter-American Development Bank.

Pacific Disaster Centre. 2006. "Bogotá, Colombia: Disaster Risk Management Profile." 3CD City Profile Series, Current Working Document.

Rogelis, M.C. 2007. "Flood Early Warning Systems Implemented in Bogotá as a Tool for Flood Management and Quality of Life Improvement." In *Water Education for a Changing World, Messages from Alumni in the Field*. UNESCO-IHE Institute for Water Education.

World Bank. 2006. "Colombia—Bogota Disaster Vulnerability Reduction Project." Project Appraisal Document. Washington, DC: World Bank.

Annex 9: Probabilistic Risk Modeling

Probabilistic risk models are built upon a sequence of modules that allow for quantifying potential losses (in financial terms) from a given hazard. Using the combination of existing land-use datasets, topographic models, and improved analysis of land use from satellite imagery, current and future land use can be evaluated to more accurately define the hazard resulting from a natural event. The value of this capability is in projecting future land use and examining the impacts of activities and policies in risk mitigation.

The hazard module defines the frequency and severity of a peril at a specific location. This is done by analyzing the historical frequency of events and reviewing scientific studies of the severity and frequency in the area of interest.

The exposure module generates an inventory of assets at risk. This inventory is created using primary data combined with remote-sensing information. When primary data is not available, secondary data sources and "proxy" approaches may be used. The module aggregates the value for each type of exposure as a product of assets at risk and the average replacement cost per unit of inventory. Exposure and inventory can be developed to the extent supported by data for the physical assets at risk, such as buildings (residential, commercial, industrial, and public), infrastructure (transportation roads and bridges), and networks (water, sewerage, power, and communications), and will detail the number, types, and distribution of assets as well as their valuation.

The vulnerability module quantifies the potential damage caused to each asset class by the intensity of a given event at a site. The development of asset classification combines parameters, including construction type (e.g., wall and roof combination), construction material, building usage, number of stories, and age. Estimation of damage is measured as a mean damage ratio (MDR). The MDR is the ratio of the repair cost divided by replacement cost of the structure. The curve that relates the MDR to the peril intensity is called a vulnerability function. Each asset class and building type will have different vulnerability curves for each peril.

The damage module calculates losses through the damage ratio derived in the vulnerability module. The ratio is translated into dollar loss by multiplying the damage ratio by the value at risk. This is done for each asset class at each location. Losses are then aggregated as required.

The loss module builds upon the first four modules and quantifies potential losses that might arise as a result of adverse natural events. Risk metrics produced by the model provide risk managers and policy makers with essential information to manage future risks. One measure is the average annual loss (AAL) and the other is the loss exceedance curve (LEC). The AAL is the expected loss per year when averaged over a very long period (e.g., 1,000 years). Computationally, AAL is the summation of products of event losses and event occurrence probabilities for all stochastic events in a loss model. The events are an exhaustive list affecting the location or region, generated by stochastic modeling. In probabilistic terms, the AAL is the mathematical expectation.

The LEC represents the probability that a loss of any specified monetary amount will be exceeded in a given year. This is the most important catastrophe risk metric for risk managers, since it estimates the funds required to meet risk management objectives (e.g., solvency criteria). The LEC can be calculated for the largest event in one year or for all (cumulative) events in one year. For risk management, the latter estimate is preferred, since it includes the possibility of one or more severe events occurring over a given timeframe.

BOX A9.1

Probabilistic Flood Hazard Analysis

A probabilistic flood hazard analysis is composed of the following steps:

1. Identification, acquisition, compilation, and review of relevant hydro-meteorological data
2. Catchment rainfall analysis: rainfall intensity-frequency-duration analysis to estimate design rainfalls for average recurrence intervals (ARI) up to

(continued next page)

BOX A9.1 *continued*

---

100 years; rainfall depth-area-duration analysis to estimate appropriate catchment rainfalls and spatial rainfall distribution for design studies

3. Hydrologic (rainfall-runoff) modeling to estimate design flows at key points in each catchment
4. Hydraulic modeling to estimate design flood levels throughout the urban agglomeration areas
5. Flood hazard mapping to show the flood extent and flood depth throughout the urban agglomeration for a range of ARI events

The catchment rainfall analysis consists of two parts:

Rainfall depth-area-duration analysis: In any given storm, the rainfall distribution over the basin is not uniform and varies from event to event. The purpose of this analysis is to identify the rainfall distribution that generates the largest flow in the river. In the probabilistic analysis, given an average rainfall over the basin, this distribution is used in the hydrologic model to estimate the river flow.

Rainfall depth-frequency-duration analysis: This analysis estimates the relationship between rainfall amount (depth), duration, and frequency. It provides the rainfall amount used in the probabilistic analysis for the selected return periods.

Hydrologic Modeling System (HEC-HMS): The HEC-HMS hydrologic model determines the flow in each drainage basin given a rainfall amount.

Model setup: Topographic maps, satellite imagery, and a digital elevation model verify the watershed delineation.

Model calibration and validation: Model calibration is the process of adjusting model parameter values until the model results match observed data based on prescribed criteria. The process is usually manual using engineering judgment to iteratively adjust hydrologic parameters and quantify the goodness of fit between the computed and observed hydrographs. Model validation is just as important as calibration because validation establishes the validity or uniqueness of the calibration parameters. The validation process is intended to ensure that the model parameters do not depend on the calibration storms. The validation process uses data that were not included in the calibration and determines the reliability of the model for other historical events.

Floodplain mapping: Based on the 10-, 25-, 50-, and 100-year flow data calculated by the hydrologic model, the boundaries of the 10-, 25-, 50-, and

(continued next page)

BOX A9.1 *continued*

100-year return period flood plains can be determined in addition to flood. The corresponding flood maps will be generated. An example of an innovative presentation of flood hazard identification is two-dimensional flood modeling in an urban setting. A floodplain map is prepared by integrating model results with geographic information system data to produce an urban floodplain map with varying depths of flow depicted in different colors. In addition, flow paths and velocities determined from the model are shown with directional arrows across the floodplain.

Source: Adapted from unpublished World Bank report on Yemen Probabilistic Risk Assessment.

Annex 10: Remote Sensing as a Tool for Assessing Urban Risk

Data capture using satellite remote-sensing tools has made large strides in the past few years. Remotely sensed images collected from space-based satellites now provide a level of detail that is beginning to rival aerial photographs taken from low-flying planes—a more expensive and cumbersome process, especially in remote or poor regions (Deichmann et al. 2011). The detail provided by these satellites is related to the size or footprint of the imagery: the larger the detail, the smaller the area captured in a single image (figure A10.1, in the color section). With the increasing prevalence of remote-sensing technologies employed in development work, city government staff and urban practitioners stand to benefit from an improved understanding of the various applications that remotely sensed satellites can have for urban areas.

The supply of satellite images is increasing and national space programs—including an increasing number in developing countries—and commercial satellite-image providers advertise earth-observation products with different characteristics satisfying many applications, including disaster management (Ehrlich et al. 2010). Currently, the use of remote sensing is often associated with disaster response through, for example, the International Charter on Space and Major Disasters (ICSMD). The ICSMD is a no-cost system for acquiring and delivering space data in case of natural or human-made disasters. The service is accessible 24 hours per day with an on-duty operator, and data is delivered to civil-protection agencies and emergency and rescue services. Increasingly, however, an additional and important function of remote sensing is the capacity to detect changes associated with slow-onset climate-related hazards (e.g., land motion and subsidence, heat-island effect, soil moisture, water levels, air pollution). Box A10.1, in the color section, highlights a recent case in Tunis, Tunisia, where remote sensing has been used to measure land subsidence.

There is general consensus that a resolution of ideally 1 m or even 0.5 m is needed for detailed urban analysis. However, even with very high resolution (VHR), important details are still lost. This underscores how several sources of data are often required to identify urban elements, as well as the need to consider combining remote-satellite imagery with aerial images of even greater resolution (i.e., 15 cm).

Very high resolutions also may lead to unforeseen challenges, such as the need for extremely high computation capability in terms of algorithms or hardware, and a balance between technological development and intended application must be found. Selected satellites with high potential in urban areas are presented in table A10.1; a related summary of detection capacity of satellite resolutions is listed in table A10.2. Prices vary for satellite products, depending on such factors as the level of preprocessing (geometric and radiometric), the data provider (worldwide or regional affiliates), whether imagery is archive or newly acquired, speed of delivery, and whether licensing applies to use by one or multiple organizations.[1]

Strengthening a city government's understanding of building features is a key input to undertaking a risk assessment. A categorization of building features typically includes construction material, building footprint, roof shape, and age of the structure. Such features can be determined through a combination of remote sensing and ground surveys, the latter serving as important verification (figure A10.2, in the color section).

Key infrastructure data can also be captured through satellite imagery, including land-use categorization spanning residential, commercial, industrial, transportation networks, green space, and utility systems, among others. Optical sensors, rather than radar, are typically used to determine land use, given the sensors' comparatively high spatial resolution, multispectral capacity, and ease of processing. A major limitation of optical sensors, however, is their inability to produce data during nighttime or through cloud cover. By the very geographic location of certain cities, such as those in the equatorial regions, persistent cloud cover necessitates the use of radar.

A key input to the analysis of vulnerabilities to hazards such as flooding and landslides is the generation of Digital Elevation Models (DEMs). DEMs consist of two types: Digital Terrain Models, which represent the topography of land (useful for landslide and flood risk); and Digital Surface Models, which include manmade infrastructure applicable to urban areas (ISU 2009). There are three steps to creating models of the built environment in urban areas: acquiring raw data, generating the model, and extracting the features of buildings through image processing. The calibration of the DEM is enhanced by using the Ground Control Points, which are determined from ground-based measurements of locations with a predetermined elevation. The combination of information collected through remotely sensed imagery with a geographic information system (GIS) can provide a highly detailed neighborhood or city-wide view. GIS is used to analyze data connected to a specific location. This can be particularly useful in improving the understanding of soils, geomorphology, vegetation, terrain slope, and orientation.

TABLE A10.1
Satellite Imagery Useful for Risk and Damage Assessment

Satellite	Spatial resolution (m)
GeoEye	0.41
	1.65
WorldView-1	0.5
QuickBird	0.6
	2.4
EROS-B	0.7
IKONOS	0.8
	4.0
OrbView-3	1.0
	4.0
KOMPSAT-2	1.0
	4.0
FORMOSAT-2	2.0
	8.0
Cartosat-1	2.5
SPOT-5	2.5
	10.0

Source: Ehrlich et al., 2010.

TABLE A10.2
Satellite Resolution and Detection Capacity

Spatial resolution	Applications
0.5–1.5 m	Identification, cartography of objects (cars, trees, urban materials)
1.5–5 m	Distinction of buildings; identification, cartography of objects (construction)
5–10 m	Location and cartography of buildings, roads, streets, agricultural lands
10–20 m	Location and geometry of large infrastructure (airports, city centers, suburbs, commercial malls, industrial areas)

Source: Weber (2008).

Remote Sensing: Satellite Descriptions, Pricing, and Application for Digital Elevation Models

Below is a brief description of three satellites: GeoEye-1, IKONOS, and City-Sphere:

GeoEye-1: A high-resolution earth-observation satellite owned by GeoEye, which was launched in September 2008. GeoEye-1 provides 41 cm panchromatic and 1.65 m multispectral imagery in 15.2 km swaths. At launch, GeoEye-1 was the world's highest-resolution commercial earth-imaging satellite. Google has exclusive online mapping use of its data. While GeoEye-1 is capable of imagery with details the size of 41 cm, that resolution will only be available to the government. Google will have access to details of 50 cm.

IKONOS: A commercial earth-observation satellite, the first to collect publicly available high-resolution imagery at 1 m and 4 m resolution. It offers imagery in multispectral at 4 m, panchromatic at 0.8 m, and pan-sharpened at 1 m.

CitySphere: Owned by DigitalGlobe, a satellite featuring 60 cm or better ortho-rectified color imagery for 300 preselected cities worldwide. These GIS-

TABLE A10.3
Pricing of GeoEye, IKONOS, and CitySphere Satellite Imagery

Product	GeoEye-1 (0.5/2.0 m)[1]	IKONOS (1.0/4.0 m)[2]
	US$/km^2	US$/km^2
Geo	25.00	20.00
GeoProfessional	35.00	33.00
GeoProfessional Precision	40.00	38.00
GeoStereo/GeoStereo Precision	Ad hoc pricing	
Archive (Geo product only)	12.50	10.00

Note: Prices are based on minimum order size of 49 km^2 for archive and 100 km^2 for all other products.

| Region | CitySphere | | | |
	Small (<1,000 km^2)	Medium (1,001–2,000 km^2)	Large (2,001–5,000 km^2)	Very large (>5,000 km^2)
U.S. and Canada	2,750	5,000	10,500	24,250
Europe and Australasia	3,850	8,250	17,250	52,500
Rest of world	7,750	16,250	34,250	84,500

Source: Eurimage Price List. WWW.eurimage.com
1. Panchromatic or pansharpened.
2. Multispectral.

TABLE A10.4
High-Resolution Data Collection for Digital Elevation Models

Technique	Description	Considerations	Mission	Resolution Horizontal	Resolution Vertical	Cost (US$/km²)
Stereoscopy	Uses binocular vision to produce overlapping photographs taken from different angles to produce a 3D model. Can be used to determine building height.	More cost-effective than Light Detection and Ranging (LIDAR) systems; however, quality of information is weather dependent. Available on select satellite missions: IKONOS (1m), Earth Resources Observation System, EROS-B, QuickBird (0.61), System Pour l'Observation de la Terre, SPOT-5 (2.5 m). Alternative option to satellite use is airborne solutions (i.e., High Resolution Stereo Camera–Airborne (HRSC-A).	Advanced Spaceborne Thermal Emission and Reflection (ASTER)	30 m	<20 m	Free
			SPOT-5	30 m	10 m	3.3
			IKONOS	5 m	<12 m	Variable
LIDAR	An alternative to radar; uses ultraviolet, visible, and near-infrared light waves. Usually installed on a small airplane.	Provides very high-resolution models with better building shape characterization, which allows for extracting fine features. Drawbacks include high cost and acquisition times and degraded images due to aerosols and clouds.	Commercial service	0.5 m	0.15 m	~250
Interferometric Synthetic Aperture Radar (INSAR)	Uses two or more Synthetic Aperture Radar images and analyzes differences in the phase of returning waves.	Current spatial resolution is low for urban areas. Limitations include scattering of building geometrics, shadowing effects, and resulting underestimation of building spatial distribution. Technology is developing in this area and approaching 1 m resolution.	Shuttle Radar Topography Mission	90 m	<16 m	Free
			TanDEM-X	12 m	<2 m	N.A.

Source: International Space University, 2009. "DREAM, Disaster Risk Evaluation and Management."

ready cities are available as off-the-shelf products and ready for immediate delivery. Each city comprises recent imagery, with initial imagery not older than 2006. The price of a CitySphere product depends on the size of the city and the continent. Importantly, the CitySphere licensing can be shared among a predefined number of customers, making the procurement of imaging more affordable if costs are shared across government agencies or departments. For example, Dar es Salaam, Tanzania, would fall into the medium-size category, given that the city's area is about 1,500 km^2.

Note

1. There would likely be preferential pricing policies if cities were able to purchase remote-sensing imagery in bulk. This pooling of cities could also yield cost savings for insurance, similar to the current national-level Catastrophe Risk Deferred Drawdown Option (Cat DDO).

References

Deichmann, U., D. Ehrlich, C. Small, and G. Zeug. 2011. *Using High Resolution Satellite Information for Urban Risk Assessment.* European Union and World Bank.

Ehrlich, D. 2009. "How High Resolution Satellite Images Can Support Urban Disaster Risk Assessment." Presentation to World Bank by Joint Research Centre.

International Space University (ISU). 2009. *Disaster Risk Evaluation and Management.* SSP Program France.

Weber, C. 2008. "Urban Remote Sensing: Recent Technological and Methodological Developments." Presentation.

Annex 11: Community-Based Institutional Mapping and Other Participatory Approaches

Pro-Poor Adaptation to Climate Change in Urban Centers: Case Studies of Urban Poor in Mombasa, Kenya, and Estelí, Nicaragua

Recently the World Bank, along with the University of Manchester, studied how poor households, small businesses, and communities cope with the impacts of climate change (experienced as increasingly variable and capricious weather patterns). The study also identified how policy and institutional systems can best build on local realities to develop pro-poor urban climate change adaptations, particularly relating to resilience.

Methodology

The study used an innovative methodology that analyzes the assets of poor individuals, households, and communities in terms of their vulnerability to severe weather, as well as their sources of resilience for dealing with the negative impacts of climate change—with the range of assets grouped under a typology of physical, financial, natural, human, and social capital. The methodology has three components: most important, an innovative new participatory climate change adaptation appraisal (PCCAA) methodology undertaken in four urban settlements in each city; an urban rapid risk and institutional appraisal (RRIA); and finally consultation and validation conducted with key selected stakeholders from government, civil society, and local communities.

Participatory Climate Change Adaptation Appraisal

The PCCAA approach uses participatory methodology to identify "bottom up" asset vulnerability to climate change, as well as strategies for asset adaptation in order to build long-term resilience, protect assets during adverse weather, and rebuild those assets. The objective of the PCCAA is twofold: first to understand the asset vulnerability of poor households, businesses, and community organizations as they relate to severe weather associated with climate change; and second to identify the types of asset adaptation strategies implemented by the same social actors to address this issue. The PCCAA comprises two components that (1) identify the links between different vulnerabilities and the poor's capital assets, and (2) explore and classify the asset-based adaptation strategies as households, small businesses, and communities develop resilience and resist, or recover from, the negative effects of climate extremes. Following is a generic methodology used in the PCCAA:

1. Selection of researchers and local teams
Foremost, participatory research requires collaborative research partnerships with researchers (and their counterparts) that have had research experience using participatory urban appraisal (PUA)/participatory rural appraisal (PRA) techniques. Constructing research teams to undertake PUAs requires skills in judging local capacities.

2. Fieldwork and research
Once all the preparation and fieldwork is completed, the actual research takes place, lasting five weeks. This breaks down into the following tasks:

- Week 1: Capacity building of local researchers to train them in the conceptual framework and participatory tools and techniques used in the study
- Week 2: Study of pilot community
- Week 3 and 4: Study of four communities
- Week 5: Analysis of data and completion of preliminary research results

3. Research techniques
The research techniques include group discussions, semi-structured interviews (one on one), direct observation, ethno-histories and biographies (one on one), and local stories, portraits, and case studies.

4. Locations for conducting a PUA in communities
Two main ways exist for implementing a PUA in a community: (1) conduct formal focus group discussions in a local community center or communal building;

and (2) conduct informal focus groups, identified while walking through the community, as well as in shops and bars, at sports fields, or outside people's houses.

5. Analysis of the research data
The analysis proceeds through four stages: creating daily field notes, developing preliminary research findings, reworking the data, and developing a final report. Apart from PCCAA, the study also relied on:

Rapid risk and institutional appraisal: A top-down review of the policy domain, in terms of the institutions tasked to deal with climate change, the relevant national, regional, and municipal policies, regulations, and mandates relating to climate change, as well as associated programs and budgets.

Consultation and validation of results: A process dependent on the level of commitment by different social actors. In Estelí, an action-planning exercise triangulated the results, allowing urban poor communities and public authorities to identify common problems, structure solutions, and negotiate collaboration. In Mombasa, consultation was more limited and prioritized information sharing and capacity building.

Findings from the Case Studies

- The studies found that the most significant asset of the urban poor (as they listed themselves) was housing. This highlighted a critical dimension of their vulnerability—weak or unclear tenure rights.
- The studies found a great variety of responses to the increasing severity of local weather patterns at the household, small business, and community level. These included asset adaptation to build long-term resilience (for example, homeowners in Ziwa La Ngombe, Mombasa, mobilized in order to seek assistance from donors, and dug water passages in case of flooding, while small-business owners constructed concrete walls to protect against flooding); asset damage limitation and protection during severe weather (such as moving temporarily to safer places or sleeping on top of houses, and placing sandbags in the doorways of houses during floods); and asset rebuilding after such weather (for example, inhabitants of Estelí replanted trees and plants, while those in Timbwani and Bofu, Mombasa, accessed weather forecasters, which informed people of severe weather).
- The RRIA revealed that the implementation of strategies for climate change adaptation at the city and country levels in both case studies was constrained. In both countries, national climate change coordinating committees, with the mandate to advise on climate policy, were located in predominantly rural ministries of environment. In addition, different legal instruments overlapped,

TABLE A11.1
Composite Matrix of Perceptions of Most Significant Natural Hazards in Mombasa and Estelí

	Mombasa*		Estelí**	
Type of weather	Ranking totals	%	Ranking totals	%
Flood/rain	166	49.8	312	69.8
Heat/sunny	105	31.4	116	25.8
Strong wind	55	16.4	20	4.4
Cold/chilly	8	2.4	-	-
Total	334	100.0	448	100.0

Sources: * Mombasa data from listing and ranking in 72 focus groups in four communities.

** Estelí data from listings and ranking in 62 focus groups in four communities.

Moser, C., et al. 2010.

and a clear mandate or effective coordination of programs was lacking within and between sector ministries, as well as among the levels of government (national, provincial, and local). Finally, the absence of concrete fiscal support seriously limited adaptation policies. Clear legal and institutional coordination and funding channels, relevant to urban areas, would make national adaptation strategies more meaningful in supporting the urban poor as they build the resilience to protect their assets.

- Results from institutional mapping in both cities showed that institutions considered important by community members were not necessarily those they perceived as assisting them against severe weather. In Mombasa, for instance, local government representatives such as chiefs and elders were identified as locally important, yet they did not take an active role in dealing with problems of severe weather, except in Tudor.

Note

This chapter was derived from Moser et al. (2010).

Reference

Moser, C., et al. 2010. *Pro-Poor Adaptation to Climate Change in Urban Centers: Case Studies of Vulnerability and Resilience in Kenya and Nicaragua.*

Annex 12: Global, National, and Local Responses to Disasters and Climate Change

At a global level, the Hyogo Framework for Action (HFA) reduces disaster losses—in lives and the social, economic, and environmental assets of communities and countries—by effectively integrating disaster risk into sustainable development policies, planning, programming, and financing at all levels of government. The HFA was adopted by 168 countries in 2005, and provides a technical and political agreement on the areas to be addressed to reduce risk. The HFA is structured around five priorities for action (table A12.1) and specific tasks related to each (box A12.1).

Key implementing agencies for the HFA include the Global Facility for Disaster Reduction and Recovery (GFDRR) and the United Nations International Strategy on Disaster Reduction (UNISDR). GFDRR provides technical and financial assistance to high-risk low- and middle-income countries to mainstream disaster reduction in national development strategies and plans to achieve the Millennium Development Goals (MDGs). UNISDR is the UN focal point to promote links between, and coordination of, disaster reduction activities in the socioeconomic, humanitarian, and development fields, as well as to support policy integration.

Climate change adaptation has a shorter history, emerging in the United Nations Framework Convention on Climate Change (UNFCCC) signed in 1992. However, the UNFCCC and the Kyoto protocol predominantly addressed climate change mitigation, as well as policies and measures to reduce the emissions of greenhouse gases. Only recently did adaptation come appear as a key concern

TABLE A12.1
Hyogo Framework Priorities for Action

Priority Action 1	Ensure that disaster risk reduction is a national and local priority with a strong institutional basis for implementation.
Priority Action 2	Identify, assess, and monitor disaster risks and enhance early warning.
Priority Action 3	Use knowledge, innovation, and education to build safety and resilience at all levels.
Priority Action 4	Reduce the underlying risks.
Priority Action 5	Strengthen disaster preparedness for effective response at all levels.

BOX A12.1

Local/City-Level Disaster Risk Reduction Tasks

Local and city governance (HFA Priority 1)
Task 1. Engage in multi-stakeholder dialogue to establish foundations for disaster risk reduction (DRR).

Task 2. Create or strengthen mechanisms for systematic coordination for DRR.

Task 3. Assess and develop the institutional basis for DRR.

Task 4. Prioritize DRR and allocate appropriate resources.

Risk assessment and early warning (HFA Priority 2)
Task 5. Establish an initiative for community risk assessment to combine with country assessments.

Task 6. Review the availability of risk-related information and the capacity for data collection and use.

Task 7. Assess capacities and strengthen early-warning systems.

Task 8. Develop communication and dissemination mechanisms for disaster risk information and early warning.

Knowledge management (HFA Priority 3)
Task 9. Raise awareness of DRR and develop education program on DRR in schools and local communities.

Task 10. Develop or use DRR training for key sectors based on priorities.

Task 11. Enhance the compilation, dissemination, and use of DRR information.

(continued next page)

BOX A12.1 *continued*

Vulnerability reduction (HFA Priority 4)

Task 12. Environment: Incorporate DRR in environmental management.

Task 13. Social needs: Establish mechanisms for increasing resilience of the poor and most vulnerable.

Task 14. Physical planning: Establish measures to incorporate DRR in urban and land-use planning.

Task 15. Structure: Strengthen mechanisms for improved building safety and protection of critical facilities.

Task 16. Economic development: Stimulate DRR activities in production and service sectors.

Task 17. Financial/economic instruments: Create opportunities for private-sector involvement in DRR.

Task 18. Emergency and public safety; disaster recovery: Develop a recovery planning process that incorporates DRR.

Disaster preparedness (HFA Priority 5)

Task 19. Review disaster preparedness capacities and mechanisms, and develop a common understanding.

Task 20. Strengthen planning and programming for disaster preparedness.

Source: Matsuoka, Shaw, and Tsunozaki (2009).

---

within the UNFCCC. The possibilities for least developed countries to develop National Adaptation Programmes of Actions (NAPA) and the Nairobi Work Program—a five-year (2005–2010) initiative under the UNFCCC—were important first steps toward enhancing the understanding of adaptation and catalyzing action on adaptation. The Bali Action Plan (BAP), agreed upon at the UNFCCC Conference of Parties (COP) in Bali, provides a roadmap toward the new international climate change agreement concluded in 2009 as successor to the Kyoto Protocol. The BAP puts adaptation on an equal footing with mitigation. In the BAP, risk management and disaster risk reduction are important elements of climate change adaptation. Further, the BAP emphasizes the importance of "building on synergies among activities and processes, as a means to support adaptation in a coherent and integrated manner" (O'Brien et al. 2008).

The GFDRR is a partnership of the International Strategy for Disaster Reduction (ISDR) system to support implementing the Hyogo Framework for Action

(HFA) and is managed by the World Bank on behalf of the donor partners and other partnering stakeholders. The GFDRR provides technical and financial assistance to high-risk low- and middle-income countries to mainstream disaster reduction in national development strategies and plans to achieve the MDGs. The GFDRR provides financing by means of three tracks to meet its development objectives at the global, regional, and country levels.

- **Track-I: Global and Regional Partnerships:** Enable leveraging country resources for *ex ante* investment in prevention, mitigation, and preparedness, particularly in low- and middle-income countries.
- **Track-II: Mainstreaming Disaster Risk Reduction in Development:** Provides technical assistance to low- and middle-income countries to mainstream disaster risk reduction in strategic planning, particularly the poverty-reduction strategies (PRSs) and various sectoral development policies.
- **Track-III: Standby Recovery Financing Facility (SRFF) for Accelerated Disaster Recovery:** Supports early recovery in low-income disaster-stricken countries to bridge the gap between humanitarian assistance and medium- and long-term recovery and development. The SRFF includes two trust funds: a technical assistance fund to support disaster damage loss, needs assessment, and planning; and a callable fund to provide speedy access to financial resources for disaster recovery.

UNISDR is the UN focal point to promote links between, and coordination of, disaster reduction in the socioeconomic, humanitarian, and development fields, as well as to support policy integration. As an international information clearinghouse on disaster reduction, it develops awareness campaigns and produces articles, journals, and other publications and promotional materials related to disaster reduction.

At the First World Congress on Cities and Adaptation to Climate Change, ISDR launched the Making Cities Resilient: My City Is Getting Ready campaign. The campaign targets more than 1,000 local government leaders worldwide and includes a checklist of ten essentials for making cities resilient (listed below) that can be implemented by mayors and local governments. Through this campaign, ISDR and the World Bank are collaborating to streamline the use of the urban risk assessment within signatory city governments.

Ten Essentials for Making Cities Resilient

1. Put in place **organization and coordination** to understand and reduce disaster risk, based on participation of citizen groups and civil society. Build local alliances. Ensure that all departments understand their role in disaster risk reduction and preparedness.

2. **Assign a budget** for disaster risk reduction and provide incentives for homeowners, low-income families, communities, businesses, and the public sector to invest in reducing the risks they face.
3. Maintain up☒to☒date data on hazards and vulnerabilities, **prepare risk assessments,** and use these as the basis for plans and decisions regarding urban development. Ensure that this information and the plans for the city's resilience are readily available to the public and fully discussed.
4. Invest in and maintain **critical infrastructure that reduces risk,** such as flood drainage, adjusted to cope with climate change.
5. Assess the **safety of all schools and health facilities** and upgrade these as necessary.
6. Apply and enforce **realistic, risk-compliant building regulations and land-use planning principles.** Identify safe land for low☒income citizens and develop upgrading of informal settlements.
7. Ensure that **education programs and training** on disaster risk reduction are in place in schools and local communities.
8. **Protect ecosystems and natural buffers** to mitigate floods, storm surges, and other hazards to which the city may be vulnerable. Adapt to climate change by building on good risk-reduction practices.
9. Install **early-warning systems and emergency-management** capacities in the city and hold regular public-preparedness drills.
10. Ensure, after a disaster, that the **needs of the survivors are placed at the center of reconstruction**, with support for them and their community organizations to design and implement responses, including rebuilding homes and livelihoods.

References

Matsuoka, Y., R. Shaw, and E. Tsunozaki. 2009. *A Guide for Implementing the Hyogo Framework for Action by Local Stakeholders.* UNISDR, Kyoto University.

O'Brien, K., et al. 2008. "Disaster Risk Reduction, Climate Change Adaptation and Human Security." Report prepared for the Royal Norwegian Ministry of Foreign Affairs by the Global Environmental Change and Human Security GECHS Project, GECHS Report 2008:3.

Annex 13: Tools for Climate Risk Assessment

Adaptation Learning Mechanism: *United Nations Development Programme (UNDP)*
The ALM draws from experiences on the ground, featuring tools and practical guidance to meet the needs of developing countries. In providing stakeholders with a common platform for sharing and learning, the ALM complements the wide range of adaptation knowledge networks and initiatives already underway. The ALM supports adaptation practices; the integration of climate change risks and adaptation into development policy; planning and operations; and capacity building.

Adaptation Wizard: *United Kingdom Climate Impacts Programme*
The Adaptation Wizard provides five steps to assess vulnerability to the current climate and future climate change, identify options to address climate risks, and develop a strategy for climate change adaptation.

Climate Change Explorer (weADAPT): *Stockholm Environment Institute (SEI)*
The Climate Change Explorer is an expanding collaboration that offers a wealth of experience, data, tools, and guidance to develop sound strategies and action on climate adaptation. weADAPT provides support for adapting to climate change by pooling expertise from a wide range of organizations that contribute to adaptation science, practice, and policy. The weADAPT partners have developed tools for undertaking steps in climate adaptation. These tools help people assess the situation and develop, implement, and evaluate measures and strategies for adaptation.

Climate Change Portal/ADAPT: *The World Bank*
The World Bank Climate Change Portal provides quick and readily accessible climate and climate-related data to policy makers and development practitioners. The site includes a mapping visualization tool (webGIS) that displays key climate variables and data.

Climate Ready: *Massachusetts Institute of Technology (forthcoming)*
Climate Ready is an interactive Web tool to help local governments and communities address the impacts of climate change. It helps users identify relevant adaptation activities, generates awareness of options and tradeoffs, promotes mainstreaming of adaptation, fosters learning and exchange, and promotes coordination, cooperation, and collaboration across stakeholders and sectors.

CRiSTAL: *International Institute for Sustainable Development (IISD)*
The Community-based Risk Screening Tool—Adaptation and Livelihoods (CRiSTAL) helps project planners and managers integrate climate change adaptation and risk reduction into community projects. The tool assists in understanding the links between livelihoods and climate in their project areas; assessing a project's impact on community adaptive capacity; and making project adjustments to improve its impact on adaptive capacity and reduce the vulnerability of communities to climate change.

SERVIR: *U.S. Agency for International Development (USAID)*
Decision makers use SERVIR to improve monitoring of air quality, extreme weather, biodiversity, and changes in land cover. SERVIR has been used 35 times to respond to environmental threats, such as wildfires, floods, landslides, and harmful algal blooms. Special attention is given to analyzing the impacts of climate change and providing information for adaptation strategies.

Note

A number of actors in the fields of science, administration, and development cooperation are developing practical approaches and instruments to assist mainstreaming adaptation to climate change. A recent GTZ (now GIZ) report, *International Workshop on Mainstreaming Adaptation to Climate Change*, describes available adaptation tools for development practitioners; also see Tanner and Guenther (2007).

Reference

Tanner, Thomas, and Bruce Guenther. 2007. "Screening Tools Geneva Workshop Report." Geneva, Switzerland, April.

Annex 14: Sample Household Urban Risk Questionnaire

This questionnaire helps communities gauge the impact of small and local disasters and household actions to minimize risk from natural hazards and climate change.

NATURAL HAZARD INFORMATION

1. In the past ten years, have you or someone in your household experienced a natural disaster such as an earthquake, severe windstorm, flood, wildfire, or other type of natural disaster?

☐ Yes
☐ No (If NO, skip to Question 2)

a. If YES, which of the hazards below have you or someone in your household

✓	Hazard	Year(s)	✓	Hazard	Year(s)
☐	Drought		☐	Wildfire	
☐	Dust storm		☐	Household fire	
☐	Earthquake		☐	Wind storm	
☐	Flash flood		☐	Winter storm	
☐	Landslide/debris flow		☐	River flood	
☐	Extreme temperature		☐	Tsunami	
☐	Storm surge		☐	Other_____	

experienced and when? (Please check all that apply.)

2. How concerned are you personally about the following hazards? (Circle the corresponding number for each hazard.)

Hazard	Extremely concerned	Very concerned	Concerned	Somewhat concerned	Not concerned
Drought	1	2	3	4	5
Dust storm	1	2	3	4	5
Earthquake	1	2	3	4	5
Flash flood	1	2	3	4	5
Landslide/debris flow	1	2	3	4	5
Extreme temperature	1	2	3	4	5
Storm surge	1	2	3	4	5
Wildfire	1	2	3	4	5
Household fire	1	2	3	4	5
Wind storm	1	2	3	4	5
Winter storm	1	2	3	4	5
River flood	1	2	3	4	5
Tsunami	1	2	3	4	5
Other _____	1	2	3	4	5

3. What is the frequency of the hazards that you have experienced? (For example, 2 times per month.)

Natural disaster	Monthly	Yearly	Cause (i.e., recurring or manmade)
Drought			
Dust storm			
Earthquake			
Flash flood			
Landslide/debris flow			
Extreme temperature			
Storm surge			
Wildfire			
Household fire			
Wind storm			
Winter storm			
River flood			
Tsunami			
Other _____			

4. What was the impact of the disasters on you or your family?

☐ Lost income   ☐ Housing damage

☐ Amount _____   ☐ Cost of repairs _____

☐ Injury or death   ☐ Disrupted services (water, electricity)

5. Following a disaster, who assists you in recovering? (For example, community association, local government, neighbors, or nongovernmental organization.)

6. Have you ever received information about how to make your family and home safer from natural disasters?

☐ Yes

☐ No (If NO, skip to Question 4)

a. If YES, how recently?

☐ Within the last 6 months   ☐ Between 2 and 5 years

☐ Between 6 and 12 months   ☐ 5 years or more

☐ Between 1 and 2 years

b. From whom did you **last** receive information about how to make your family and home safer from natural disasters? **(Please check only one.)**

☐ News media
☐ Government agency
☐ Insurance agent or company
☐ Utility company

☐ Red Cross
☐ Other nonprofit organization
☐ Not sure
☐ Other (specify)_____

7. Whom would you most trust to provide you with information about how to make your family and home safer from natural disasters? **(Please check all that apply.)**

☐ News media
☐ Government agency
☐ Insurance agent or company
☐ Utility company

☐ Red Cross
☐ Other nonprofit organization
☐ Not sure
☐ Other (specify)_____

8. What steps, if any, have you taken to minimize the impact of changing weather or a natural disaster?

Other comments:

Annex 15: PAGER[1] Construction Types Used for Development of Building Inventory

Construction type	Description
Adobe	Owners and local builders typically build these types of houses from raw and processed earth. Such houses often perform poorly in earthquakes.
Wood	There are many forms of wood housing: bamboo frame; plank, beam, and post; and engineered timber. Their quality varies, depending on the level of technical input.
Stone masonry	This housing form appears worldwide. The main materials in the walls are blocks of natural stone, like granite, laterite, sandstone, and slate. There are stone masonry houses with and without mortars; when mortars are used, they are either mud- or cement-based. The houses have various types of roofs, including tiled roofs supported on wood trusses, asbestos or steel sheets on steel trusses, and reinforced concrete slab.
Brick masonry	This construction type, appearing worldwide, uses clay mud to form regular-sized masonry bricks. These bricks are sometimes burnt in a kiln, and simply sun-dried. Brick masonry houses are made with and without mortars; when mortars are used, they are either mud- or cement-based. The bricks are the main materials used in the walls. The houses have various roofs, including tiled roofs supported on wood trusses, asbestos or steel sheets on steel trusses, and reinforced concrete slab.

(continued next page)

Construction type	Description
Confined masonry	This type of housing has been practiced in many vernacular forms worldwide, particularly along the Alpine-Himalayan belt. They are load-bearing masonry houses improved with the help of wood or concrete frames to reduce the masonry walls into smaller panels more capable of withstanding earthquake shaking. The masonry could be made with either stone or brick. This type is far superior to the traditional load-bearing masonry houses. The houses have various roofs, depending on the geographic region of construction.
Reinforced concrete frame	This type of housing is increasingly popular across the world, particularly for urban construction. It employs beams (long horizontal members), columns (slender vertical members), and slabs (plate-like flat members) to form the basic backbone for carrying the loads. Vertical walls made of masonry or other materials fill between the beam-column grids to make functional spaces. These houses are expected to be constructed based on engineering calculations; however, in a large part of the developing world, such buildings are built with little or no engineering calculations.
Reinforced concrete shear walls	This type of housing is the same as the reinforced concrete frame building but provided with additional thin vertical plate-like reinforced concrete structural walls, positioned in bays. The construction requires a high level of engineering. This type of building, with structural walls, shows superior seismic performance during earthquakes compared to reinforced concrete frame buildings without shear walls.
Precast concrete	The building consists of individual high-quality factory-made components connected at site. There are two styles of construction: (a) the components consist of the reinforced concrete frame building alone, i.e., beams, columns, structural walls, and slabs; and (b) the components consist of large-panel prefabricates of walls and slabs only, and not of beams and columns. This type of house construction is in limited use in urban areas or mass housing projects.
Advanced technologies	Some wood houses and reinforced concrete frame houses have been built using base-isolation technology. Here, the building is rested on flexible bearing pad-like devices, which absorb part of the earthquake energy transmitted from the ground to the building, thereby reducing damage to the building. This type of construction is expensive, but such houses perform well during earthquakes.
Vernacular	Many housing types found around the world today are based on technology handed over from one generation to the next, usually by word of mouth. Impressively, these construction schemes often address the prevalent local conditions of temperature and other natural effects (like earthquake shaking). There is much to learn from these housing practices.

Note

1. Prompt Assessment of Global Earthquakes for Response (PAGER).

Annex 16: Urban Risk Assessment Template

City/metropolitan area, country

Map

City Profile

What are the distinct characteristics of the city area and urban population? Where is the city expanding? What are the geographic characteristics of the city's location? (Include physical setting, topography—e.g., coastal, near mountain, inland plains, inland plateau, near a river—and seismic activity.)

CITY SNAPSHOT
(From Global City Indicators)
Total city population in year
Population growth (% annual)
Land area (km²)
Population density (per km²)
Country's per capita GDP (US$)
Percentage of country's population
Total number of households
Dwelling density (per km²)
Avg. household income (US$)
Percentage of country's GDP
Total budget (US$)
Date of last Urban Master Plan

Describe predominant features of the built environment and provision of basic services. (Include infrastructure, water supply, energy networks, transport, waste, management, road, and housing.) What are the priorities and main development challenges of the city?

Pillar 1—Institutional Assessment

Describe briefly which agencies are involved in disaster risk management or climate change adaptation. How are they involved? What is their function? Is their role clearly reflected in their mandates, work plans, and staff job descriptions? How are the agencies or institutions active in the fields of disaster risk management and climate change related to each other?

Name relevant policies and legislation—related to disaster risk management or climate change adaptation—available to the agencies or institutions mentioned above, or if there is any under preparation.

What are the most important ongoing programs and projects related to disaster risk management or climate change adaptation? What resources are available to support these programs? Is there a disaster response system in the city, and is it comprehensive? Is the system regularly tested and updated?

Are there any shortcomings in current disaster risk management or climate change adaptation management tools, policies, or programs that need to be addressed?

Is there a leading agency coordinating the disaster risk management activities of the city? Does the agency have sufficient financial, technical, and human resources to lead the activities? Does it have a legal backing?

Institutional Snapshot
Leading agency coordinating Disaster Risk Management efforts
Government staff trained in early warning, preparedness, and recovery
Disaster Risk Management budget under different agencies
Non-governmental organizations involved in Disaster Risk Management

What is being done to mainstream risk reduction activities, including prevention and preparedness?

What are estimated levels of spending on pro-poor services and infrastructure, on climate mitigation and resilience (public and private)? How is this spending estimated?

Pillar 2—Hazard Impact Assessment
In the past, which have been the most significant natural disasters? Include information such as total affected population (dead, wounded, and those suffering material and economic loss); affected geographical area; estimated amount of damage and losses (assets, production, and increased spending); and economic impacts (changes in GDP, exports, imports, and tourism).

What are the city's main climate hazards based on historical data and scenarios using available climate projections?

Which specific urban areas (infrastructure and buildings) and populations at high risk of disasters and climate change impacts have been identified? (Include hazard exposure maps, if available.)

Is there information on the magnitude, distribution, and probability of potential losses due to each of the most relevant projected hazards? (Include information on the probabilistic risk assessment methodology used and vulnerability curves.)

Natural Hazards Snapshot		
	Y /N	Date of last major event
Earthquake		
Wind storm		
River flow		
Flood, inundation, and waterlog		
Tsunami		
Drought		
Volcano		
Landslide		
Storm surge		
Extreme temperature		

- Additional background on most relevant historical hazards, include if available picture, graphs, maps, etc.

_____

_____

_____

- Additional information on most relevant projected hazards, include if available picture, graphs, maps, etc.

_____

_____

_____

Pillar 3—Socioeconomic Assessment

Which areas within the city have the highest population exposure to hazards? (Use data on land use, ecosystems, geophysical properties, socioeconomic factors, and infrastructure.)

Indicate the location of urban poor settlements. (Include poverty maps.) What is the level of exposure of the settlements to climate and natural hazards?

What are the characteristics of slums (informal settlements or similar)? (Include information on geospatial, socioeconomic, and environmental characteristics, as well as access to basic services, tenure, and social capital.)

Does the city have good practices in addressing urban poverty, and if so what are they? Can these practices be referred to as climate smart?

What are the key lessons in terms of constraints and opportunities to address urban poverty in a climate-smart way for the city?

What is the urban carbon footprint of the city? What are the main assumptions underlying these numbers? What are the trends?

Social Assessment Snapshot
Percentage of city population below poverty line
Social inequality (Gini index)
Unemployment (percentage of total labor force)
Areal size of informal settlements as a percent of city area
Percentage of city population living in slums
Percentage of households that exist without registered legal titles
Percentage of children completing primary and secondary education: survival rate
Human Development Index
Predominant housing material

Annex 17: Key Definitions[1]

Adaptation

The adjustment in natural or human systems in response to actual or expected climatic stimuli or their effects, which moderates harm or exploits beneficial opportunities.

Comment: This definition addresses the concerns of climate change and is sourced from the secretariat of the United Nations Framework Convention on Climate Change (UNFCCC). The broader concept of adaptation also applies to non-climatic factors such as soil erosion or surface subsidence. Adaptation can occur autonomously, for example through market changes, or as a result of adaptation policies and plans. Many disaster risk reduction measures can directly contribute to better adaptation.

Capacity

The combination of all the strengths, attributes, and resources available within a community, society, or organization to achieve agreed goals.

Comment: Capacity may include infrastructure and physical means, institutions, societal coping abilities, as well as human knowledge, skills, and collective attributes such as social relationships, leadership, and management. Capacity also may be described as capability. Capacity assessment is a term for when the capacity of a group is reviewed against desired goals, and the capacity gaps are identified for action.

Climate Change

(a) The Intergovernmental Panel on Climate Change (IPCC) defines climate change as "a change in the state of the climate that can be identified (e.g., by using statistical tests) by changes in the mean and/or the variability of its properties, and that persists for an extended period, typically decades or longer. Climate change may be due to natural internal processes or external forcings [*sic*], or to persistent anthropogenic changes in the composition of the atmosphere or in land use."

(b) The UNFCCC defines climate change as "a change of climate which is attributed directly or indirectly to human activity that alters the composition of the global atmosphere and which is in addition to natural climate variability observed over comparable time periods."

Comment: For disaster risk reduction, either of these definitions may be suitable, depending on the context. The UNFCCC definition is more restricted as it excludes climate changes attributable to natural causes. The IPCC definition can be paraphrased for popular communication as "a change in the climate that persists for decades or longer, arising from either natural causes or human activity."

Climate Risk

Denotes the result of the interaction of physically defined hazards with the properties of the exposed systems—that is, their sensitivity or social vulnerability. Risk can also be considered as combining an event, its likelihood, and its consequences—that is, risk equals the probability of climate hazard multiplied by a given system's vulnerability.[2] Climate risk management, on the other hand, implies climate-sensitive decision making in dealing with climate variability and change, and promotes sustainable development by reducing vulnerabilities associated with climate risk.

Community-Driven Development (CDD)

Broadly defined, an approach that gives community groups and local governments control over planning decisions and investment resources. CDD empowers rural communities to play a stronger role in directly providing basic services, and to hold government more accountable in assisting communities to address their needs.

Coping Capacity

The ability of people, organizations, and systems, using available skills and resources, to face and manage adverse conditions, emergencies, or disasters.

Comment: The capacity to cope requires continuing awareness, resources, and good management, in normal times as well as during crises or adverse conditions. Coping capacities contribute to reducing disaster risks.

Critical Facilities

The primary physical structures, technical facilities, and systems that are socially, economically, or operationally essential to the functioning of a society or community, both in routine circumstances and in emergencies.

Comment: Critical facilities are elements of the infrastructure that support essential services in a society. They include such things as transport systems, air and sea ports, electricity, water, communications systems, hospitals and health clinics, and centers for fire, police, and public administration services.

Disaster

A serious disruption of the functioning of a community or a society involving widespread human, material, economic, or environmental losses and impacts, which exceeds the ability of the community or society to cope using its own resources.

The Centre for Research on the Epidemiology of Disasters (CRED) defines a disaster as a "situation or event, which overwhelms local capacity, necessitating a request to national or international level for external assistance." The CRED maintains an emergency events database (EM-DAT),[3] which has information on the occurrence and effects of many types of disasters in the world from 1900 to the present. For a disaster to be entered into EM-DAT, at least one of the following criteria must be fulfilled:

- 10 or more people reported killed
- 100 people reported affected
- Declaration of a state of emergency
- Call for international assistance

Comment: Disasters are often described as a result of combining the exposure to a hazard; the conditions of vulnerability present; and insufficient capacity or measures to reduce or cope with the potential negative consequences. Disaster impacts may include loss of life, injury, disease, and other negative effects on human physical, mental, and social well-being, together with damage to property, destruction of assets, loss of services, social and economic disruption, and environmental degradation.

Disaster Risk

The potential disaster losses, in lives, health status, livelihoods, assets, and services, which could occur to a particular community or a society over some specified future time period.

Comment: The definition of disaster risk reflects the concept of disasters as the outcome of continuously present conditions of risk. Disaster risk comprises different types of potential losses that are often difficult to quantify. Nevertheless, with knowledge of the prevailing hazards and the patterns of population and socioeconomic development, disaster risks can be assessed and mapped, in broad terms at least.

Disaster Risk Management

The systematic use of administrative directives, organizations, and operational skills and capacities to implement strategies, policies, and improved coping capacities in order to lessen the adverse impacts of hazards and the possibility of disaster.

Comment: Disaster risk management extends the more general term "risk management" in addressing disaster risks. Disaster risk management aims to avoid, lessen, or transfer the adverse effects of hazards through activities and measures for prevention, mitigation, and preparedness. Disaster management implies emergency management and response, whereas disaster risk management implies all four phases of disaster risk reduction, preparedness, response, and post-disaster reconstruction.

Disaster Risk Reduction

The practice of reducing disaster risks through systematic efforts to analyze and manage the causes of disasters, including through reduced exposure to hazards, lessened vulnerability of people and property, wise management of land and the environment, and improved preparedness for adverse events.

Comment: A comprehensive approach to reduce disaster risks is set out in the United Nations-endorsed Hyogo Framework for Action, adopted in 2005, whose expected outcome is "The substantial reduction of disaster losses, in lives and the social, economic and environmental assets of communities and countries." The International Strategy for Disaster Reduction (ISDR) system provides a vehicle for cooperation among governments, organizations, and civil society to assist in implementing the framework. Note that while the term "disaster reduction" is sometimes used, the term "disaster risk reduction" better recognizes the ongoing nature of disaster risks and the ongoing potential to reduce these risks.

Disaster Risk Reduction Plan

A document prepared by an authority, sector, organization, or enterprise that sets out goals and specific objectives for reducing disaster risks together with related actions to accomplish these objectives.

Comment: Disaster risk reduction plans should be guided by the Hyogo Framework and coordinated within development plans, resource allocations, and program activities. National plans need to be specific to each level of administrative responsibility and adapted to the social and geographical circumstances present. The plan should specify the timeframe and responsibilities for implementation and the sources of funding. Linkages to climate change adaptation plans should be made where possible.

Early-Warning System

The set of capacities for generating and disseminating timely and meaningful warnings to enable individuals, communities, and organizations threatened by a hazard to prepare and act appropriately and quickly enough to reduce the possibility of harm or loss.

Comment: This definition encompasses the range of factors to achieve effective responses to warnings. A people-centered early-warning system comprises four key elements: knowledge of the risks; monitoring, analysis, and forecasting of the hazards; communication of alerts and warnings; and local capabilities to respond to the warnings. The expression "end-to-end warning system" is used to emphasize that warning systems need to span all steps from hazard detection to community response.

Exposure

People, property, systems, or other elements present in hazard zones and subject to potential losses.

Comment: Measures of exposure include the number of people or types of assets in an area. These can be combined with the vulnerability of the exposed elements to a particular hazard to estimate the quantitative risks associated with that hazard in the area.

Geological Hazard

Geological condition or occurrence that may cause loss of life, injury or other health impacts, property damage, loss of livelihoods and services, social and economic disruption, or environmental damage.

Comment: Geological hazards include internal earth processes, such as earthquakes and volcanic emissions, as well as related geophysical processes, such as mass movements, landslides, rockslides, surface collapses, and debris or mud flows. Hydrometeorological factors contribute to some of these processes. Tsunamis are difficult to categorize; although undersea earthquakes and other geological events trigger tsunamis, they are an oceanic process manifested as a coastal water-related hazard.

Greenhouse Gases

Gaseous constituents of the atmosphere, both natural and manmade, that absorb and emit radiation of thermal infrared radiation emitted by the Earth's surface, the atmosphere, and clouds.

Comment: This is the definition of the IPCC. The main greenhouse gases are water vapor, carbon dioxide, nitrous oxide, methane, and ozone.[4]

Hazard

A dangerous phenomenon, substance, human activity, or condition that may cause loss of life, injury or other health impacts, property damage, loss of livelihoods and services, social and economic disruption, or environmental damage.

Comment: The hazards of concern to disaster risk reduction as stated in footnote 3 of the Hyogo Framework for Action are "hazards of natural origin and related environmental and technological hazards and risks." Such hazards arise from a variety of geological, meteorological, hydrological, oceanic, biological, and techno-logical sources, sometimes acting in combination. In technical settings, hazards are described quantitatively by the likely frequency of occurrence of different intensities for different areas, as determined from historical data or scientific analysis.

Land-Use Planning

The process by public authorities to identify, evaluate, and decide on options for the use of land, including consideration of long-term economic, social, and environmental objectives and the implications for different communities and interest groups, and the subsequent formulation and promulgation of plans that describe the permitted or acceptable uses.

Comment: Land-use planning is important to sustainable development. It involves studies and mapping; analysis of economic, environmental, and hazard data; formulation of alternative land-use decisions; and design of long-range plans for different geographical and administrative scales. Land-use planning can mitigate disasters and reduce risks by discouraging settlements and construction of installa-tions in hazard-prone areas, including consideration of service routes for transport, power, water, sewage, and other critical facilities.

Natural Hazard

Natural process or phenomenon that may cause loss of life, injury or other health impacts, property damage, loss of livelihoods and services, social and economic disruption, or environmental damage.

Comment: Natural hazards are a subset of all hazards. The term describes actual hazard events as well as the latent hazard conditions that may give rise to future events. Natural hazard events can be characterized by their magnitude or intensity, speed of onset, duration, and area of extent. For example, earthquakes have short durations and usually affect a small region, whereas droughts are slow to develop and fade away and often affect large regions. In some cases hazards may be coupled, as in the flood caused by a hurricane or the tsunami created by an earthquake.

Resilience

The ability of a system, community, or society exposed to hazards to resist, absorb, accommodate to, and recover from the effects of a hazard in a timely and efficient manner, including through the preservation and restoration of its essential basic structures and functions.

Comment: Resilience means the ability to "resile from" or "spring back from" a shock. The resilience of a community in respect to potential hazard events is determined by the degree to which the community has the necessary resources and is capable of organizing itself both before and during times of need.

Retrofitting

Reinforcement or upgrading of existing structures to become more resistant and resilient to the damaging effects of hazards.

Comment: Retrofitting requires considering the design and function of the structure, the stresses that the structure may be subject to from particular hazards, and the practicality and costs of different retrofitting options. Examples of retrofitting include adding bracing to stiffen walls, reinforcing pillars, adding steel ties between walls and roofs, installing shutters on windows, and improving the protection of important facilities and equipment.

Risk

The combination of the probability of an event and its negative consequences.

Comment: This definition closely follows the definition of the ISO/IEC Guide 73. The word "risk" has two distinctive connotations: in popular usage the emphasis is usually placed on chance or possibility, such as in "the risk of an accident"; in technical settings the emphasis is usually placed on the consequences, in terms of "potential losses" for some particular cause, place, and period. People do not necessarily share the same perceptions of the significance and underlying causes of different risks.

Risk Assessment

A methodology to determine the nature and extent of risk by analyzing potential hazards and evaluating conditions of vulnerability that together might harm exposed people, property, services, livelihoods, and the environment on which they depend.

Comment: Risk assessments (and associated risk mapping) include: a review of the technical characteristics of hazards, such as their location, intensity, frequency, and probability; the analysis of exposure and vulnerability, including the physical social, health, economic, and environmental dimensions; and the evaluation of the effectiveness of prevailing and alternative coping capacities in respect to likely risk scenarios. This series of activities is sometimes known as a risk analysis process.

Risk Management

The systematic practice of managing uncertainty to minimize potential harm and loss.

Comment: Risk management comprises risk assessment and analysis, and the implementation of strategies and actions to control, reduce, and transfer risks. It is widely practiced by organizations to minimize risk in investment decisions and to address operational risks such as those of business disruption, production failure, environmental damage, social impacts, and damage from fire and natural hazards. Risk management is a core issue for sectors such as water supply, energy, and agriculture whose production is directly affected by extremes of weather and climate.

Risk Transfer

The process of formally or informally shifting the financial consequences of risks from one party to another, whereby a household, community, enterprise, or state authority will obtain resources from the other party after a disaster occurs, in exchange for ongoing or compensatory social or financial benefits provided to that other party.

Comment: Insurance is a well-known form of risk transfer, where an insurer provides coverage of a risk in exchange for ongoing premiums. Risk transfer can occur informally within family and community networks where there are reciprocal expectations of mutual aid by means of gifts or credit, as well as formally where governments, insurers, multilateral banks, and other large risk-bearing entities establish mechanisms to cope with losses in major events.

Structural and Nonstructural Measures

Structural measures: Any physical construction to reduce or avoid the impacts of hazards, or application of engineering techniques to achieve hazard resistance and resilience in structures or systems.

Nonstructural measures: Any measure not involving physical construction that uses knowledge, practice, or agreement to reduce risks and impacts, in particular through policies and laws, public awareness raising, training, and education.

Comment: Common structural measures for disaster risk reduction include dams, flood levies, ocean wave barriers, earthquake-resistant construction, and evacuation shelters. Common nonstructural measures include building codes, land-use planning laws and their enforcement, research and assessment, information resources, and public awareness programs. In civil and structural engineering, the term "structural" is restricted to mean just the load-bearing structure, with other parts such as wall cladding and interior fittings termed nonstructural.

Urban

An urban area is typically defined by country statistics offices as a nonagricultural production base and a minimum population size (often 5,000). There are substantial differences in practice across countries (UN Statistics Division).[5]

Comment: Urban areas include continuously built-up inner city areas, as well as transitional or peri-urban areas between fully built-up and predominantly agriculture use or rural areas. However, there is debate on a universal definition of urban areas. In practice, countries define urban areas differently.

Vulnerability

The characteristics and circumstances of a community, system, or asset that make it susceptible to the damaging effects of a hazard.

Comment: There are many aspects of vulnerability, arising from various physical, social, economic, and environmental factors. Examples include poor design and construction of buildings, inadequate protection of assets, lack of public information and awareness, insufficient official recognition of risks and preparedness measures, and disregard for wise environmental management. Vulnerability varies significantly within a community and over time. This definition identifies vulnerability as a characteristic of the element of interest (community, system, or asset), which is independent of its exposure. However, in common use the word is often used more broadly to include the element's exposure.

Notes

1. UNISDR (2009a). Definitions are adopted from the disaster risk and climate change scientific and policy literature (UNISDR, IPCC, UNFCCC, etc.). In some cases the

definitions differ in the literature, so a comment follows selected definitions in order to better explain their use in this report.

2. http://beta.worldbank.org/climatechange/content/adaptation-guidance-notes-key-words-and-definitions.
3. http://www.emdat.be/.
4. IPCC negotiations focus on six greenhouse gases: carbon dioxide (CO_2), methane (CH_4), nitrous oxide (N_2O), hydrofluorocarbons (HFCs), perfluorocarbons (PFCs), and sulphur hexafluoride (SF_6).
5. http://unstats.un.org/unsd/demographic/sconcerns/densurb/Defintion_of%20Urban .pdf.

Reference

United Nations International Strategy for Disaster Reduction. 2009. *Global Assessment Report on Disaster Risk Reduction*. Geneva, Switzerland: United Nations.

Figure 1.1 Large Cities Exposed to Cyclones and Earthquakes

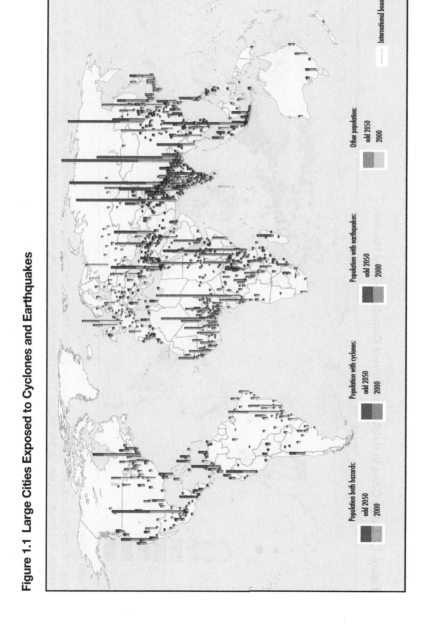

Population both hazards:
2050
2000

Population with cyclones:
2050
2000

Population with earthquakes:
2050
2000

Other population:
2050
2000

—— International boundaries

Figure 1.2 Large Cities in Relation to Current Climate-Related Hazards

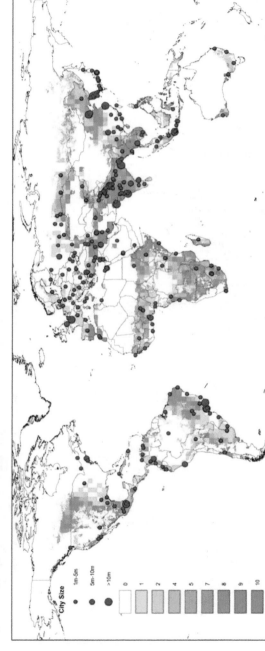

Source: De Sherbinin and Romero-Lankao (2011) in UN-HABITAT (2011).

Note: The urban areas included in this figure have populations greater than 1 million. The hazard risk represents a cumulative score based on risk of cyclones, flooding, landslides, and drought. "0" denotes "low risk" and "10" denotes "high risk." Hazard risk represents a cumulative score based on risk of cyclones, flooding, landslides, and drought.

Original source data include: For cities: Center for International Earth Science Information Network (CIESIN), *Global Rural-Urban Mapping Project* (GRUMP), 2006, alpha version, http://sedac.ciesin.columbia.edu/gpw/. For hazards, see Dilley et al. (2005).

Figure 3.1 Built-up Areas of Dakar Threatened by Hazards (2008)

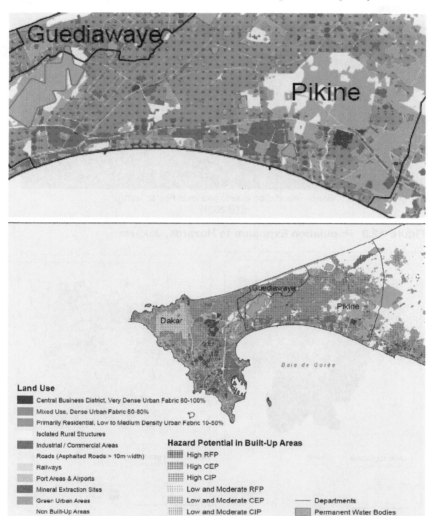

Land Use

◼ Central Business District, Very Dense Urban Fabric 80-100%

◼ Mixed Use, Dense Urban Fabric 50-80%

◼ Primarily Residential, Low to Medium Density Urban Fabric 10-50%

◼ Isolated Rural Structures

◼ Industrial / Commercial Areas

◼ Roads (Asphalted Roads > 10m width)

◼ Railways

◼ Port Areas & Airports

◼ Mineral Extraction Sites

◼ Green Urban Areas

◼ Non Built-Up Areas

Hazard Potential in Built-Up Areas

▦ High RFP

▦ High CEP

▦ High CIP

▦ Low and Moderate RFP

▦ Low and Moderate CEP

▦ Low and Moderate CIP

—— Departments

◼ Permanent Water Bodies

Figure A2.2 Impact of Sea-level Rise on North Jakarta with Business as Usual

Blue = inundation due to sea level rise at 1cm/yr
(ITB 2007)

Figure A2.3 Population Exposure to Hazards, Jakarta

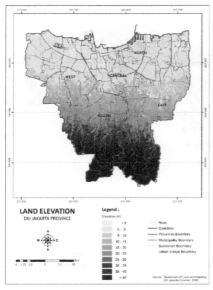

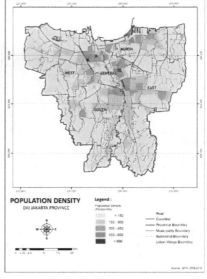

Figure A2.4 Slum Areas, Flooding, and Unregistered Land, Jakarta

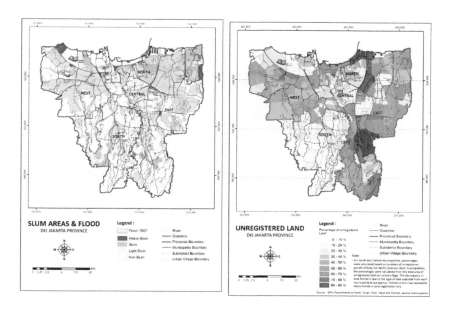

Figure A3.2 Urban Expansion of Mexico City Metropolitan Areas, 1950–2005

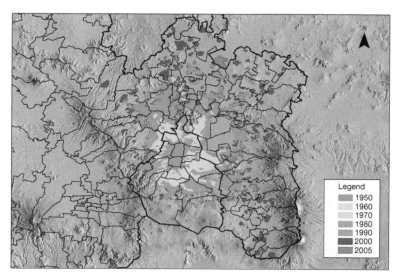

Figure A3.5 Vulnerable Areas in Terms of Population and Housing,
Mexico City

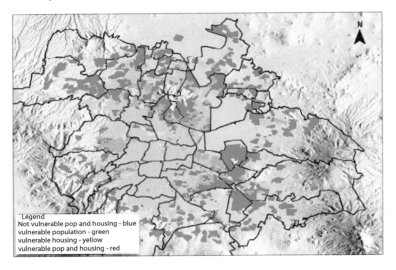

Figure A4.4 São Paulo´s Topography and Main Waterways

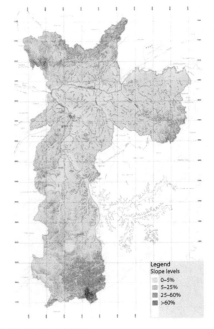

Source: PMSP—São Paulo Environmental Atlas.

Figure A5.1 Hotspots of Social Exposure with High Population Growth and High Hazard Potentials, Dakar

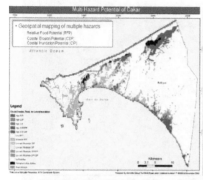

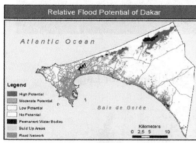

Figure A5.2 Areas of Multiple and Single Hazards Dakar

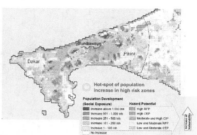

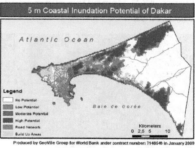

Produced by GeoVille Group for World Bank under contract number: 7148548 in January 2009

Figure A6.1 Legazpi Study Area

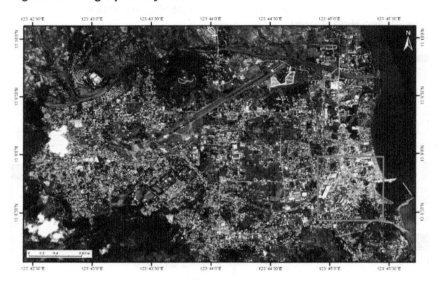

Figure A6.2 Using Pan-sharpened QuickBird Imagery for Legazpi Study Area

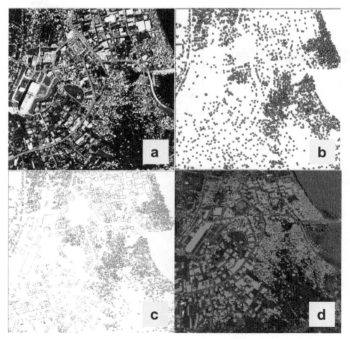

Figure A6.3 Building Typology and Qualification in Legazpi

Figure A6.5 Simulation for Inundation Caused by Tsunami 4 m High

Figure A7.2 Flood Hazard Map for Sana'a

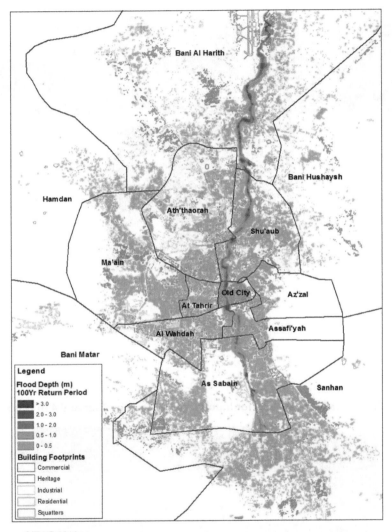

Source: GFDHR 2010.

**Figure A7.3 Flood Risk Zone for 10- and 25-Year Return Periods over
Building Footprints**

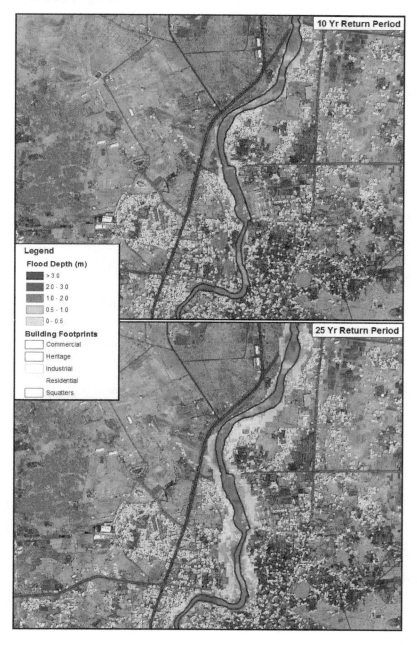

Figure A8.2 Exposure Characterization for Bogota (Building by Building)

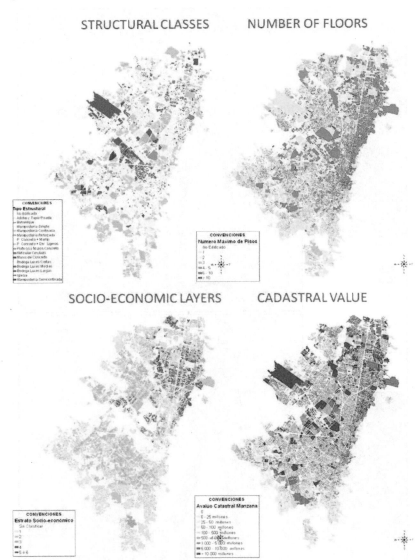

STRUCTURAL CLASSES   NUMBER OF FLOORS

SOCIO-ECONOMIC LAYERS   CADASTRAL VALUE

Source: Cardona 2010.

Figure A8.3 Physical Seismic Risk for Bogota

Physical Seismic
Risk

**Building by building,
(graphic by blocks of the city)**

**Scenarios of damage for
disaster risk management**

FRONTAL FAULT M=6

FRONTAL FAULT M=7

FRONTAL FAULT M=7.6

Figure A8.4 Physical Landslide Risk (City Blocks)

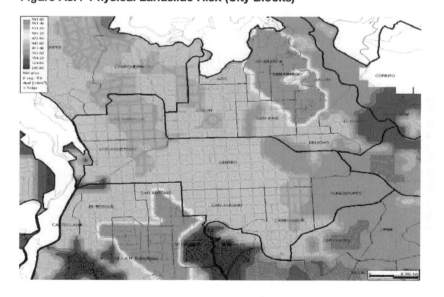

Figure A8.6 Day and Night Injuries

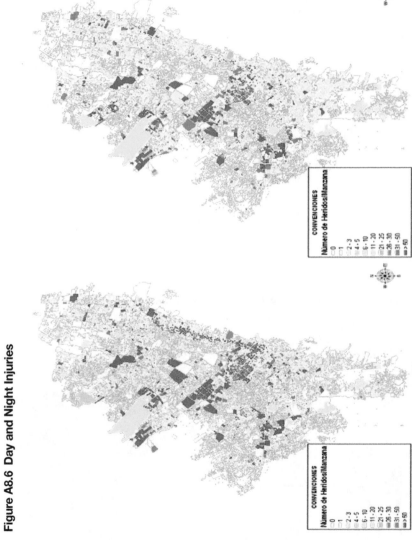

BOX A10.1

Land Subsidence in Tunis, Tunisia

In support of a World Bank study on coastal cities in the Middle East and North Africa, the European Space Agency measured land subsidence in the central area of Tunis. The red dots show a very high rate of subsidence of more than 5 m per year.

While the ongoing deformation within the city was a known fact, having it measured in an objective and incontrovertible way provides the needed entry point for city management to initiate actions to prevent further subsidence.

Source: European Space Agency

Figure A10.1 Examples of Satellite Resolution

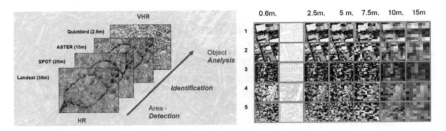

Figure A10.2 Spectral Fusion

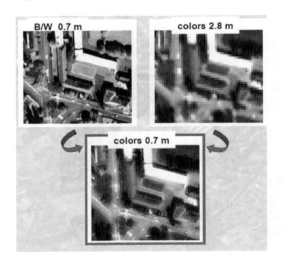

CPSIA information can be obtained at www.ICGtesting.com
Printed in the USA
LVOW02s1633151013

357039LV00018B/39/P

9 780821 389621